MAR 8 1995

SHELVED WITH NEW BOOKS

DISCARDED
from the Public Library of Nashville & Davidson Co.

DISCARDED
from the Public Library of Nashville & Davidson Co.

Property of
The Public Library of Nashville
and Davidson County
225 Polk, Nashville TN 37203

THOMPSON LANE

Library

D1064301

15,~

AN AMERICAN COLLECTION
Paintings and Sculpture
from the
National Academy of Design

AN AMERICAN

COLLECTION

Paintings and Sculpture from the National Academy of Design

Abigail Booth Gerdts, curator

National Academy of Design
New York

Cheekwood Fine Arts Center
Nashville, Tennessee

October 7–January 7, 1990

North Carolina Museum of Art
Raleigh, North Carolina

March 4–April 24, 1990

Emory University Museum
Atlanta, Georgia

May 30–July 15, 1990

Triton Museum of Art
Santa Clara, California

August 15–October 31, 1990

Terra Museum of American Art
Chicago, Illinois

May 18–July 14, 1991

Washington University Gallery of Art
St. Louis, Missouri

September 6–November 3, 1991

Denver Art Museum
Denver, Colorado

November 1991–January, 1992

*An American Collection: Paintings and Sculpture from
the National Academy of Design* copyright © 1989 by National Academy of Design.

All rights reserved.
For information contact the publisher:
National Academy of Design
1083 Fifth Avenue
New York, New York, 10128

Library of Congress Catalog Card Number: 89:061821

Printed in Japan

*An American Collection:
Paintings and Sculpture from the
National Academy of Design*
was produced for the National Academy of Design
by Perpetua Press, Los Angeles

Edited by Barbara Krulik
Designed by Dana Levy
Color photographs by David Allison, New York
Typeset in Electra by Wilsted & Taylor, Oakland
Printed and bound by Dai Nippon, Tokyo

CONTENTS

NATIONAL ACADEMY OF DESIGN

Council
Richard McDermott Miller, *President*
Will Barnet, *First Vice President*
Clare Romano, *Second Vice President*
Robert White, *Corresponding Secretary*
Morton Kaish, *Assistant Corresponding Secretary*
Jane Wilson, *Recording Secretary*
Wolf Kahn, *Treasurer*
Sidney Simon, *Assistant Treasurer*

Charles Cajori
Stephen Greene
Lester Johnson
Mervin Jules
Leo Manso
Richard Mayhew

Museum Board
Mr. Garett Albert
Mrs. Douglas Auchincloss
Mrs. George Delacorte
Mrs. Daniel Fraad
Prof. William H. Gerdts
Mr. Brendan Gill
Mr. Robin Graham
Mr. Mark Hampton
Mrs. Alfred Harrison
Mr. Robert S. Hutchins
Mr. Richard Manney
Mr. Leonard Milberg
Mrs. Samuel Newhouse
Prof. Barbara Novak
Mr. John Pierrepont
Mrs. Lee Radziwill
Mr. Andrew Rose
Mr. Clifford Ross
Mr. Wilbur Ross, *Chairman*
Mr. Robert Schoelkopf
Mr. Dave Williams, *Chairman, Executive Committee*
Mr. Thomas Zacharias
Mr. Richard McDermott Miller, *ex officio*

President's Foreword

TWO CENTURIES IN DIALOGUE

On viewing "An American Collection" in its premier installation at the National Academy of Design, I was struck by the remarkable colloquy between works of artists of the past and from the present. It was as though I was surrounded by a gathering of esteemed colleagues in deep conversation with one another. Although the majority of the works—and even some of the artists' names—were unfamiliar, I felt myself very much among friends. Somehow, the artists responsible for this seemingly unrelated aggregation of paintings and sculptures managed to coalesce into a kind of visual definition of the National Academy itself.

It is easy to see in this exhibition that the outlook of Academy members has undergone continuous change. The styles, tastes, and ideas about art as reflected here have inevitably swung this way and that since our founding in 1825. As our list of members gradually changed over the generations, so have our notions about art. But there has been no sudden break, no closing our eyes to the past. We and our predecessors share a common goal of achieving excellence.

The special manner in which these works were acquired provides this continuity and accounts for the special character of the collection. The fact that each of these works was selected by its own creator makes the National Academy collection unique. These are the presentation pieces required for Academy membership. For the most part the artists chose what they considered their best work as a way of representing themselves to their fellow artists.

The eternal question—What is our best?—is a primary topic in the dialogue between the works in this exhibition. However varied the tastes and times they represent may be, these paintings and sculptures speak freely to one another. Through them we can witness artists addressing each other: we can see both nineteenth- and twentieth-century painters and sculptors mingled together in a great conversation about important values in art.

RICHARD McDERMOTT MILLER
President
National Academy of Design

Sponsor's Preface

Support of the arts is a tradition at Northern
Telecom. Thus we are particularly proud to
have enabled the restoration and exhibition
of the works of the National Academy of
Design that make up *An American Collection*.

Roy Merrills
President
Northern Telecom Inc.

DIRECTOR'S STATEMENT

An American Collection, a project of several parts, has been under discussion for more than five years. Its earliest incarnation was a proposal to the Henry Luce Foundation for the support of a catalogue of our painting and sculpture collections. With the support of the Luce Foundation in hand Abigail Gerdts, curator of paintings and sculpture, selected graduate assistants and was well on her way when a second idea emerged. We would celebrate this noble venture, this grand catalogue, with an exhibition from the painting and sculpture collections.

At this juncture Kevin Grogan, Director of the Cheekwood Fine Arts Center, Nashville, Tennessee, stepped forward. He introduced the National Academy of Design to Northern Telecom, also of Nashville. Northern Telecom agreed to sponsor *An American Collection* on its tour across the United States and to support the conservation and preparation of the works in the exhibition. This is an example of extraordinary generosity for which the National Academy is very grateful. Northern Telecom has been an ideal partner. Their goal and ours is the introduction of the Academy's collection to a wide audience, and this is being accomplished.

Abigail Gerdts has been the tireless shepherd of this project since its inception. The success of *An American Collection* and that of the catalogue of the collections, which will follow the exhibition, are due to her hard work and determination.

JOHN H. DOBKIN
Director
National Academy of Design

INTRODUCTION

The foundation of the collection of the National Academy of Design is Rule 23 of its first constitution and by-laws, approved on December 16, 1826:

> Every Academician shall, during the first year after his election, present to the Academy a specimen of his own production in the Arts of Design, to be preserved in the Gallery of the Academy. A failure to comply with this rule, unless an excuse for delay satisfactory to the Academicians shall be given, shall make void the election of the candidate elect.

The deposit of a "specimen of production" by members, along with the rest of the structure of the Academy, was modeled explicitly on the principles and regulations of England's Royal Academy. The revision of the constitution and by-laws instituted April 24, 1839, however, introduced the novel ruling: "Every Associate shall, during the first year after his election present to the Academy his own portrait."[1] These regulations have been retained without substantial alteration through every subsequent revision of the constitution to the present day and in the intervening century and a half have been the source of the overwhelming majority of the 2,224 paintings and sculptures by 1,100 artists of which the Academy's collection is presently comprised.[2]

Although grown so great, the collection started slowly and small. Of the twenty-six Founders of the Academy one had died before the first constitution was enacted; three moved out of the city within a short time; fourteen were inactive in management, but for the most part amply supported the new organization by contributing work to its annual exhibitions. This left but eight (and John L. Morton, who could not be among the Founders, as he was not an artist by profession at the time) who devoted time and energy to the survival of the fledgling association: Samuel F. B. Morse, Asher B. Durand, Henry Inman, Charles Ingham, Thomas S. Cummings, William Dunlap, Thomas Cole, and Frederick Agate. While these few men regularly set and reset deadlines for themselves for delivery of their Academic "specimens"—and threatened each other with dread penalties for failure to comply—they also uniformly ignored their own rulings and resolutions.

It is not surprising that the threat of expulsion for failure to comply was not exercised: to have done so would have meant dissolution of the Academy itself. Why did the Founders fail to comply? Academy minutes are silent on the point. (Indeed, to historians' great frustration, minutes never digress into motivations and consequences of any Council business.) Even after 160 years, however, it is not difficult to venture some guesses. The mainstay of most of these artists was portraiture; commissioned portraits could not be given to other than the patrons. The landscape and subject pictures they executed were the important work that if not also done on commission, needed to be held for exhibition with the possibility of sale. To offer up something less than a fully realized composition to the judgement of peers and—if they took their places in history into consideration—to posterity could be embarrassing. Probably also among the excuses, as they were men as well as artists, were "too busy"; "I forgot, but will bring it next time"; and "the piece now on my easel is the best I've ever done. I'll give it when it's finished."

None of the Founders presented a diploma work to the Academy, with the possible exceptions of John Frazee and Morse. Frazee's bust self-portrait in plaster was his contribution to the Academy's second annual exhibition in 1827. When the Academy first published a listing of its holdings "of Statues, Busts, Bas Reliefs, Books, Engravings and Paintings" in 1843, his self-portrait was included, annotated as a presentation of the artist. It was, however, listed amidst the records of casts from antique sculptures, the part of the collection primarily associated with the operation of the Academy school. When Frazee made the presentation, and with what intent—whether to fulfill his obligation as a member, as a contribution to the school, or both—is unknown. In March 1827 the Council, to show its appreciation and respect to Dr. Frederick Gore King for having served as the first lecturer in anatomy for its school, requested him to sit to Morse. The resulting portrait was shown in the next year's annual exhibition, noted as Morse's diploma presentation (and is in the present exhibition), which indicates it fulfilled both the Council's "commission" and Morse's obligation.

Even with the addition to the body of Academicians by election the situation did not improve much: the first artist elected to join the Founders, George Catlin, resigned a year later. None of the twenty-one Academicians elected over the next fifteen years had presented a diploma work by 1843 when the listing of Academy property was published. Yet none were expelled from the organization.

To be fair, in this period no records were made of acquisitions as they arrived, other than gifts of casts from the antique, engravings, and a few European paintings, all considered as contributions primarily of benefit to the school. The portraits of Henry Inman by Edward Mooney, and of James Freeman and of John L. Morton, both by James Whitehorne, which were among the twelve American paintings on the 1843 collection list, could well have been presented as NA diploma works by their artists, who were among those twenty-one Academicians. Later, others from among the twenty-one would present portraits to the collection, which were probably also considered to be their artists' NA diploma works, as the sitters had been elected Associates before the initiation of the ruling requiring ANAs to present portraits: Daniel Huntington, a portrait of Thomas Cole; John Gadsby Chapman, a portrait of Alexander Anderson; William Page and the brothers William Sidney Mount and Shepherd Alonzo Mount, self-portraits. Although never a stated policy, the accrual of portraits of members elected before the 1839 regulation requiring Associate portraits, clearly indicates that the Academy sought to fill that gap in its collection. Portraits of those pre-1839 entrants would have been appropriate, and especially welcomed, diploma presentations.

While the record-making improved little, Associates' and Academicians' response to the requirements of their elections picked up considerably as the 1840s progressed. The Academy again published an inventory of its property in 1852. By then it counted eighteen American subject paintings, of which fifteen were identified as Academic diploma works; seventy-seven portraits, of which three were identified as Academic presentations; and the remainder as Associate presentations—although several, such as Morse's Dr. King, Huntington's Cole, and the others just noted, were surely not. The collection of sculpture by members had doubled: Frazee's bust self-portrait had been joined by Henry Kirke Brown's NA diploma presentation, a bust portrait of Thomas Cole. (This bust of Cole was likely also a plaster and probably a victim of the fate of much work in that fragile medium: it long ago disappeared from the collection, probably as fragments tossed into a dustbin.)

If in its first quarter century of existence the Academy's development of a collection of members' works seems lethargic, it may be explained by several factors. One was certainly pragmatic: the NAD periodically moved from one to another rented quarters that had to serve as school rooms and also as display galleries for the annual exhibition; the less there was to pack and store the better. From 1826 to 1852 the Academy relocated four times. (There is no indication that the collection ever was "preserved in the Gallery of the Academy," that is, hung for display.) Also, despite their enthusiasm for the institution, the Founders and near followers had to harbor a feeling that its survival was precarious. Was it really worthwhile to assemble permanent property that did not contribute directly to the good of the school? It was with laudable wisdom that their first priorities steadfastly remained the school and the annual juried exhibition of contemporary American artists's works; maintaining quarters and enlarging the cast collection on which the former depended; organizing the presentation of the latter and encouraging artists to submit their best work, so the shows would be fresh, interesting, and critically approved, thus holding and increasing an audience from year to year. In this period the Academy's operation was financed entirely from the admission charges yielded by each year's exhibition.

It was 1911 before the permanent collection was again inventoried and announced in a published checklist. By this time it had grown to 830 paintings and sculptures, nearly nine times its size in the mid-nineteenth century. The addition of new generations of members certainly accounts for most of the growth, but those members' new alacrity in securing their elections as Associates and Academicians, and concern for the character of their representation in the collection contributed to its development.

The sixty years between the second and this third publication of a collection list was a period of ever-growing glory for the Academy. Its annual exhibitions had early acquired the status of premier arena for native artists to show their accomplishments. As the nineteenth century progressed, for an artist to have a work accepted by the jury of Academicians for inclusion in an annual was for many the launching point of a career; to be awarded any of the substantial cash prizes, introduced into the annuals in 1884, was to attain instant celebrity; to be elected to Associate membership was to be certified as among America's most promising, and to Academician, as among America's best. Academicians were among the leaders, if not instigators, of all the many manifestations of the rising thirst for the arts in New York, such as the establishment of the Metropolitan Museum of Art. They also wielded considerable influence elsewhere. They were the directors and teachers of many of the art schools opening in cities all across the country. Most of the artists who directed the design of America's first world's fair, the Columbian Exposition held in Chicago in 1893, were Academicians.

Arguably a major force in the Academy's advancing prestige was the attainment of its first really permanent home (a previous building had become the property of creditors almost as soon as it was erected) and the character of the building itself. Also of significance is that by the 1860s there was a sufficient body of wealthy business and professional men in New York with an interest in the advancement of the fine arts to be tapped for the funds to erect such a building. They responded to a remarkable fund-raising project, the Fellowship Fund, in numbers and with enough generosity to pay for the "Doge's Palace," as it was called, to go up on the corner of Twenty-third Street and Fourth Avenue in just two years. The Fortieth Annual Exhibition inaugurated the grand new headquarters in April 1865. This Venetian Gothic Revival–style edifice would remain one of New York's favorite sightseeing attractions until its demolition in the early years of the twentieth century.

Permanent quarters provided stability and space for the school and the exhibitions. The Doge's Palace provided the most space for art to be displayed—and displayed to advantage—of any building in New York. All that space went to show the work of contemporary American artists. (Although the point was never made overtly, the Academy galleries were also among the few sales rooms in town until late in the century.) New York's growth as the center of American wealth and power brought with it a rise in numbers and aspirations of a patronage class. That many of the most prominent representatives of this class had a vested interest in the Academy as Fellows for Life or In Perpetuity (depending on size of donation) enhanced the attraction for artists of exhibiting in Academy annuals. Being among the exhibitors was also the only way to be eligible to be considered for membership in the Academy.

While it didn't get a share of gallery walls, the Academy's collection was surely one of the major beneficiaries of the new building: it gained the security of permanence and space, albeit for storage. As the membership broadened, so did the collection of diploma presentations. Few electees delayed or ignored the rules, which would have risked forfeiture of the precious rank of Associate or Academician. While they generally still did not part with a major, current work, neither were they careless about the standard of product they offered for review of Council; rejection of a work as too slight or "not representative" was not unknown. Storage was surely then, as always, something of a problem. The size for ANA portraits was constitutionally stipulated, but there seems also to have been an unwritten regulation concerning NA diploma works that, though they were to be representative, they should be fairly small.

The centennial of the American Revolution had given Americans a realization that they had a history and the inspiration to explore and preserve it. The Academy was no exception to this growing movement. Gradually it began to see itself, and to be seen, as an embodiment of the continuum of America's history in the fine arts. Late in the century diploma presentations began to be larger in scale and importance within an artist's oeuvre. But of more significant impact on the nature of the permanent collection was the addition of gifts, from persons generally unconnected with the Academy, of American paintings and even a few sculptures. In 1865 the Academy had received by bequest James Suydam's important collection of approximately one hundred American and European paintings. Suydam, besides being a perceptive patron, was an amateur painter turned professional and an Academician. Relatives and friends of members of the Academy had given works to the collection, often as a gesture of honor to the artist of the work or subject of a portrait. Over a period of about twenty years beginning in the mid-1890s, however, a number of works were received so they might be preserved in the preeminent artistic institution devoted to American art. Certainly among the most distinguished of these gifts were *Robert Rait* by Charles Loring Elliott, *Morning of Life* and *Evening of Life* by Asher B. Durand, and *War News From Mexico* by Richard Caton Woodville, all of which are included in the present exhibition.

By the end of the century the Academy had outgrown its building, sold it (and, more to the point, the land it occupied), and optimistically launched on the project to build a great Beaux Arts–style structure in a new, more fashionable neighborhood. A supposedly temporary building to house the school, Academy offices, and collection was erected at 109th Street and Amsterdam Avenue; exhibitions were held in the galleries of the Fine Arts Building on West 57th Street. But the plans for the new headquarters met with constant and multiple frustrations, not the least of the obstacles being the members' inability to agree on which neighborhood of spreading New York was, indeed, the most desirable for the NAD's purposes. The collection continued to grow, as did indication in Council minutes of the members' respect and care for it. Early in the new century George Maynard, NA, became unpaid custodian of all the collections; it was he who oversaw the research preliminary to publication of the 1911 checklist of the collection. The "historical" paintings were put into commercial storage in the 1920s for their protection. Judging from old photographs of the 109th Street building, the Associate portraits were hung, edge-to-edge, in the school studios, a kind of simultaneous storage solution and encouragement to greatness for the students.

Forty years passed before the parts and functions of the Academy were reassembled under the roof of a permanent headquarters. Philanthropist Archer Huntington's Fifth Avenue townhouse, which he gave to the Academy, continues to be its home today. Where in 1865 the Doge's Palace had been inaugurated with the resplendent Fortieth Annual Exhibition, in January 1942 the new headquarters opened with an exhibition drawn from the permanent collection and titled by its proud owners, *Our Heritage*. It should not be inferred that the Academy then, or ever, subordinated its annual exhibitions to its permanent collection, but rather that the artist-members seized upon their first real opportunity in nearly half a century to recognize the significance of the work of generations of colleagues and of the unique assemblage of "specimens" in their possession.

Between 1911 and the present, when the results of the latest exhaustive review of the collection is nearing publication in a comprehensive catalogue, the collection of paintings and sculpture nearly tripled in numbers. This is partly a result of the passage of time, but is also a reflection of the expanded limitation on the numbers of members.[3] The period over which these nearly 1,400 works have been added to the collection has seen the healthy proliferation of museum institutions and exhibiting organizations—and the rise to ascendancy of an aesthetic alternative to the academic tradition. The Academy gradually ceased to be "the only game in town," but as its particular basis of acquisition did not change, its collection accrued works representative of the still living—if temporarily unpopular—artistic values rooted in the Renaissance. In recent years, as those values have come to a mode

of synthesis with abstractionism, the Academy's membership and, consequently, its collection, has continued to reflect the times.

While the Academy collection has been much revered by historians of American art—virtually the only persons much acquainted with it until recent years—it has also been much misunderstood. It is routinely categorized with the great museum assemblages of American art. These institutions, working from the vantage point of a present viewing a past, seek to select (with relative objectivity) and preserve for posterity a record of the most important examples in terms of content as well as quality of the primary artists and schools of American art. But the Academy's collection was formed and continues to grow from an entirely different, but no less intriguing perspective: that of artists.

Associate diploma portraits are informal images, frequently of artists as they saw themselves (and wanted their fellow artists to see them), such as the portraits of Thomas Eakins, Gertrude Fiske, Edwin Dickinson, and Wayne Thiebaud seen in this exhibition. Almost as frequently they are by the husbands, wives, children, mentors, close friends, or coworkers of the sitters, as are the portraits of Timothy Cole, Cass Gilbert, Robert Blum, George Bellows, and Charles Curran, also in this exhibition. Some Academicians such as Winslow Homer, George Inness, and Charles Hawthorne are represented in the Academy collection with examples of work presented and current at the time of their elections and presentations, which eventually prove not to be perfectly representative of their careers. Some, as seen in the examples by William Merritt Chase, Kenyon Cox, and Philip Pearlstein in the present exhibition, gave works that marked a particular moment in the development of their careers well before election. Some, such as Augustus Saint-Gaudens and Will Barnet, gave works both stylistically representative and imbued with special significance for the community of American artists. This gives the collection its special character, flavor, and insight into American art and artists. The Academy holds some master works, certainly, and just as certainly some minor works. It offers a look at many of the faces of the most famous and of the most forgotten of our artists from the past 160 years. Most of all it provides a view of American art passed down to the future by its makers.

ABIGAIL BOOTH GERDTS
Curator of Paintings and Sculpture
National Academy of Design

NOTES

1. Election to membership in the Academy—whether entering as Associate or advancing to Academician—has always been separated from actual achievement of membership. Submission to the Academy's governing body, the Council, and Council acceptance of an electee's portrait or representative "specimen" is mandatory before he or she may enter upon the duties and privileges of membership, including appending of the initials ANA or NA to signature. Upon acceptance of the so-called qualifying work, the electee received a certificate or, as it was initially termed, a "diploma," in confirmation of membership. These presentations, upon which actual membership is based, are thus designated "diploma portraits" and "diploma works."

Although Academy regulations require that diploma presentations be submitted within one year of election, Councils have always been liberal in granting extensions and in recent years have tended to honor the time-limit rule in theory only. Consequently there may be lengthy gaps between dates of election and attainment of functional membership. However long that gap, the date of initiation of membership is always considered to be the member's date of election, not the date of confirmation by acceptance of the diploma piece.

2. At its founding in 1826 the Academy was to be comprised of artists practicing in the four acknowledged branches of the fine arts: painting, sculpture, engraving, and architecture. By the twentieth century the definition of "engraving" had been broadened to embrace all the graphic arts, and in 1944 the Academy officially recognized watercolor painting as a distinct form by establishing a fifth membership category for artists specializing in that medium. Until the major constitutional revision of 1906, each year's nominees for Associate membership could only come from among exhibitors in the NAD annual exhibiton of the same year. Paintings in oil dominated the exhibitions, with sculptures a relatively rare but welcome enhancement; engraving or other works in graphic art were sparsely exhibited in annuals and architectural renderings hardly seen at all. Thus, in the eighty years between founding and the elimination of the "exhibitor" rule—or the first half of the NAD's history—only five graphic artists and no architects were elected Academicians, which precluded much development of a collection of diploma works on paper. However, drawings, sketchbooks, some master prints, and many fine reproductive engravings were presented to the Academy during this period. After 1906 this aspect of the collection grew significantly by the portfolios of prints, specimens of architectural rendering, and watercolor paintings presented by Academicians in these classifications, as well as from continued gifts. The NAD's collection of prints, drawings, watercolors, and architectural renderings presently totals approximately 4,500 items and is in the process of being thoroughly catalogued.

3. In the nineteenth century the maximum number of Academicians was thirty to fifty; it is now set at one hundred and twenty-five painters and fifty sculptors; the number of Associates is not limited, but is held in proportion to Academicians.

The following abbreviations are used throughout the catalogue:

NAD   National Academy of Design
NA   National Academician
ANA   Associate National Academician
PNAD   President of the National Academy of Design

Dimensions are in inches and are stated in order: height, width, depth.

NOTE ON REFERENCES:

Only documentary references that specifically support, or are especially pertinent to, individual biographical summaries and commentaries on works are cited following these sections. Material held in the Academy archives, published biographical dictionaries, exhibition indexes, and other standard reference works in American art history were basic research sources underlying preparation of all catalogue entries. To avoid extensive repetition of identical texts, these are not cited within each entry. References cited AAA refer to papers held by the Archives of American Art, Smithsonian Institution. Two publications of the National Academy of Design are frequently cited in abbreviated form as: NAD: *From All Walks*, 1979; and NAD: *Next to Nature*, 1980. Full titles for these are: *From All Walks of Life: Paintings of the Figure from the National Academy of Design*, 1979; and *Next to Nature: Landscape Paintings from the National Academy of Design*, 1980.

AN AMERICAN COLLECTION

Paintings and Sculpture
from the
National Academy of Design

CATALOGUE AUTHORS

John Davis
David B. Dearinger
Abigail Booth Gerdts
Jonathan P. Harding
Mary A. Lublin
Robert H. Luck
Ruth Pasquine

SAMUEL FINLEY BREESE MORSE

Founder 1826; PNAD 1826–45; 1861–62
Charlestown, Massachusetts 1791–1872 New York

Of the Founders of the National Academy of Design, perhaps none was more influential in its creation and in shaping its successful survival than Samuel F.B. Morse.

Morse was the eldest child of the Reverend Jedidiah Morse, a prominent preacher and minister of the First Congregational Church of Charlestown, a suburb of Boston, from 1789 to 1819. As befitted the intellectual aristocracy of his background, Morse was educated at Phillips Academy, Andover, Massachusetts, and Yale College, New Haven, Connecticut. He aspired to a life of distinction, one in which he would at once serve God and society and win honor and at least some wealth. While still in college he began painting miniatures and determined upon art as the calling in which he might best attain his ambition. Back in Boston in 1810 he met and became a student of Washington Allston, who was twelve years his senior and already greatly respected in Boston for the moral idealism of his landscapes and figure subjects. Allston, who would become America's most revered artist of the first half of the nineteenth century, was the ideal mentor for Morse. He was a model of the kind of artist Morse intended to become, a painter of imaginative, complex compositions expressive of the great moral lessons of humanism and Christianity: a History Painter. Morse accompanied Allston to England in July 1811. He immediately began to prepare to enter the Royal Academy's school and was admitted on his first try that October. Like many of his contemporaries, Morse also benefited from the advice and encouragement of the Royal Academy's president, the expatriate American Benjamin West. Morse advanced rapidly; within a year he was at work on an eight by six foot canvas, *Dying Hercules* (Yale University Art Gallery, New Haven, Connecticut), which was highly praised by West and the London critics when it was exhibited at the Royal Academy's annual exhibition of 1813.

Morse was back in Boston by the close of 1815, very well trained, with demonstrated accomplishments in his profession, and convinced of his calling to elevate American art and the artistic perceptions of the American public. Opportunities to pursue his career as a historical painter were rare in America, however; he turned to portraiture to make his living. Gilbert Stuart dominated Boston in this speciality, and in the circumstances Morse saw little hope of prompt success. He began to travel in search of commissions: Concord, Hanover, and Portsmouth in New Hampshire, in 1816; Charleston, South Carolina, in the winters of 1817–18, 1818–19, 1819–20, and 1820–21. He was an active participant in the founding of the South Carolina Academy of the Fine Arts, but eventually became disillusioned with its administration by businessmen and slowly withdrew his support.

Late in 1821 Morse was in Washington, D.C., at work on a large painting of the interior of the congressional chamber in the Capitol. This was to be part of a tripartite composition that would show the president and cabinet flanked by the two houses of Congress. The other two canvases were not begun. Instead, in 1823 Morse toured his painting, *The House of Representatives*, (Corcoran Gallery of Art, Washington, D.C.) to New Haven, Boston, and finally New York. Its exhibition gained Morse considerable praise from important sources, but nearly nothing in the way of reward from the admission charge. After a short return to New Haven, where his family now lived, Morse again took up the life of an itinerant portraitist.

In the autumn of 1824 he settled in New York and established connections with the leading literary and intellectual figures of the day, including James Fenimore Cooper, William Cullen Bryant, and Fitz-Greene Halleck. The ease with which Morse's intellectual and social background allowed him to move in such circles, as well as the demonstrated excellence of several portraits done after his arrival in New York, contributed to his receiving the coveted commission from the city's Common Council to paint a portrait of the Marquis de Lafayette, then making a tour of the country whose independence he had helped secure. The commission and the resulting monumental painting, completed in 1826 (City Hall, New York), established Morse among America's foremost artists.

Morse's status in New York's artistic, political, and social world made him the ideal rallying point for the growing dissatisfaction of a rising young generation of artist with the failure of the American Academy of Fine Arts to provide the kind of opportunity for sophisticated training it had promised. The members of the American Academy, founded in 1802, were the city's most prominent business and social leaders; a few artists were included, and its president was the formidable John Trumbull. In November 1825 the younger artists, along with the established professionals Henry Inman, Asher B. Durand, William Dunlap, Charles Ingham, and a number of gentlemen amateurs, formed the New-York Drawing Association. They met three evenings a week to draw from casts of classical sculpture. Morse was elected president of what was essentially a self-help group. Several attempts to consolidate the two groups were misunderstood on both sides, and tempers grew short. Instead of effecting an amicable liaison, in January 1826, at Morse's suggestion and with his guidance on the specific form the organization should take, the Association confirmed its independence by reconstituting itself as the National Academy of Design.

The keystone of Morse's concept of the Academy was that its membership be limited to professional artists and, consequently, that the arbiters of all its actions on behalf of American art and artists would be those best qualified for the authority, the artists themselves. He was explicit in identifying London's Royal Academy as his model for the structure of the American organization.

As president of the National Academy, Morse was its eloquent spokesman, defender, and wise guide through the first critical decades of its existence. He was not always present in person to oversee Academy practice, for he continued his active role as a painter and in 1829 brought to fruition a long-planned return to Europe. With the support of a fund of $3,000 subscribed by friends and patrons, he passed three years of travel and study abroad, visiting London, Paris, northern Italy, Rome, and Switzerland; he often enjoyed the company of American fellow artists who were abroad for varying lengths of time. In addition to executing his own compositions, he made some copies of old masters as ordered by his sponsors. The last year of the trip Morse spent in Paris, developing the very large *Gallery of the Louvre* (Terra Museum of American Art, Chicago), to which he put the finishing touches after his return to New York late in 1832. Near the end of the following year Morse put the painting on public display. His experience with the *House of Representatives* was repeated: *Gallery of the Louvre* was admired by the knowledgeable, but shunned by the paying public. Morse continued to paint portraits, and in 1835 New York University named him its first Professor in the Literature of the Arts of Design.

The single greatest hope of aspiring American history painters in the second quarter of the nineteenth century were the eight huge places for paintings around the interior of the U.S. Capitol rotunda. John Trumbull had filled four of them by 1824, but had been denied the commission for the remaining four, which remained blank for over another decade. Much lobbying was done on behalf of various artists, including Morse, who had applied for a commission himself. It was the concensus of cultured New York that he would be among the chosen artists; indeed, he considered his second period of European study a specific preparation for undertaking a composition for the Capitol. When the commissions were announced in 1836, however, Morse was not among the honored four. The reason for his rejection was likely his conspicuous and unpopular political activity; in 1836 he had made an unsuccessful run for the New York mayoralty on the xenophobic Native American ticket.

Morse's disappointment and humiliation were overwhelming. His career as a painter had not truly gone beyond portraiture, and now all hope of attaining his artistic ambition was at an end. As an educated man Morse had long had a practical knowledge and curiosity in the sciences. He had begun to experiment with the concept of telegraphy at about the time of his return from Europe. With the closure of his future in art, Morse turned to science as a route to attain the distinction he sought. He sent the first successful telegraphic communication early in 1838.

Morse's withdrawal from the art world occurred gradually over the next several years as his involvement with development of the telegraph increased. He continued to attend as diligently as possible to Academy affairs, although he was frequently absent from New York on matters related to his invention. The first public demonstration of the telegraph occurred in 1844 and the following year Morse declined reelection to the presidency of the Academy.

Asher B. Durand became the Academy's second president, but in 1861, when he refused to continue in the post and divisive fighting for the controlling position seemed imminent, the now-venerable Morse was asked to return to it. He agreed, but on condition that his service be limited to one year. In expressing his reluctance, he wrote the Academy: "There are many reasons, of mainly a personal nature, which make me unfeignedly reluctant to accede to your request. I have been so long out of the traces of Art, that I am conscious of inability to fulfill the duties of the position either to my own or your satisfaction."

Although Morse turned away from the practice of art, he never lost his interest in the Academy, nor failed to support it—substantively, as well as in spirit. When the Fellowship Fund was created in 1863 to raise the money to build the Academy headquarters, Morse led off the subscriptions with a contribution of $1,000, and two years later, just before the opening of that building, he made a gift to the Academy of a portrait of Washington Allston by his old friend and fellow Allston protégé, Charles Robert Leslie.

Morse's death was solemnly noted around the world. On April 3, 1872, a special meeting of the Academy's Council was called to enter into record its memorial:

In common with the rest of the World, it becomes our painful duty to recognize the passage away from among us of Prof. Saml. F.B. Morse our first president, we may almost say the very founder, of our institution, a man endeared to many of us by still closer ties. The last of a trio of painters from whom have proceeded during the past century, perhaps the three most remarkable inventions of the age, in their widespread and still spreading influence upon mankind; for Fulton, Daguerre and Morse are names which hereafter associate themselves in the mind of men, to a very remote stretch of time. . . . We cannot but feel some pride in the share which the study of our common profession must have had in developing those faculties with which he wrought the great telegraphic plan that makes his name forever famous and though he has secured such a lasting name by other than the pursuit of that Art with which he set out in his life, had he confined himself thereto, there is little doubt among the best judges in Art matters, but that he would even then have left his among the role of the names not born to die.

ABG

REFERENCES

Thomas S. Cummings, *Historic Annals of the National Academy of Design, New-York Drawing Association, etc., with Occasional Dottings by the Way-side, from 1825 to the Present Time* (Philadelphia: George W. Childs, Publisher, 1865; reprint New York: Kennedy Galleries, Inc., Da Capo Press, 1969).

NAD minutes, April 3, 1872.

Samuel Irenaeus Prime, *The Life of Samuel F.B. Morse, LL.D., Inventor of the Electro-Magnetic Recording Telegraph* (New York: D. Appleton and Company, 1875).

Edward Lind Morse, ed., *Samuel F.B. Morse: His Letters and Journals*, (Boston and New York: Houghton, Mifflin, and Co., 1914; reprint New York: Kennedy Galleries, Inc., Da Capo Press, 1973).

Carlton Mabee, *The American Leonardo: A Life of Samuel F.B. Morse*, (New York: Alfred A. Knopf, 1943; reprint New York: Octagon Books, 1969).

Grey Art Gallery and Study Center, New York University: Paul J. Staiti and Gary A. Reynolds, *Samuel F.B. Morse*, 1982.

NAD: Paul J. Staiti and Nicolai Cikovsky, Jr., *Samuel F.B. Morse: Educator and Champion of the Arts in America*, 1982.

Nicolai Cikovsky, Jr., ed., *Lectures on the Affinity of Painting with the Other Fine Arts by Samuel F.B. Morse* (Columbia, Missouri, and London: University of Missouri Press, 1983).

Carrie Rebora, "American Academy of Fine Arts and the National Academy of Design," paper delivered at NAD symposium, June 1, 1989.

DR. FREDERICK GORE KING [1827–28]
Oil on canvas, 34½ × 27½
By order of NAD Council; and NA diploma presentation, 1827

King was born in England in 1801 and brought to America during his youth. He attended college in Massachusetts and pursued the study of medicine under a Dr. Post in New York. After practicing for a brief period, King became demonstrator of anatomy at the New York College of Physicians and Surgeons. In 1828 he compiled and published *Catalogue of the Anatomical Museum in the College of Physicians and Surgeons New-York*.

At just the same time late in 1825 that the New-York Drawing Association was being formed, King was appointed lecturer in anatomy by the American Academy of Fine Arts. It is difficult to imagine to whom he would have lectured under that appointment. Upon the founding of the National Academy, King offered to assume the all-important position of anatomy instructor in its newly established school. The Academy was pleased to appoint him immediately to that lectureship. His tenure was sadly brief, as he died in 1829.

The Academy was also grateful for King's pioneering support. In March 1827, following the close of the first full school year, the Council showed its appreciation by requesting King to sit to Morse for his portrait. When the painting was shown in the Academy's next annual exhibition, it was noted as "[Morse's] Academician picture," suggesting the artist made a presentation of the portrait to the Academy, letting it serve as his diploma work, rather than considering the assignment a formal commission, which the Academy could then ill afford.

REFERENCES
NAD minutes, March 2, and 23, 1827

Cummings, 1865 (1969), 37.

ASHER BROWN DURAND

Founder 1826; PNAD 1845–61
Jefferson Village [Maplewood], New Jersey 1796–1886 Jefferson
Village

Durand early displayed his artistic talents in his engraving work on the watches and silver manufactured by his father. In 1812 he was apprenticed to the engraver Peter Maverick in Newark, New Jersey. He so excelled in the medium that after completing his apprenticeship in 1817, Maverick immediately made him his partner; Durand established an office for the firm in New York. His only training in art was during this period when he would occasionally draw from the casts at the American Academy of the Fine Arts. Three years later John Trumbull engaged Durand to engrave his painting, *The Signing of the Declaration of Independence*. Relations with Maverick became strained as Durand's skills gained admirers, and when such a major commission went independently to the junior partner, Maverick dissolved their association. The large plate reproducing Trumbull's painting was completed in 1823; its publication in the same year brought Durand immediate acclaim and established his reputation as one of the leading engravers working in the United States. Durand then set up in business for himself, maintaining a firm under various partnership names until 1831, producing bank notes, book illustrations, and especially reproductive engravings after portraits of celebrated men.

He continued to work in engraving, executing nineteen of the plates for *The National Portrait Gallery of Distinguished Americans*, published between 1832 and 1840, but his last significant effort in the medium came in 1834. In 1831 Durand had purchased John Vanderlyn's remarkable painting of the female nude, *Ariadne Asleep on the Island of Naxos*, 1814 (Pennsylvania Academy of the Fine Arts, Philadelphia). He made his engraving after it using his own small-sized oil copy as well as Vanderlyn's original as models. The print, published in 1835, was immediately recognized as his finest work in the engraving medium.

In the same year, however, the assured patronage of Luman Reed allowed Durand to turn fully to painting. Working as a painter was not new to him. Although professionaly identified in the Academy's publication of its founding and its first exhibition catalogue as an engraver, Durand contributed portrait and landscape paintings along with his engravings to its first six annual exhibitions, 1826 thorugh 1832. When he gave up engraving work in the mid-1830s, he concentrated on painting portraits, but in the summer of 1837 he determined to focus on landscape as his theme, following the leadership of Thomas Cole in idealistic interpretation of the subject and becoming the other major figure in the group of artists commonly called the Hudson River School. In 1837 he began the landscape painter's habit of passing at least part of each summer in travel to scenic locales to sketch subjects for later development, and that first of many such excursions was made in the company of Thomas Cole. Durand continued to show a few portraits among many landscapes in Academy annuals through 1844, but thereafter, to his last participation in an annual fifty years later, showed only landscapes.

Durand, with Samuel F. B. Morse, Henry Inman, John Frazee, and Thomas Cummings formed the activist core of artists seeking substantive change in the art establishment of New York, which resolved in the founding of the National Academy of Design in 1826. Always central to activities of the Academy, he was a member of the Council from that body's establishment in December 1826 to 1828, and was again on the Council holding the office of recording secretary from 1832 to 1838. Following a year spent abroad, predominately in Italy, he was returned to the Council for the year 1842–43; in 1844 he was elected vice president, and at the next year's election succeeded Samuel F. B. Morse as the Academy's second president.

In the spring of 1869 Durand left New York for a home and studio he had newly built on the family's land in Jefferson Village; there he continued to paint for another nine years and live for an additional eight. At its first meeting of the season, October 18, 1886, the earliest opportunity following Durand's death, the Council passed a lengthy resolution of respect. At the next annual meeting of the Academicians, May 11, 1887, President Daniel Huntington included in his annual address the formal eulogy:

> The death of the venerable ex-President Asher B. Durand on the 17th of September last, at the age of ninety, is a memorable event in the history of our Institution, as well as of the Arts of our country. In early life he obtained a high reputation as an engraver, and the admiration his prints received from his contemporaries has suffered no diminution as those works have been compared, critically, with the masterpieces of earlier or of recent times. The admirably engraved portaits of Colden; of Dr. Mason; of Washington (for the "Life," by Jared Sparks); of Marshall; of Carroll, Trumbull and many others, maintain their supremacy and take rank with the greatest examples in that department. His principal work, "The Ariadne," from Vanderlyn's famous painting, is still, and must always be, a delight to all who can appreciate beauty and grace of lines; this delicate expression of form; the sweet diffusion of light; the tremendous depth of shadow and that combination of softness and subtlety, with precision and force in the execution, which renders this engraving one of the masterpieces of modern times. Time would fail to give an adequate expression to the long and interesting career of this distinguished artist. For many years his principal works in landscape were objects of attraction in our Exhibitions and are now treasured in collections. It is not generally known that he was the first of our landscape painters who habitually made exact and finished studies from nature in the fields. Our earlier landscape painters were contented to make drawings in pencil, often with written hints descriptive of the color or effects; or at best slight water-color, or tepid drawings as material to work from. Durand was a resolute pioneer in a practice, which has been followed by most of our Artists, and which has contributed so greatly to the preeminent merit of our Landscape Art. For several of his latter years, Durand had ceased to paint, saying that his hand would not obey his wish. His last work was a recollection of a sunset over an Adirondack lake, in which, the gentle radiance of a declining sun, aptly prefigured his own peaceful departure to another world.

ABG and JPH

REFERENCES

Daniel Huntington, *Asher B. Durand. A Memorial Address*, printed for The Century Association, New York, 1887.

John Durand, *The Life and Times of A. B. Durand*, (New York: Charles Scribner's Son, 1894; facsimile reprint New York: Da Capo Press, 1970).

Frederick A. Sweet, "Asher B. Durand," *Art Quarterly* 3 (Spring 1945): 141–60.

David B. Lawall, *Asher B. Durand: His Art and Art Theory in Relation to His Times* 4 vols. (Ann Arbor, MI: University Microfilms, 1966).

Montclair (New Jersey) Art Museum: David B. Lawall, *A. B. Durand, 1796–1886*, 1971.

Hudson River Museum, Yonkers, NY: *Asher B. Durand: An Engraver's and a Framer's Art*, 1983.

THE MORNING OF LIFE, 1840
Inscribed lower left: *A. B. Durand / 1840*
Oil on canvas, 49⅝ × 84⅛
Gift of Mrs. Frederick J. Betts, 1911

THE EVENING OF LIFE, 1840
Inscribed lower left: *A. B. Durand / 1840*
Oil on canvas, 49⅝ × 83⅜
Gift of Mrs. Frederick J. Betts, 1911

This pair of paintings was first exhibited in the Academy annual of 1840 under the titles *Landscape, Composition, Morning* and *Landscape, Composition, Evening*, suggesting Durand, or Frederick J. Betts who commissioned the works, was not as interested in the allegorical nature of his paintings as in stressing their claim to the picturesque landscape tradition of such artists in Claude Lorrain. The critic for the *New-York Mirror* grasped this intention while noting their close affinity with Thomas Cole's *Departure* and *Return* (Corcoran Gallery of Art, Washington, D.C.) which had been exhibited at the Academy in 1838:

> [Durand's] "Morning" and "Evening," lately finished, and now exhibiting at the National Academy, are his greatest works. They abound in many beauties and some faults. In the first place, the idea is too much like Cole's "Departure" and "Return," to be original. He imitated very successfully the coloring of Cole, and tried, though without success, to use his pencil. . . . If Durand devotes his attention to landscape-painting alone, and studies nature more, he will eventually become a first-rate artist in this interesting branch. . . . The large group of trees in the first [*Morning*] are admirable, excepting that they are a little too top-heavy. Those in the second [*Evening*] could not be improved. It was customary with Claude to throw over his foregrounds a dark mass of shadow, and it is this which adds to the beauty of his perspectives.

The critic for the *New-Yorker* noted: "Durand has materially changed his style. . . . He seems to have depended altogether on memory and imagination." And the *Knickerbocker's* reviewer, after calling the two paintings "very fine," but faulting a few details of coloring, concluded, "Mr. Durand recently sailed for Europe, and we are satisfied . . . no one will avail himself more closely of the privilages there offered. . . . He has surprised every one, year after year, by his steadily progressive improvement; and should his life be spared, we may predict that Mr. Cole will sooner encounter him as a rival than any other artist now among us."

In all their iconographic details Durand certainly intended that the *Morning* and *Evening* lead spectators to contemplation of contrast of youth and age, hope and patience, the pagan world of the antique and Christian world of the Middle Ages. Despite the contemporary complaint of imitation of his friend and mentor, Thomas Cole, Durand demonstrates a remarkable degree of independence in that he has made such didacticism subservient to the overall pastoral theme of the idealized composite landscape. At this early stage of his career as a landscapist Durand seems more drawn to the long-standing traditions of such art than the innovations being pursued by his closest colleague.

Durand would certainly have been familiar with Cole's five-painting series *The Course of Empire* of 1836 (New-York Historical Society) and clearly quoted details from it; also Cole was completing his four-canvas series, *The Voyage of Life*, in the Academy's rooms at the same time Durand was painting the *Morning* and *Evening*, with their not dissimilar subtext of passage from youth to old age. Yet the distinction in the two artists' conception of the primary function of their serial compositions is clear when it comes to presenting them to an audience. Cole's two great series require proximity and specific order in their hanging if they are to be properly understood. Durand's *Morning* and *Evening* need not be read as a pair, and, indeed, appear somewhat compositionally awkward when hung side-by-side. From their catalogue numbering in their debut showing at the Academy—where Durand would have been able to dictate their placement—they were not hung immediately adjacent to each other.

REFERENCES

New-Yorker 9 (June 20, 1840): 222.

Knickerbocker 16 (July 1840): 81.

New-York Mirror 18 (July 18, 1840): 30.

David B. Lawall, *Asher B. Durand: A Documentary Catalogue of the Narrative and Landscape Paintings*, (New York: Garland Publishing, Inc., 1978): 30–32.

Montclair (New Jersey) Art Museum: David B. Lawall, *A. B. Durand, 1796–1886*, 1971, 54–55.

Kathie Manthorne, in NAD: *Next to Nature*, 38–41.

ASHER BROWN DURAND

THE MORNING OF LIFE, 1840
Inscribed lower left: *A. B. Durand / 1840*
Oil on canvas, 49⅝ × 84⅛
Gift of Mrs. Frederick J. Betts, 1911

THE EVENING OF LIFE, 1840
Inscribed lower left: *A. B. Durand / 1840*
Oil on canvas, 49⅜ × 83⅜
Gift of Mrs. Frederick J. Betts, 1911

RICHARD CATON WOODVILLE
Baltimore, Maryland 1825–1855 London, England

Woodville probably received his earliest instruction in art from Samuel Smith and Joseph Hewett who gave drawing classes at Saint Mary's College, the Baltimore boys' school he attended. He may also have had contact with Alfred Jacob Miller. In Baltimore he surely would have had the opportunity to see private collections of old master paintings—including Dutch genre subjects—especially in the collection of Robert Gilmor, considered the finest in America at the time. In 1842 he began studying medicine at the University of Maryland, but soon abandoned his studies in favor of pursuing his aspirations to become an artist. Even at this early stage of his career Woodville worked almost exclusively in genre.

His *Scene in a Bar-room* (unlocated) received great praise when shown in the Academy's annual exhibition of 1845, including the best criticism of all, its purchase from the exhibition by a major New York collector. This was the only occasion on which Woodville showed a work at the Academy. The success of this debut undoubtedly contributed to his prominent family's endorsement of his future in art, for it was only a little later that year that, with their permission, he embarked for Europe.

Although he initially planned to pursue his studies in Italy, Woodville abandoned this idea in favor of Düsseldorf in Germany. Upon his arrival he enrolled in the Düsseldorf Academy's antique class. He then continued his studies with private instruction from the portraitist Carl Ferdinand Sohn. During this period Woodville frequently sent his genre paintings to the exhibitions of the American Art-Union in New York. Upon concluding his studies under Sohn in 1851, he departed Düsseldorf for Paris. There, the following year, he completed his last major genre painting, *The Sailor's Wedding* (Walters Art Gallery, Baltimore, Maryland). The remainder of Woodville's short life was divided between Paris and London. He never revisited the United States, yet the majority of his genre scenes were given American contexts and characters, which may have been a canny response to his American base of patronage or reflected genuinely fond memories of the surroundings and experiences of his youth.

Woodville's death was the result of an overdose of morphine.

JPH

REFERENCES
Francis Grubar, *Richard Caton Woodville: An American Artist, 1825–1855* (Ann Arbor, MI: University Microfilms, 1966).

Corcoran Gallery of Art, Washington, D.C.: Francis Grubar, *Richard Caton Woodville: An Early American Genre Painter*, 1967.

WAR NEWS FROM MEXICO [1848]
Oil on canvas, 27×25
Gift of John D. Crimmins, 1897

In the spring of 1849 John G. Boker opened his Düsseldorf Gallery in New York. The exhibition of the paintings by German artists working in that city attracted constant attention and brought about a major interest in artists of the Düsseldorf School, which extended to American artists working in Düsseldorf. When Woodville's *War News from Mexico* was exhibited at the American Art-Union in the same year, its success was enhanced by the popularity of Boker's display. In 1850 the American Art-Union engaged Alfred Jones to do two engravings of the painting: one in small scale for publication in the Art-Union's April 1851 *Bulletin*, the other in large format for distribution to the union's 14,000 members at the end of the same year.

Woodville's scene is set on the porch of a generic American Hotel in an anonymous American city. The eleven people who crowd the shallow stagelike space represent a cross-section of American society. The eagerness with which they await the news of a battle embodies the nationalistic enthusiasm that the annexation of Texas and the subsequent war with Mexico inspired. Although the scene Woodville depicts is thoroughly American, the histrionic poses of the figures, the meticulous attention to detail, and the fine finish of the painting are characteristics of the academic style associated with Düsseldorf, that Americans so much admired.

According to family tradition, the elderly gentleman seated at the right is a posthumous portrait of Woodville's great-uncle and the woman in the window is his friend, Miss Maria Johnson. Much has been written about Woodville's exceptional sensitivity in the presentation of the figures of the Black man and child, who are nonetheless positioned as separated and below the central group.

REFERENCES
Bulletin of the American Art-Union 2 (May 1849): 9–10.
Grubar, 1967.

EDWARD LUDLOW MOONEY
ANA 1839; NA 1840
New York 1813–1887 Upper Red Hook, New York

Mooney enrolled in the Academy school's antique class in 1835; at the close of that year's season he was awarded the first prize, an inscribed gold-washed miniature palette, in the competition for the best original drawing of a single figure. Academy classes were held in the evenings, and during the days Mooney supported himself by working as a sign and ornament painter and by copying portraits by other artists. In about 1837 he entered the studio of Henry Inman. He possibly remained his assistant for the remaining nine years of Inman's life and certainly benefited greatly from the guidance of New York's foremost portraitist.

Mooney first exhibited in an Academy annual in 1838, and continued to be represented in these shows, hardly missing a year through 1874. The Academy exhibitions were virtually the only venue he used to display his work. Of the ninety-two paintings he exhibited in annuals over his working lifetime only two were not conventional portrait likenesses: *Return From a Walk*, presumably a genre subject, shown in 1840; and *Armenian in Old Style of Turkish Costume*, shown in 1849.

From the exhibition of his portrait of "Achmet Ben Aman" in the Academy annual of 1841, Mooney's career as a portraitist advanced steadily. His eulogy entered into Academy minutes took special note of his portraits of the New York mayors ordered for the City Hall collection and of his large-scale portrait of Governor William Seward in the Albany state capital. Mooney executed approximately twenty portraits of faculty for Princeton University, earning him a particular identification with that school. While his career was essentially confined to New York, in its later years he several times passed his winters working in Columbus and Savannah, Georgia. After 1874 he retired to his country home in Upper Red Hook.

In her lifetime his daughter Ella established the Mooney Traveling Scholarship in her father's memory, which around the turn of the century began to afford selected students of the Academy school the opportunity to study abroad for two years. She also gave the Academy Mooney's gold palette award and in her will directed a number of paintings be presented to its collection.

ABG and JPH

REFERENCES
Clara Erskine Clement and Laurence Hutton, *Artists of the Nineteenth Century and Their Works*, 2 vols. rev. ed., 1884 (Saint Louis: North Point, Inc. reprint, 1969), 2:125.

NAD minutes, October 10, 1887.

New York Daily Tribune, 23 July, 1887.

New York Evangelist, 14 August, 1887.

ARMENIAN IN OLD STYLE OF TURKISH COSTUME [1848–49]
Oil on canvas, 42 × 36
Bequest of Ella Mooney in memory of her father, Edward Mooney, 1906

Mooney's reputation was established when his portrait of Ahmad bin Na'aman bin Muhsin bin Abdulla Al-k'abi al Bahraini, emissary of the Iman of Muscat and Zanzibar, was purchased by the New York Common Council for its gallery of images of distinguished visitors to and personages associated with the city. The Iman's ship the *al-Sultanah* appeared in New York harbor on April 30, 1840. While this trade mission was not altogether unexpected by certain Washington officials, no advance notice had been given New York, and such exotically garbed and customed visitors as the Ahmad bin Na'aman, the officers, and crew of the ship caused great excitement. Mooney's portrait (New York City Hall; replica, Essex Institute, Salem, Massachusetts) was inevitably as colorful and exotic as its sitter.

Mooney's practice as a painter seemed nearly limited to commissioned portraits of American men of various substantial social and professional stations. Memories of the aesthetic opportunity of portraying the very different character and costume of an Oriental dignitary could well have combined with a desire to remind his public of his past triumph and caused him to execute a figure piece in exotic trappings and background similar to those of the Iman of Muscat's emissary. *Armenian in Old Style of Turkish Costume*, shown at the Academy in 1849, was likely such a speculative venture; a buyer for such a subject could not have been expected. It also seems likely that the work Mooney showed in Brooklyn nearly two decades later, under the title *An Eastern Courtier*, was the same painting rather than another essay in this specialized genre. By the early years of the twentieth century when Mooney's daughter listed her collection in her will, this painting was being called *Turkish Courtier*, seemingly an elision of the two exhibition titles, and a further suggestion that the 1849 exhibition work is the painting that remained in the artist's and his daughter's possession until its bequest to the Academy.

John Thomas Peele
ANA 1846
Peterborough, England 1822–1897 London, England

Sources are at odds on whether Peele was two or twelve years of age when his parents brought him to the United States. The family lived in Buffalo, New York. Although Peele's only training as an artist seems to have been an opportunity to watch an itinerant portrait painter, he set up his own practice as a portraitist. By 1840 he had moved to New York, for in that year he enrolled in the Academy's antique school and exhibited for the first time in its annual, a *Pastoral Landscape*. He seems to have gone to Albany, New York, within the year to work as a portrait painter, remained in Albany for two years, and then passed several years in London. He could not afford to study there in any regular way; however, he surely must have polished his skills by observation and copying.

Peele was back in New York by the spring of 1845, when he made his second appearance in an Academy annual. He then commenced a career as a specialist in ideal subjects, almost always featuring children, which by their quality as well as charm of subject gained him quick success. In late 1851 or early 1852 he chose to return to England to pursue his career. He was in London to about 1856 and then moved to Liverpool for a stay of two years. He next settled on the Isle of Man, where he remained until about 1866; thereafter he lived in London. He maintained a favorable reputation for his ideal pictures of children and also seems to have returned successfully to portraiture, but, not surprisingly, also as a specialist in children. His works were frequently exhibited at the British Institution, the Royal Academy, and the Society of British Artists; however, he also continued to send his paintings to America, especially to the Academy's annual exhibitions, where his work was last seen in 1885. He last exhibited in London in 1891.

ABG and JPH

REFERENCES

James Dafforne, "The Work of John T. Peele," *The Art Journal* n.s. 2 (1876): 137–40.

Clara Erskine Clement and Laura Hutton, *Artists of the Nineteenth Century and Their Works*, 2 vols., rev. ed. 1884 (Reprint, St. Louis: North Point, 1969), 2: 169–70.

The Pet, 1853
Inscribed lower right: *J. T. Peele* / 1853
Oil on canvas, 36×28
Bequest of James A. Suydam, 1865

Another version of *The Pet* is in the collection of the Parrish Art Museum, Southampton, New York. It is also signed and dated 1853 and is a near duplicate of the Academy's painting, the only significant variations being elements of the background. No doubt has ever been raised that either painting is not by Peele, although which might be termed the replica is impossible—and essentially irrelevant—to know.

Peele's sole contribution to the Academy's 1854 annual exhibition was titled *Girl and Kitten*; whether it was acquired by Suydam from the annual and rechristened by him must remain a matter of speculation. At the Royal Academy's annual spring exhibition of the same year he showed *Girl and Kittens*. It is possible to speculate further that, given Peele's continued interest in both the British and American markets, he had executed two versions of the same composition to allow exhibition and possible sale on both sides of the Atlantic.

FREDERIC EDWIN CHURCH
ANA 1848; NA 1849
Hartford, Connecticut 1826–1900 New York

The son of a wealthy Hartford businessman, Church received early artistic training from Benjamin H. Coe and Alexander H. Emmons, but far more important was the period, 1844–46, that he spent in Catskill, New York, as a student of Thomas Cole, the only pupil Cole ever accepted. Following this apprenticeship with Cole, Church went first to Hartford and then New York, where he took a studio in the Art-Union Building, and registered for the 1846–47 term in the Academy's antique school. Church spent the next several summers studying the landscape of Virginia, New York, New England, and Canada. Recognition came quickly for Church; he sold a number of early paintings to the American Art-Union, and was represented in every Academy annual between 1845 and 1857. Church was one of four Associates elected in 1848 and advanced to Academician the following year. The others, John F. Kensett, Junius B. Stearns, and Edwin D. White, were from eight to sixteen years older than Church, and he remained the youngest Academician until 1859. He served on the Academy Council for the year 1851–52 and was appointed a Visitor to the school for the following year.

Church's life was changed by an 1853 trip made to South America with Cyrus W. Field. Two years later he began exhibiting tropical landscapes, and he continued to produce this type of scene throughout most of his career. He returned to Ecuador in 1857, this time in company with Louis R. Mignot, and it was this experience that resulted in his monumental *Heart of the Andes*, 1859 (Metropolitan Museum of Art, New York). Church advanced his fame by independently presenting his blockbuster pictures such as *Heart of the Andes* as individual exhibitions. Subsequent trips to Labrador and the North Atlantic, in 1859, and Europe and the Middle East, 1867–69, in turn yielded large-scale, crowd-attracting canvases.

Beginning in 1860, the year of his marriage to Ohioan Isabel M. Carnes, Church began spending time on his Hudson, New York, estate, situated just across the river from the home of Thomas Cole, where he had been a student. In the wake of his trip to the Middle East, he started building a lavish, Islamic-inspired home, Olana, atop a great hill on the property. He gradually withdrew from the New York art world, and he became less involved with the Academy. Gerald L. Carr has demonstrated how Church used early Academy annuals to develop his reputation (see Kelly and Carr, 15), yet after his success with the separate exhibition of his works, his

contributions became more sporadic, ending in 1878. That year he was elected vice president of the Academy, but he declined the office. His name had previously been mentioned as a candidate for president, but nothing had ever come of the idea.

In later years rheumatism made it difficult for him to paint, and when not at Olana, he sought relief for his condition in Mexico. Although he never taught in a formal art school, Church sometimes gave instruction and criticism to younger friends such as Jervis McEntee, William J. Stillman, Lockwood de Forest, and Howard R. Butler, all of whom became members of the Academy.

JD

REFERENCES
David C. Huntington, *The Landscapes of Frederic Edwin Church* (New York: Braziller, 1966).

National Collection of Fine Arts, Smithsonian Institution, Washington, D.C.: David C. Huntington, *Frederic Edwin Church*, 1966.

Smithsonian Institution Traveling Exhibition Service, Washington, D.C.: Theodore E. Stebbins, Jr., *Close Observation: Selected Oil Sketches by Frederic E. Church from the Collections of the Cooper-Hewitt Museum*, 1978.

Barbara Novak, *Nature and Culture: American Landscape and Painting, 1825–1875* (New York: Oxford University Press, 1980).

Dallas Museum of Fine Arts: Gerald L. Carr, *Frederic Edwin Church: The Icebergs*, 1980.

Hudson River Museum, Yonkers, NY: Elaine Evans Dee, *To Embrace the Universe: Drawings by Frederic Edwin Church*, 1984.

National Museum of American Art, Smithsonian Institution, Washington, D.C.: Katherine Manthorne, *Creation and Renewal: Views of Cotopaxi by Frederic Edwin Church*, 1985.

Franklin Kelly and Gerald L. Carr, *The Early Landscapes of Frederic Edwin Church, 1845–54* (Fort Worth, TX: Amon Carter Museum, 1987).

SCENE ON THE MAGDALENE, 1854

Inscribed lower left: *F. Church 1854*
Oil on canvas, 28¼×42
Bequest of James A. Suydam, 1865

Scene on the Magdalene was one of four South American works that Church selected to introduce the public to his new tropical subject matter in 1855. When the paintings were exhibited at the Academy that year, their radiant light, balmy atmospheric effects, and lush foliage generated enthusiastic praise from most critics. The reviewer for *The Albion* announced, "Mr. Church has adventured, and with brilliant success, into an entirely new range of subjects. He has recently made extensive travels through the finest regions of Central and Southern America, whose matchless colours and glowing atmosphere are precisely suited to his style."

Studies for *Scene on the Magdalene* were made two years earlier, in May 1853, when Church and his friend Cyrus Field ascended the Magdalena River (in present-day Colombia) by steamer and canoe. In his Spanish diary and letters to relatives (quoted in *Next to Nature*, 108–10), the artist voiced his astonishment at the rich profusion of plant life visible along the shores of the Magdalena. The impact of Church's river voyage can be gauged by the fact that his first tropical easel picture completed after his return to New York was the related *Scenery of the Magdelena River, New Granada, South America* (Corcoran Gallery of Art, Washington, D.C.). Of the several Magdalena views that he produced, however, the closest to the Academy's painting is *Summer in South America* (Vassar College Art Gallery, Poughkeepsie, NY), a small oil study that is the prototype for *Scene on the Magdalene*. In moving from the study to the finished work, Church made several changes, increasing the distance to the hills and mountain, deleting a sailboat and cattle, and further emphasizing the bulbous silhouette of the foliage-encrusted tree at center.

The juxtaposition of snow on the distant mountain peak and steamy jungle undergrowth within the same scene was doubtless appreciated by Church, who was sensitive to the climatic extremes of the region. He stresses the natural elements of weather, greenery, and wildlife, relegating man to the bottom right corner where two natives appear dwarfed and marginalized by the wall of towering trees above.

Most reviews of the 1855 Academy annual discuss the four South American pictures as a group or concentrate on the two larger works Church showed. Several writers, however, made specific mention of *Scene on the Magdalene*, the most extensive appearing in *The Albion*: "In *La Magdalena*, No. 131, you may see the most elaborate and apparently most truthful portraiture of that marvellous [sic] tropical vegetation, which bedecks the riverbanks, although the gigantesque is not so obvious as might have been expected. In it, too, the waters have more transparency than Mr. Church generally obtains even in the most admired of his pictures." Several years after the painting entered the Academy collection, it was included in the Academy's winter exhibition of 1869–70. Critics generally chafed at the practice of showing old paintings by contemporary artists; fifteen years after its execution, *Scene on the Magdalene* was praised in cooler and more historical terms for "all that calculating preraphaelistic minutia of detail" (*New York Tribune*, November 4, 1869). As late as 1880, however, Academy records show that *Scene on the Magdalene* was still considered the gem of the Suydam Collection. An insurance report of that year valued it at $800, twice as much as any other of the sixty-three paintings by American artists in the bequest.

REFERENCES

"Fine Arts, The National Academy of Design," *The Albion* 14 (March 24, 1855): 141.

"Exhibition of the National Academy of Design," *New York Tribune*, May 7, 1855.

"National Academy of Design, Winter Exhibition," *New York Tribune*, November 4, 1869.

David C. Huntington, "Landscapes and Diaries: The South American Trips of F. E. Church," *Brooklyn Museum Annual* 5 (1963–64): 65–98.

Kate Nearpass, in NAD: *Next to Nature*, p. 108–11.

Franklin Kelly, "Frederic Church in the Tropics," *Arts in Virginia* 27 (1987): 16–33.

Information provided by Gerald L. Carr, December 27, 1987.

Franklin Kelly, *Frederic Edwin Church and the National Landscape* (Washington, D.C.: Smithsonian Institution Press, New Directions in American Art Series, 1988), 77–78.

National Gallery of Art, Washington, D.C.: Franklin Kelly, Stephen J. Gould, and James Ryan, *Frederic Edwin Church*, 1989.

SCENE ON THE MAGDALENE,
1854
Inscribed lower left: *F. Church 1854*
Oil on canvas, 28¼×42
Bequest of James A. Suydam, 1865

33

JONATHAN EASTMAN JOHNSON
ANA 1859; NA 1860
Lovell, Maine 1824–1906 New York

Eastman Johnson was raised in Fryeburg and Augusta, Maine. He early demonstrated a marked talent for drawing, but none for the dry goods business in which his father first placed him. Consequently, in about 1840 he was sent for a year to Bufford's lithography shop in Boston to learn that trade. He turned the experience to launching a career as a crayon portraitist, first back in Augusta, and then ranging into Massachusetts and Rhode Island in pursuit of commissions. In the winter of 1844–45 Johnson was in Washington, D.C. with permission to use a Senate committee room in the Capitol as a studio to take the likenesses of distinguished persons living in and visiting the city; the following year he went to Boston on the urging of Henry Wadsworth Longfellow and there set up a studio in the Tremont Temple. Among Johnson's sitters during these years were Dolley Madison, Daniel Webster, John Quincy Adams, Nathaniel Hawthorne, and Ralph Waldo Emerson.

In 1849 Johnson, who had made some tentative tries at working in color, went to study in Düsseldorf, Germany. He first attended the Düsseldorf Royal Academy and then in early 1851 entered the studio of Emanuel Leutze. At the end of that year he went to live in The Hague, the Netherlands, where he remained, with some excursions around northern Europe, studying the Dutch old masters and painting portraits, into 1855. He then went to Paris, where he took up study with Thomas Couture; however, the death of his mother prompted his return to America in the autumn of 1855. The next two and a half years Johnson passed chiefly in Washington, D.C., and in Cincinnati, Ohio. In the spring of 1858 he opened a studio in New York.

Johnson had sent paintings from Washington to the Academy annual exhibitions of 1856 and 1857; these were subjects related to his European experience. He was not represented in 1858; but in the annual of 1859, along with three crayon drawings, a painting belonging to William W. Corcoran of Washington, and *The Sketch Book*, he showed the painting that established his fame: *Negro Life at the South* (New-York Historical Society), which came to be known as *The Old Kentucky Home*. This large scene, based on observations of slave quarters in Washington's Georgetown section, brought him recognition as the major painter of American genre of the day. Nevertheless, he maintained and indeed enhanced his reputation as a consummate painter of both individual and group portraits for the rest of his long career.

In the 1860s, in addition to a number of Civil War–related subjects, Johnson was at work on a large, complex scene of maple sugaring in Fryeburg, that resulted in a number of studies, but no fully resolved version. In 1871 he acquired property on Nantucket Island, where he summered for the rest of his life. Nantucket was the source of an extended series of studies of cranberry harvesting done in the latter half of the 1870s; and in the 1880s a number of images of the elders of Nantucket singly and in groups conversing around a potbellied stove in a shop interior. In the 1880s, however, Johnson worked less in genre subjects and increasingly in portraiture.

In addition to sustaining active participation in Academy annual exhibitions throughout the second half of the nineteenth century, Johnson was elected to the Council from 1866 to 1870, vice-president 1874 to 1876, and again to Council, 1890 to 1893. He was appointed a Visitor to the Academy school for the seasons of 1867–68 and 1868–69. He was also a member of the Society of American Artists and a trustee of the Metropolitan Museum of Art.

When he died in 1906, the Academy's formal memorial to him recalled:

> Eastman Johnson, entering our ranks about the time of the Civil War, brought to the Academy a solid accomplishment as a draftsman and painter, the fruit of a long sojourn as a Student in Holland. For many years in the Academy Exhibitions Johnson's compositions representing phases of American life were examples to our painters and when in 1877 the now historic Society of American Artists was formed the mature painter, without severing his loyalty to the Academy, gave hearty welcome to the newer outlook of the younger men.
>
> To the end of his career Johnson maintained his enthusiasm for good painting rendered significant by his own practice to which we owe in his later years a series of portraits viril in characterization and color.

DBD

REFERENCES

NAD minutes, May 13, 1874; June 4, 1906.

"In Memoriam: Eastman Johnson," *Academy Notes* (Albright Art Gallery, Buffalo, NY) 2 (June 1906): 13–14.

William Walton, "Eastman Johnson, Painter," *Scribner's Magazine* 40 (August 1906): 263–74.

Brooklyn (New York) Museum: John I. H. Baur, *An American Genre Painter: Eastman Johnson 1824–1906*, 1940.

Whitney Museum of American Art, New York: Patricia Hills, *Eastman Johnson*, 1972.

Patricia Hills, *The Genre Painting of Eastman Johnson: The Sources and Development of His Style and Themes* (Ann Arbor, MI: University Microfilms, 1973).

THE ART LOVER, n.d.
Oil on canvas, 12⅜ × 15½
Bequest of James A. Suydam, 1865

There exists a highly finished pencil drawing titled *The Picture Book* (New York art market, 1987), identical in composition, and nearly identical in dimensions, to this painting. It is signed and dated June 15, 1855, and therefore would have been executed in Europe, probably in The Hague, a location further borne out by the wooden shoes worn by the child. The character of the drawing, combined with its precise signature and dating, suggest Johnson considered it a finished work in its own right, not a study preliminary to some other work. The painting would then be a somewhat later work in which Johnson turned to his own drawing for a source. (Another drawing of the same composition, this one undated and done in charcoal, was in the New York market in 1972.)

The painting may be the work shown at the Academy's 1859 annual exhibition under the title *The Sketch Book*. If so, then it would be likely James Suydam purchased it from that exhibition.

SANFORD R. GIFFORD, n.d.

Inscribed center left: *E. J.*
Oil on canvas, 26 ½ × 22 ¼
Gift of Mrs. Eastman Johnson, 1907

Johnson was a close friend of Sanford Gifford and painted at least two other portraits of him, both of which show him at about the same age. One was in Gifford's widow's possession and eventually passed into the collection of the Metropolitan Museum of Art, New York; the other is in the collection of the Pennsylvania Academy of the Fine Arts, Philadelphia. The Metropolitan Museum's portrait, which is dated 1880, is especially close to the Academy's portrait in pose and manner of execution. Gifford was fifty-seven years of age at his death in August 1880. Ila Weiss has suggested that both the Metropolitan's and the Pennsylvania Academy's portraits were executed after his death, from memory with the assistance of studies presumably made in Gifford's lifetime, surely including this portrait of his friend retained by Johnson.

REFERENCES

Natalie Spassky, et al., *American Paintings in the Metropolitan Museum of Art. Volume II: A Catalogue of Works By Artists Born between 1816 and 1845* (Princeton, NJ: Princeton University Press, 1985), 232–33.

Ila Weiss, *Poetic Landscape: The Art and Experience of Sanford R. Gifford* (Newark: University of Delaware Press; London and Toronto: Associated University Presses, 1987), 163, 167.

John Frederick Kensett
ANA 1848; NA 1849
Cheshire, Connecticut 1816–1872 New York

Kensett's father, Thomas, an engraver, emigrated to America from England in about 1800. The son, at the age of twelve, entered the engraving shop run by his father and uncle, Alfred Daggett, in New Haven, Connecticut. Throughout the 1830s he pursued his career as an engraver, working in Albany and New York as well as New Haven. He had higher ambitions, however: to be a painter of landscapes and as such he made his debut in the Academy annual exhibition of 1838. Two years later, in company with fellow engraver-painters, Asher B. Durand, John W. Casilear, and Thomas P. Rossiter, he went to Europe.

For two years from his arrival in the summer of 1840, Kensett was based in Paris, first sharing quarters with Rossiter and later with Benjamin Champney. He was fully occupied in studying from the old masters in the Louvre, painting scenes of the the countryside near the city, and working at engraving as a means of supporting himself. The next two years he was in London, where he maintained much the same regimen. When he returned to the Continent in June 1845, the business that had held him in England, collection of a modest inheritance, had relieved him from further need to pursue engraving work. After a summer touring Germany and Switzerland, Kensett settled in Rome, where he remained for another two years. He passed the summer of 1847 in Florence and Venice, and then, after final visits to Paris and London, he returned to America, arriving in New York just at the close of the year.

During this extended stay abroad Kensett regularly sent his work back to New York for exhibition and sale. He was well represented in the Academy annuals of 1845 and 1847; the American Art-Union acquired eight of his paintings in 1846. He had consequently attained some standing in the artistic community by the time he established his studio in the New York University Building in 1848, and that position rapidly grew. The works he showed in the Academy annual of that year attracted great popular and critical admiration and placed him securely in the first ranks of American landscape painters. The paintings that continued to result from his annual summer sketching trips to the Catskill and Adirondack mountain regions, Niagara Falls, and Lake George in New York; the White Mountains in New Hampshire; Narragansett Bay and Newport in Rhode Island (and occasional excursions to the West, in the areas of the Missouri and Mississippi Rivers) sustained and expanded that reputation throughout his life.

Kensett was also singularly loved and respected for his personal qualities: his support of his fellow artists, general sweetness of nature, and energy and skill in assuming a public role in the arts. In 1859 he was appointed, with Henry Kirke Brown and James R. Lambdin, to the presidential advisory commission on the decoration of the Capitol building. At about the same time he was active in the founding of the Artists' Fund Society. He chaired the Art Committee of the New York Sanitary Fair, held in 1865 to raise funds for the medical needs of the Union Army; and in 1870 he was among the organizers of the Metropolitan Museum of Art. At the Academy Kensett served on the Council 1850–51, was a Visitor to the school for the 1852–53 season, was returned to the Council for terms 1858–59, 1861–62, and from 1863 to 1866. During the latter period he was among the most active Academicians in raising the money to erect the Academy's building at Twenty-third Street and Fourth Avenue, which opened in April 1865.

Kensett did not take students in a formal sense, but his characteristic generosity of spirit caused him to be helpful to a number of rising landscapists whose work shared his particular affinity for expansive, but undramatized, light-filled views.

The essential cause of Kensett's untimely death was characteristic of his life. His unsuccessful attempt to save the artist Vincent Colyer's wife from drowning in the waters of Long Island Sound, off Darien, Connecticut, led to pneumonia, and he died from heart failure shortly thereafter.

The unusual emotionalism of the Academy's eulogy reflected the shock of the loss:

> Resolved that on the death of J. F. Kensett, N. A. we the Academicians, both as artists and as friends, have suffered one of the severest wounds yet inflicted on us by the Scythe of Time, which has cut off from our body one of the most earnest and eminent of us Academicians, from the profession one of our most brilliant ornaments, and from Society at large a singularly amiable and acccomplished gentleman.
>
> Resolved that we hold in the highest admiration, and will endeavor to emulate the disinterested zeal, stopping at no personal sacrifice, with which he labored for the welfare of the Academy and other institutions.
>
> Resolved that we shall always remember with the kindest regard, his affection and self-sacrificing devotion to his brother artists, his gentle and loving heart, his unswerving integrity, and the many virtues of his noble character.

JPH

REFERENCES

Henry T. Tuckerman, *Book of the Artists. American Artist Life* (New York: G. P. Putnam & Son, 1867), 510–14.

NAD minutes, December 16, 1872.

American Federation of Arts, New York: John K. Howat, *John Frederick Kensett 1816–1872*, 1968.

Worcester (Massachusetts) Art Museum: John Paul Driscoll and John K. Howat, *John Frederick Kensett: An American Master*, 1985.

The Bash-Bish, 1855
Inscribed lower right: *JFK 55*
Oil on canvas, 36 × 29
Bequest of James A. Suydam, 1865

During the nineteenth century Bash-Bish Falls near South Egremont, Massachusettts, was considered one of the most beautiful cascades in the country and was a major attraction for both tourists and artists. Kensett returned to South Egremont frequently during his career and between 1852 and 1860 he painted the falls at least five times. The Academy's version can be most closely associated with another view executed in the same year (Museum of Fine Arts, Boston).

REFERENCES

Sally G. Shafto, in NAD: *Next to Nature*, 121–23.

Carol Troyen, in Metropolitan Museum of Art, New York: *American Paradise: The World of the Hudson River School*, 1987, 151–53.

Sanford Robinson Gifford

ANA 1850; NA 1854
Greenfield, New York 1823–1880 New York

The son of a well-to-do owner of an iron works, Sanford Gifford grew up in Hudson, New York, near the home of Thomas Cole. After attending the Hudson Academy he studied at Brown University, Providence, Rhode Island, for two years, 1842–44. Determined to become an artist, he left college for New York, where he took lessons in portrait painting from John Rubens Smith, was enrolled in the Academy's antique and life classes from 1846 into 1849, and studied anatomy at the Crosby Street Medical College, New York. Time spent in the Catskill Mountains of New York, however, convinced the young artist to abandon figure painting and take up the study of landscape. Regular summer hikes in the mountains of the Northeast provided Gifford with his subjects, and he was soon selling works. His first appearance in an Academy annual exhibition was in 1847; and he would show in the annuals every year excepting 1869 and 1875 through the year of his death.

Gifford left for Europe in 1855, spending two years in Britain, Northern Europe, Switzerland, and Italy. During his trip he met John Ruskin, Charles R. Leslie, and Jean-François Millet and spent time with Albert Bierstadt and Worthington Whittredge. He was greatly impressed by the tonal unity of the Barbizon landscape school; thereafter, he became increasingly sensitive to atmospheric effects. Upon his return to New York, Gifford moved into studio number 19 in the Tenth Street Building, which he occupied for the rest of his life. His routine of summer fishing and sketching trips and winter studio work was broken only by the Civil War, in which he served in the Seventh Regiment, New York State National Guard, from 1861 to 1864. During the war he was able to paint several military scenes, a genre he abandoned soon after.

The artist's second trip abroad occurred in 1868–69; he visited Europe, Egypt, Palestine, Turkey, and Greece. While there, he spent time with Jervis McEntee, Frederic E. Church, and George Yewell. On this journey he also had an assignment from the Academy to purchase photographs of drawings, paintings, and statues by the old masters for the school with 1,000 French francs entrusted to him. The year after his return, Gifford was traveling again—to Colorado and Wyoming with Whittredge, John F. Kensett, and the explorer Ferdinand V. Hayden. He returned to the West in 1874, visiting San Francisco and journeying as far north as Alaska.

In 1875 Gifford's genial relationship with the Academy and most of its members was temporarily marred by his resignation in protest of a policy that excluded one of his paintings from the annual exhibition. The painting in question had already received a semiprivate viewing at a New York club, and thus—according to strict interpretation of the Academy constitution which forbade works previously seen in New York from being accepted into its exhibitions—was ineligible for display. The dispute seems to have been based on principle rather than animosity, for exactly one week after he resigned, the ever-generous Gifford contributed five hundred dollars to the Academy's Mortgage Fund. At the annual meeting held within a month of the exhibition opening, he was publically asked by the Academicians to withdraw his resignation, which he apparently did.

Gifford married late in life in 1877. Three years later he became ill while on a trip to Lake Superior and was brought back to New York, where he died. His death was seen as a great tragedy for American art. He was memorialized by the publication of a series of addresses given at the Century Association, the organization of a large retrospective exhibition at the Metropolitan Museum of Art, and the compilation of an exhaustive catalogue raisonné.

JD

References

AAA, Sanford Robinson Gifford "Journal," D21.

NAD minutes, March 27, 1869; April 26, 1875.

University Art Museum, University of Texas at Austin: Nicolai Cikovsky, *Sanford Robinson Gifford*, 1970.

Ila Weiss, *Sanford Robinson Gifford (1823–1880)* (New York: Garland Press, 1977).

Alexander Gallery, New York: Ila Weiss, *Sanford R. Gifford*, 1986.

Ila Weiss, *Poetic Landscape: The Art and Experience of Sanford R. Gifford* (Newark: University of Delaware Press; London and Toronto: Associated University Presses, 1987).

Mount Mansfield, Vermont, 1859

Inscribed lower left: *S. R. Gifford 1859*
Oil on canvas, 10½ × 20
Bequest of James A. Suydam, 1865

This small landscape is from a series of up to twenty paintings inspired by Gifford's trip in August 1858 to Mount Mansfield, a popular tourist site in the Green Mountains of Vermont. In particular, it occupies a place in the smaller group of studies leading to his greatest depiction of the peak, *Mansfield Mountain*, 1859 (private collection), which he exhibited at the Academy annual of 1859. It shares compositional and stylistic features with much of Gifford's work of the period: a brightly lit, laterally sloping rock promontory in the foreground distinctively lacking the rose-tempered haze of the middle- and backgrounds, a low basin of calm water, a single rearing distant peak, and a structure of overlapping parallel planes unified by a glistening atmospheric veil.

Ila Weiss has discussed the two Indians who appear in the foreground, noting that they are Gifford's first depiction of

Native Americans in his painted work (*Sanford Robinson Gifford*, 179). Attention is focused on the tiny figures through the red cloak at left, which intensifies and draws to a point the pervasive orange-pink tonality of the canvas. With their backs to the viewer, they gaze across the misty valley to the vague forms of Mount Mansfield. Weiss has examined this repeated progression in Gifford's work from a clear, hard-edged foreground to an ethereal, elevated, slightly blurred distance, likening it to a transcendental passage into a vaporous future, more poetic and indeterminate than the present. While permitted this suggestive vision, Gifford's viewers usually remain physically rooted on the firm and stable edge of the material world.

REFERENCES

Cikovsky, 24.

Ila Weiss, *Sanford Robinson Gifford*, (1823–1880) (New York: Garland Press, 1977), 178-80, 420–21.

Robert Hull Fleming Museum, University of Vermont, Burlington: William C. Lipke, "Changing Images of the Vermont Landscape," in *Vermont Landscape Images 1776–1976*, 1976, 38.

Weiss, *Sanford R. Gifford*.

Kevin Avery, in NAD: *Next to Nature*, 44–45.

Weiss, *Poetic Landscape*, 209–10.

CHARLES LORING ELLIOTT
ANA 1845; NA 1846
Scipio, New York 1812–1868 Albany, New York

From youth Elliott displayed pronounced ambitions to become an artist. His father, an architect, initially sought to dampen his enthusiasm. When the family moved to Syracuse, New York, in 1827, he was placed as a clerk in a local store, then sent to a private school, and finally taken into his father's office. None of these alternatives deflected his artistic desires, and in 1829 Elliott was allowed by his father to go to New York to seek formal training. He arrived with a letter of introduction to John Trumbull and seems to have passed a month or two as Trumbull's student, but as Trumbull was consistently discouraging, he began working in the studio of John Quidor. Elliott remained in Quidor's studio for a brief six months before deciding to return to the Syracuse area and commence a career as a portraitist.

Elliott's practice and reputation grew slowly. He found much patronage in the village of Skaneateles, just west of Syracuse, where he also executed several landscape paintings. In 1833 he was commissioned to paint the faculty of Hamilton College in Clinton, New York, and there met and encouraged a Hamilton student, Daniel Huntington. He first exhibited in an Academy annual exhibition in 1836; in 1839 he showed a portrait and a landscape at the Academy, and later that year made the move back to New York. Among his four works in the annual of 1840 were two portraits of members of the Vanderbilt family. Elliott was not represented in the succeeding three annual exhibitions, but in 1844 he was represented by five portraits, including a full length of William H. Seward. Throughout the remaining twenty-four years of his life Elliott's portraits—in quantity—were seen in every annual excepting those of 1861 and 1867.

Shortly before his death in 1846, Henry Inman was reported to have said of Elliott: "When I am gone that young man will take my place. He has the true idea of portrait painting. If it were possible for me to live my life over again, in some respects I would change my style." Whether that prediction from New York's preeminent portraitist of the 1830s and '40s was apocryphal or not, it proved true. Elliott quickly became the leading portraitist working in New York and held that position until his death. He spent the majority of his remaining years residing in the city, but commissions allowed him to travel extensively in the eastern United States. He painted many of the United States's most prominent personalities, including James Fenimore Cooper, Washington Irving, and presidents Andrew Johnson and Ulysses S. Grant.

Elliott was apparently as widely loved and admired for his sweetness of nature, his geniality and kindness, as he was respected for the excellence of his artistic performance. Oddly, he was also well known for his fondness for drink, which seems only to have been conquered by his taking the pledge the year before his death. Perhaps the only fully reported instance of this abberant aspect of his life occurred at the Academy. In mid-afternoon, April 12, 1860, Elliott appeared in the galleries of the annual exhibition "in a drunken intoxicated condition, acting in a disorderly manner and making use of abusive and improper language in the presence of ladies" and proceeded to try to cut one of his own works from its frame in complaint of its hanging position. Police were summoned to assist in subduing and removing him from the premises. The Academy brought suit against him, but eventually an apology was made and the suit dropped. Elliott had served on the Council from 1847 to 1848 and from 1852 to 1854; he again was elected to a year's term on the Academy's governing body in 1866.

Elliott's death, August 25, 1868, brought forth an exceptional public response: long articles reviewing his life and accomplishments appeared in the press; a call was made to erect a monument to him in Central Park. He had died at a home lately purchased in Albany. The body was brought to New York, escorted by Erastus Dow Palmer, Charles Calverley, Samuel P. Avery, and a number of other friends and distinguished subjects of his portraits, and taken to the Academy. There it lay in state for admirers to pay respects until the funeral rites arranged by the Academy and burial in Brooklyn's Greenwood Cemetery. A retrospective exhibition of thirty-six of Elliott's paintings was presented by the Academy within its winter exhibition of 1868–69, and at the Academy annual meeting of May 12, 1869, he was eulogized:

> For Elliott we must all deeply lament. It is sad to remember that we shall no more grasp his cordial hand or hear the mellow tones of his voice ever ready for a kindly greeting, or meet the frank and manly glance of that glowing eye: an eye and a brow which told clearly of a strong intellect, a generous temper, and a warm heart. In him were marvellously blended a man's vigour, a woman's tenderness, and the gaiety and freshness of a child. He has passed away, but his name will be forever associated with the brilliant lifelike portraits which have so often graced our walls.
>
> JPH

REFERENCES

"Art and Artist of America, Charles Loring Elliott," Graham's Magazine 44 (June 1854): 564–68.

NAD minutes, April 16, April 20, October 29, 1860; October 12, 1868; November 16, 1868; May 12, 1869.

Henry T. Tuckerman, Book of the Artists. American Artist Life (New York: G. P. Putnam & Son, 1867), 300–305.

T[homas] B. Thorpe, Reminiscences of Charles L. Elliott, Artist (pamphlet reprint of articles in New York Evening Post, September 30, and October 1, 1868).

C. E. L[ester], "Charles Loring Elliott," Harper's New Monthly Magazine 38 (December 1868): 42–50.

Theodore Bolton, "Charles Loring Elliott: An Account of his Life and Work," Art Quarterly 5 (Winter 1942): 59–84.

Theodore Bolton, "A Catalogue of the Portraits Painted by Charles Loring Elliott," Art Quarterly 5 (Winter 1942): 85–96.

ROBERT RAIT, 1860
Inscribed lower right: Elliott 1860
Oil on canvas, 40×30
Gift of Francis Dashwood, 1894

The date of Rait's birth in Edinburgh, Scotland, is not known. He emigrated to the United States in 1833, settling in New York, and immediately opened one of the city's first jewelry stores, which he maintained until his retirement in 1856. He was well known in the New York business community for his geniality. Presumably he was also quite successful in his business, as judging from this portrait he must have been able to afford to give up active engagement in business in middle age. Rait died in 1870 while on a visit to Britain.

GEORGE INNESS
ANA 1853; NA 1868
Newburgh, New York 1825–1894 Bridge-of-Allan, Scotland

Inness's family moved to New Jersey when he was a boy. His long, peripatetic, and prolific career began with studies under the itinerant artist John Jesse Barker, a year working in New York in the shop of a map engraver, and a brief period of study under the French emigré painter Regis F. Gignoux. By 1846, when Inness registered in the Academy school, his name could be annotated "landscape painter," an indication that he already had attained professional status. Indeed, he had exhibited a number of landscape compositions in Academy annuals for the previous three years.

Inness made his first trip to Europe in 1851, passing a year in Italy, but it was his second, taken in 1853, again for about a year, that had a lasting impact on his art. On this visit he was predominantly in France. His landscapes thereafter took on attributes of the French artists working in and around Barbizon whose work Inness had experienced first-hand. Perhaps most striking of the changes in Inness's art, accountable to his study of France's progressive painters was the use of a lighter, freer brushstroke that spoke more of atmosphere than of form. This vigorous, expressive use of paint supported his intention in representing nature to communicate feelings and sentiments from mind and heart, rather than specific, realistic detail.

By now married and with children, Inness returned from France and settled in Brooklyn, New York. Here he enjoyed the patronage, as well as the acquaintance, of Henry Ward Beecher. Always plagued by delicate health and an acutely sensitive, nervous temperament, his state of health and mind dictated removal to the calm of Medfield, Massachusetts, a suburb of Boston, in 1860.

He moved his family again in 1864, this time to Eagleswood, near Perth Amboy, New Jersey, the site of a former Utopian colony. From childhood Inness was always much preoccupied with metaphysics, philosophy, and theoretic premises of religion, and brought his intense religious convictions to his painting of landscape. William Page also took up residence at Eagleswood, and the force of this senior, distinguished artist's intellect had great influence over Inness. It was Page who introduced him to the Swedenborgian faith — to which he was a committed convert by the time he left Eagleswood in 1867. Inness was especially receptive to Swedenborgianism's tenet that all material objects have a spiritual significance and correspondence, both in form and color.

Inness returned to Europe in 1870, settling in Rome for five years. On coming back to America he went again to live in Medfield and set up a studio in Boston; a few years later he returned to New York, until in 1878, he finally came to rest in Montclair, New Jersey. His son lived there also, and the house occupied by his daughter and son-in-law, the sculptor Jonathan Hartley, adjoined his. Although he attained some measure of peace and contentment in these years, his physical health remained a problem, and his continued travels to every part of North America, from Niagara Falls to Florida, from the Yosemite Valley to Mexico City, had much to do with seeking respite in beneficial climates.

Thomas B. Clarke began to represent and advise Inness in the the later 1870s, and partly from this assistance his work began to enjoy broad acceptance and admiration and the accompanying material rewards. In 1877 he was among the founders of the Society of American Artists. A younger generation of artists and, most certainly, prevailing taste finally had caught up with his vision of landscape as a vehicle of emotional expression.

Despite long absences from New York, Inness had remained a consistent exhibitor in Academy annuals and otherwise kept strong ties with the Academy. This fact is no better proved than that the venerated landscapist's funeral was held in the Academy on August 23, 1894. The appropriateness of these proceeding was remarked upon in the Academy minutes, which also eulogized Inness's "intense individuality, manifested in his positive utterances, his enthusiasm, and devotion to his work."

The Inness Gold Medal for landscape painting, instituted by the artist's son, George Inness, Jr., was awarded in Academy annual exhibitions from 1901 through 1918.

DBD

REFERENCES

NAD minutes, May 8, 1895.

Alfred Trumble, *George Inness, N. A.: A Memorial of the Student, the Artist, and the Man* (New York: "The Collector," 1895).

Nicolai Cikovsky, Jr., *The Life and Work of George Inness* (New York and London: Garland Publishing, Inc, 1977).

LeRoy Ireland, *The Works of George Inness: An Illustrated Catalogue Raisonné* (Austin and London: University of Texas Press, 1965).

Oakland Museum Art Department: Marjorie Dakin Arkelian and George W. Neubert, *George Inness Landscapes: His Signature Years, 1884–1894*, 1979.

Los Angeles County Museum of Art: Nicolai Cikovsky, Jr. and Michael Quick, *George Inness*, 1985.

LANDSCAPE, 1860
Inscribed lower right: G. *Inness* 1860
Oil on paper, mounted on panel, 16¼ × 24
NA diploma presentation, May 3, 1869

This work was executed while Inness and his family were living in Medfield, and the scene shown, although not in any way topical, might have been inspired by the landscape of that area. Whatever the case, *Landscape* shows the influence of the French Barbizon school on the young Inness who, just at this time, was moving away from the clarity and detail of his earlier Hudson River School aesthetic.

REFERENCES

AAA, LeRoy Ireland Papers, "Owners of Paintings by George Inness," 993, fr. 592.

Ireland, 46.

Kevin Avery, in NAD: *Next to Nature*, 77–78.

SAMUEL COLMAN

ANA 1854; NA 1862
Portland, Maine 1832–1920 New York

While still a boy, Colman moved to New York where his father became a publisher and seller of books and prints. Young Colman thus grew up on familiar terms with the artists who frequented the family shop on Broadway. The aesthetic atmosphere seems to have affected his sister as well: she married painter Aaron Draper Shattuck, long a close friend of Colman.

Few facts are known about Colman's education; however, tradition has the teenager studying with Asher B. Durand around 1850. In 1851, his first work was accepted at an Academy annual. Years later in 1859, when already an Associate and established as a rising young landscape painter, Colman registered for the Academy school's life class.

Colman went abroad in 1860, visiting France, Spain, and Morocco. He was struck by the Moorish landscapes in the south and by the old master paintings he saw in Paris and elsewhere. He retained an interest in these two subjects, as demonstrated by his continued exploitation of North African scenes and the 1870 entries in the Academy Library Register that show Colman signing out books by Leonardo da Vinci and Sir Joshua Reynolds.

Returning to the United States in 1862, Colman became active in the New York art world. In 1866 he helped found the American Society of Painters in Water Colors and served as its first president. The following year he experimented with etching, a medium that, like watercolor, would become more interesting to him in later years. At the Academy he served two years on the Council, 1866–68. He was again a member of the Council for the year 1876–77 just prior to participating in founding the rival Society of American Artists, a group composed predominately of younger, European-trained painters. He also joined the New York Etching Club at this time.

During these years much of Colman's time was devoted to travel. His first trip to the American West may have occured in 1870. Subsequent visits took place in the 1880s and, for long periods of time, around the turn of the century. A second, four-year trip to Europe and North Africa began in 1871. The many sketches Colman made in Egypt, Algeria, and Morocco no doubt provided models for his exotic decorative designs after his return to the United States. By 1878 he was an associate of Louis Comfort Tiffany; Colman's own Newport, Rhode Island, house, designed by McKim, Mead, and White in the early 1880s, served as a showcase of his ideas for interior decoration. He also developed a taste for Oriental art, which along with Barbizon painting, he collected and displayed in his home.

Colman's other interests began to leave little time for painting, and in 1882 he resigned from the Academy, citing his inability to exhibit (Colman to Dielman, NAD archives). His resignation was apparently not accepted. He did continue to paint in later years, frequently in watercolor. After a ten-year absence from Academy annual exhibitions, his paintings were again shown in 1892, 1895, and 1896.

In 1902 he sold his large Oriental collection—there were over 1,200 lots—at auction. He had periodically conducted auctions of his work throughout his career; late in life, he seems to have been anxious to dispose of his collection by making gifts to favorite institutions. In 1903 the Academy received a gift of books, travel photographs, and prints, which included a suite of Mary Cassatt drypoints. Fourteen years later Colman gave the art museum in Portland, Maine, the city of his birth, twenty-seven of his own sketches. Colman's last major expansion of his capacities was the writing and publishing of two books on art theory: *Nature's Harmonic Unity* was issued in 1912, and *Proportional Form* appeared just before his death.

JD

REFERENCES

NAD archives, Samuel Colman to Frederick Dielman, March 15, 1882.

Henry T. Tuckerman, *Book of the Artists. American Artist Life* (New York: G. P. Putnam & Sons, 1867), 559–60.

"Paintings by Samuel Colman," Critic 22 (n.s. 19) (1 April 1893): 208.

Nancy Dustin Wall Moure, "Five Eastern Artists Out West," *American Art Journal* 5 (November 1973): 15–37.

Wayne Craven, "Samuel Colman (1832–1920): Rediscovered Painter of Far-Away Places," *American Art Journal* 8 (May 1976): 16–37.

Barridoff Galleries, Portland, MN: *Samuel Colman: East and West from Portland*, 1981.

Kennedy Galleries, New York: *The Romantic Landscapes of Samuel Colman*, 1983.

THE GENESEE VALLEY, NEW YORK [1862–63]

Inscribed lower right: *S. Colman*
Oil on canvas, 15 × 24
NA diploma presentation, February 9, 1863

The scenery of New York's Genesee Valley provided Colman with subject matter for a long series of sketches and finished oil paintings. Following the appearance of the present work in the 1865 Academy annual, Colman exhibited two other Genesee scenes in annuals of 1866 and 1880. In addition, his auction sales of 1864, 1872, and 1893 each contained several Genesee studies.

The Genesee Valley, New York was likely painted shortly after Colman returned from Europe in 1862, when his work was growing increasingly delicate and atmospheric. It was this aspect of his landscapes, in fact, that most critics emphasized. Kevin Avery has discussed Colman's debt to George Inness in this picture, and indeed its intimate, pastoral qualities and summary execution have much to do with Inness's Barbizon-inspired work.

Colman's other contribution to the 1865 annual was the large *Hill of the Alhambra, Granada* (Metropolitan Museum of Art, New York), and although most press notices concentrated on this more spectacular work, the reviewer of the *New York Times* was captivated by the Academy's smaller work:

A delicious landscape is contributed by Mr. SAMUEL COLMAN, N.A. It is . . . so slumbrous and unpretending that one might pass it without notice. . . . The perspective is not remarkable, nor can much be said for the atmosphere. The charm of the work is found in its perfect repose, and in the depth and steady swell of the river. Moving as the latter does in leaden shadow, the pearly translucent depths are singularly truthful. There is good work in the trees, and the grassy slope to the water is daintily painted. No one knows better than Mr. COLEMAN [sic] how to stain the earth with a tender growth of grass. He is apt, indeed, to carry this European characteristic to excess, but in the present work it is refreshing, effective, and only sufficient.

REFERENCES

"National Academy of Design, North Room," *New York Times*, 29 May 1865.

Tuckerman, 560.

James W. Lane, "The Heritage of the National Academy," *Art News* 40 (January 15–31, 1942): 15.

Memorial Art Gallery, Rochester, NY: Howard S. Merritt, *The Genesee Country*, 1976, 89.

Kevin Avery, in NAD: *Next to Nature*, 67–69.

JOHN QUINCY ADAMS WARD
ANA 1862; NA 1863; PNAD 1873–1874
Urbana, Ohio 1830–1910 New York

Although raised in a rural setting where opportunities to be introduced to the sculptural arts were rare, Ward showed an early interest in plastic expression and was encouraged to give it vent in the workshop of a local potter. At the age of nineteen he went to Brooklyn, New York, where he was apprenticed to the sculptor Henry Kirke Brown. He remained in Brown's employ until 1856. The most important of Brown's projects on which Ward worked during these years was the equestrian statue of George Washington for Union Square, New York. Ward's first major independent work was *The Indian Hunter*, designed about 1857. Its showing in the Academy annual exhibition of 1862 probably contributed to Ward's election to Associate that spring.

Ward's career was soon assured. During the 1860s he executed portrait busts and several monumental works including *The Seventh Regiment Memorial* in New York's Central Park. The 1870s opened with a commission for a statue of Shakespeare, also in Central Park, and closed with the unveiling of the equestrian figure of Major General Thomas in Washington, D.C.

In the same period Ward was becoming increasingly involved in the art organizations of New York, especially the Academy. In 1865 he was hired by the Academy to supervise the repair of its plaster casts and busts and to make copies of the classical casts where appropriate. He was appointed a Visitor to the Academy school for the 1867–68 season. In 1870 and 1871 he was elected vice-president of the Academy and continued to serve on its Council the next year; in 1873 he was elected president, the first sculptor to hold the post. His generosity to the Academy was manifest on several occasions. Besides making several monetary donations over the years, he acquired plaster casts for the use of Academy students on his trips to Europe in 1872 and 1887; in the latter year, Academy minutes record his gift of ten plasters. In 1909 his donation of seventeen small bronze figures of nudes to be used for anatomical study was noted.

By the late 1870s Ward's artistic talents were in great demand and he was usually the first choice for the execution of monumental sculpture. Among his most well-known works of the 1880s and 1890s are the statue of George Washington for Federal Hall, New York; *James Garfield Memorial*, the Mall, Washington; *Horace Greeley*, City Hall Park, New York; and *Henry Ward Beecher*, Cadman Plaza, Brooklyn. Ward had by now fully earned the title "Dean of American Sculptors" and, as Lewis Sharp has pointed out, his productivity continued unabated almost until his death.

DBD

REFERENCES
NAD minutes, February 3, 1868; May 14, 1873; October 31, 1887; May 12, 1909.

NAD archives: J. Q. A. Ward, "Report of Committee on Mangement of Casts," October 9, 1865.

Lewis I. Sharp, *John Quincy Adams Ward: Dean of American Sculpture* (Newark: University of Delaware Press, 1985).

THE FREEDMAN [1862]
Inscribed front of base: *J. Q. A. Ward / 1863*
Bronze, 20 × 14¾ × 7
NA diploma presentation

On October 14, 1863, Ward's diploma work, a plaster bust of Henry Peters Gray, was accepted by the Council. The work had been shown in the Academy annual exhibition of 1862. The bust, which was the only cast known of the work, was evidently destroyed or damaged beyond repair sometime around the turn of the century, for about 1900, Ward presented the Academy with a recently made bronze cast of *The Freedman* to replace the destroyed bust. It seems likely that the sculptor chose this piece, not only because of its enduring popularity, but because it represented his work of the period in which he was elected Academician.

As Lewis Sharp has noted, the exact date of the conception of *The Freedman* is not known. It was probably begun after September 1862, when President Lincoln issued the Emancipation Proclamation, which must certainly have served as an inspiration for the piece. The *Boston Evening Transcript* announced in January 1863 that Ward had completed the sculpture. The model of the work was shown in the Academy annual of that year and doubtless contributed to Ward's elevation to Academician at the annual meeting held shortly after the exhibition opened. This fact made it even more appropriate that, years later, Ward should choose a cast of the particular work to replace his original diploma presentation.

Sharp records eight casts of *The Freedman*, including one probably spurious, that are known today. Of the authenticated pieces, four were made in the 1860s; two, including the Academy's, in the 1890s; and one in 1910.

REFERENCES
NAD minutes, October 14, 1863.

AAA, Gorham Company, Bronze Division Papers, "Identification Assigned to Statuary & Bronzes, 1906–1930" (p. 157), 3680.

Sharp, 152, 153–56.

John George Brown

ANA 1861; NA 1863
Durham, England 1831–1913 New York

Brown spent his early years in England and Scotland, where he studied glass cutting as well as painting. He was inspired to come to America in 1853 by a song about immigrant life that he heard in a music hall. He settled in Brooklyn, New York, where he worked for the glass-cutting firm of William Owen, who would become his father-in-law. Realizing his young employee's true ambitions, Owen encouraged him to pursue his art study in the evenings. Brown attended the Academy's antique and life classes for the year of 1857–58 and with two portraits made his debut in an Academy annual exhibition that opened at the end of the school year. He continued in the life class for 1858–59 and again was represented in the spring Academy annual exhibition; this time with two portrait subjects and a genre subject.

By 1861 Brown had taken a studio in the Tenth Street Studio Building, occupying the rooms being vacated by George H. Boughton, who was leaving soon for Europe. Before he left, however, Brown observed Boughton at work on a painting of a group of boys, an experience that seems to have influenced Brown's future. It was in the Tenth Street building that Brown began his lifelong concentration on this same theme: children. Earlier in his career his children were of the country, and his paintings were part of the mid-century preoccupation with the innocence of pastoral life, which was fast slipping away as America became an industrial power. Brown increasingly turned to the urban scene for his subject matter and eventually made a specialty of images of bootblacks, newsboys, and other youths who made their livings—and sometimes their homes—in city streets. Brown's proficiency at presenting this sad by-product of an overcrowded, underemployed New York as a quaint attribute of city life made his art extremely popular. His prodigious output of paintings and shrewd marketing practices in copyrighting them and issuing reproductive prints made him a wealthy man.

Brown was a consistent participant in Academy exhibitions, missing hardly a year from his first appearance in 1858 to his death. He also was actively involved in the administration of the Academy and its school. He served on the Council from 1872 to 1877, 1879 to 1883, 1885 to 1888, 1895 to 1898, and then was returned to the Council as the Academy's vice president from 1899 to 1903. He was made a Visitor to the school in what was perhaps the most difficult year of its history, 1875–76; in the winter of 1881 the students of the portrait class engaged him as their teacher "at their own expense." In 1902 he sponsored a twenty-five dollar prize in the illustration class.

Not surprisingly, Brown was also an active exhibitor at the Brooklyn Art Association. In addition to his obviously considerable time devoted to his painting and his work for the Academy, Brown also managed to serve as president of the American Watercolor Society for many years and as president of the Artists' Fund Society for a decade; he was also chairman of the National Art Committee and was a member of the jury of awards at the 1893 Columbian Exposition.

DBD

References

NAD minutes, December 20, 1875; January 24, 1881; May 14, 1902.

S. G. W. Benjamin, "A Painter of the Streets," *The Magazine of Art* 5 (1882): 165–70.

Obituaries, *New York Herald*, February 9, 1913, and *New York Times*, February 9, 1913.

American Art Association, NY: *Catalogue of the Finished Pictures and Studies Left by the Well-Known American Artist the Late J. G. Brown, N. A.*, 1914.

Rolayn Lana Tauben, "John George Brown, Painter of Street Children 1831–1913: A Critical Evaluation," Master's thesis, George Washington University, Washington, D.C., 1974.

Robert Hull Fleming Museum, University of Vermont, Burlington: *John George Brown, 1831–1913: A Reappraisal*, 1975.

George Walter Vincent Smith Art Museum, Springfield, MA: Martha Hoppin, *Country Paths and City Sidewalks: The Art of J. G. Brown*, 1989.

BOY AND GIRL, 1863
Inscribed lower right: *J. G. Brown* / 1863
Oil on canvas, 15¼ × 12
NA diploma presentation, May 11, 1864

JOHN LEWIS FREDERICK JOSEPH LA FARGE
ANA 1863; NA 1869
New York 1835–1910 Providence, Rhode Island

La Farge was born of wealthy, cultured French emigré parents who maintained a home in the Washington Square area of New York. As a child he received his first lessons in drawing from his maternal grandfather, a painter of miniatures, and had some lessons in watercolor painting from an unidentified Englishman while a student at the Columbia Grammar School. Beginning in 1850 he attended Mount Saint Mary's College, Emmitsburg, Maryland, and Saint John's College (now Fordham University) in New York, graduating from the Maryland college in 1853. He then took up the study of his intended profession, the law, in New York; however, he also began to study painting. By April 1856, when he left for a year-and-a-half stay abroad, he had turned his mind to the pursuit of the arts. He was first in Paris, where he studied briefly with Thomas Couture, copied in the Louvre, and met Parisian intellectual leaders including Jean-Léon Gérôme, and Pierre Puvis de Chavannes. He also visited Brittany, Belgium, and Denmark before returning to New York in 1857.

Within a few months La Farge had taken a studio in the newly erected Tenth Street Studio Building, although he also was practicing law as a means of livelihood. The architect Richard Morris Hunt encouraged him to give up the law and turn his full attention and talents to art, which he did in the spring of 1859 by going to Newport, Rhode Island, for further art instruction from the architect's brother, William Morris Hunt. The next three years were taken up in study and an independent effort to master landscape and still life painting; travel; and the complicated matter of persuading Margaret Mason Perry, a daughter of the prominent naval family, to convert to Catholicism and marry him. These events occurred late in 1860, and the following year, happily settled in Newport, La Farge began his first productive period of painting, his primary subject being floral still lifes. The annual exhibition of 1862 marked his debut at the Academy with a decorative study of water lillies and a portrait study.

La Farge's activities over the next fifteen years defined the principal focuses of his life. While continuing to paint in oil, he took up the watercolor medium, becoming a member of the American Society of Painters in Water Colors in 1868; he also began increasingly to accept commissions to execute architectural decorative work. In 1874 he essayed his first (initially unsuccessful) designs for stained glass windows. Parallel to his practice as an artist was his role as writer and lecturer. Long interested in Japanese art, he began to collect it in 1863; in 1870 his "Essay on Japanese Art" was published. In 1871 La Farge was appointed university lecturer in composition in art at Harvard College. In 1875 he was a member of the committee to establish the school of the Museum of Fine Arts, Boston.

A major turning point in La Farge's career came in 1876 when he began his participation in designing the decoration of H. H. Richardson's Trinity Church in Copley Square, Boston. His principal assignment was the stained glass, but this project was intentionally a cooperative venture, much in the spirit of the interlocking of the plastic arts as practiced in the Renaissance. A co-worker on Trinity Church was the sculptor Augustus Saint-Gaudens with whom La Farge would execute a number of joint commissions. La Farge had begun manufacturing stained glass shortly before the Trinity commission, but this work gave impetus to his experimentation in the medium he would bring to new heights in beauty and technology.

From the late 1870s, although he would continue to execute easel paintings and many watercolors, La Farge gave his primary attention to the designing and execution of murals and, especially, stained glass decorative schemes for private homes, churchs, and public buildings. A selection of these demonstrates the ever-increasing prestige of his commissions: 1879, a peony window for Newport home of John P. Marquand; 1880, decorations for the dining room of the Union League Club, New York; 1881, windows and decorations for Vanderbilt family mansions in New York; 1893 (installed 1898), a mural for Bowdoin College, Brunswick, Maine; 1896, the skylight for the Vanderbilt mansion, The Breakers, Newport; 1900, windows for the Wellesley (Massachusetts) College Chapel; 1904–05, murals for the Supreme Court Room, Minnesota State Capitol; 1906–07, murals for the Baltimore (Maryland) Court House, and windows for the Columbia University Chapel, New York.

Two major travel excursions reflect the adventurousness of La Farge's intellect, as well as aesthetic sensibility. In June

1886, in company with his lifelong friend Henry Adams, La Farge made a six-month's tour of Japan, which resulted in paintings, and "An Artist's Letters from Japan," serialized in *Century Magazine*, 1890–93. A full year, 1890–91, was passed—again with Adams's company—in touring the islands of the South Pacific, with stops in Australia, Ceylon, and Java. This trip led to an ambitious body of paintings in oil and watercolor, based on sketches and photographs made on the sites, which was were exhibited at Doll and Richards Gallery, Boston, and Durand-Ruel, New York, in 1895.

La Farge continued to be a highly regarded lecturer and author. In 1893 he was appointed instructor in color and composition at the Metropolitan Museum of Art, New York, and delivered a series of six lectures there entitled "Considerations on Painting." His six Scammon Lectures on the subject of the Barbizon School painters, delivered at the Art Institute of Chicago, were published in *McClure's Magazine*. That journal also published in serial his "One Hundred Masterpieces" between 1903 and 1908. The esteem in which La Farge was held as an intellectual was testified by the honorary degrees awarded him by Yale University in 1896 and 1901 and by Princeton University in 1904.

La Farge had a long, but not altogether peaceful relationship with the Academy. The early rumblings of dissent among certain artists, which eventually led to the creation of the Society of American Artists, might be heard in La Farge's letter to the Academy Council in 1874 in which he complained about the rejection of his works for the annual exhibition. La Farge was among the founding members of the Society, participated in its first exhibition in 1878, and later served as its president. Having hardly missed a year since 1862, his last appearance in an Academy annual exhibition was 1879. But he was certainly reconciled with the Academy by the time the two organizations merged in 1906. Perhaps not coincidentally, La Farge donated a set of books, "the complete literary works of John La Farge," to the Academy in that year. In 1907 he was recommended by the once-offending Council for a professorship of decorative arts at Columbia University. La Farge, in turn, showed his magnaminity in bequeathing a number of casts to the Academy.

In rememberance of this long history of affiliation, the Academy Council entered the following tribute to La Farge in its minutes of November 21, 1910.

> Resolved, That the Officers of the National Academy of Design, who are also the Officers of the Society of American Artists, desire to register their sense of the loss to the United Body in the death of John La Farge, a highly honored member of the Academy, who was also president of the Society of American Artists for many years, and until the union of the two Societies. Whether as a painter, a writer, or a man of subtle intellect and wide culture, he was one who reflected credit upon the profession of Art, and who did, perhaps, more than any man of his generation to place that profession, in the eyes of the world, among intellectual pursuits worthy of occupying the attention of serious minds.

DBD and ABG

REFERENCES

NAD minutes, April 27, 1874; May 13, 1874; October 25, 1906; May 8, 1907; November 18, 1907; Novmber 21, 1910; April 17, 1911.

H. Barbara Weinberg, *The Decorative Work of John La Farge* (New York: Garland Publishing, Inc., 1977).

James L. Yarnall, *The Role of Landscape in the Art of John La Farge* (Ann Arbor, MI: University Microfilms, 1981).

Henry Adams, Kathleen A. Foster, Henry A. La Farge, H. Barbara Weinberg, Linnea H. Wren, and James L. Yarnall, *John La Farge* (New York: Abbeville Press, 1987).

SELF-PORTRAIT [1864]
Oil on canvas, 30×25
Gift of Mr. and Mrs. Willard G. Clark, in memory of Henry La Farge, 1987

La Farge was elected an Associate of the Academy on May 13, 1863. Academy regulations then gave him one year, or essentially to the next annual meeting, to submit a portrait of himself or his election would be voided. That next annual meeting convened at 2 p.m., May 11, 1864. The Council met at noon of the same day to accept several Associate Elects's portrait presentations, including La Farge's, so those members might take their seats at the afternoon meeting. La Farge's portrait is not again noted in Academy records; and the portrait was not in the collection when it was inventoried in 1910, in preparation for publication of a checklist the following year.

This self-portrait remained among those of La Farge's works not included in the sale of his estate in the spring of 1911. It was probably withheld—as his executrix, Grace Edith Barnes, wrote to Robert C. Vose on January 15, 1912, in offering it for sale—because "It is incomplete and rather unfinished but it is very interesting. He did it when he was about twenty-five or thirty years old." The Vose Galleries did not purchase the portrait; however, Alden Sampson, of Washington, D.C., apparently did, along with a number of minor works remaining in the estate. Sampson's collection passed to his son, Edward Sampson, of Princeton, New Jersey, in 1925. Edward Sampson's estate, including the La Farge Self-Portrait, was auctioned in 1978. The portrait then changed hands several times until it was again sold at auction at Christie's, New York, October 24, 1979, at which time it was acquired by Mr. and Mrs. Clark.

When the portrait appeared in the market, it attracted the attention of a leading La Farge scholar, James L. Yarnall, who has noted that its "unusual scale and overall formality of the rendering [were] hard to relate to any other works in La Farge's oeuvre." In communicating with the Academy and discovering that La Farge's diploma portrait was long missing, however, the explanation for the scale—the Academy's mandatory thirty by twenty-five inches—and formality became clear.

It was not uncommon for members-elect to submit unfinished works as diploma presentations in order to meet deadlines for securing of elections and then to request that their works be returned on loan for purposes of completion. It is possible La Farge reclaimed his unfinished portrait in this way on the very day he presented it. The artist's relationship with the Academy thereafter was not close or notably friendly, and in 1910, at the time of the first thorough collection inventory in over fifty years, La Farge was seriously ill and then died late in the year. Had it occurred to the Academy to press for the return of the portrait, there were good reasons to forego such a request.

On this circumstantial evidence it came to be believed that this unfinished portrait, which remained in La Farge's studio at his death, is the work accepted by the Academy in May 1864. Mr. and Mrs. Clark's conclusion that such is the history of the portrait prompted their generous offer to place—or replace—it in the collection. The Academy is also especially indebted to Mr. Yarnall for sharing his full documentation on the painting prior to its publication.

REFERENCES
James L. Yarnall, "John La Farge's *Portrait of the Painter*, and the Use of Photography in His Work," *American Art Journal* 18 (no. 1, 1986): 5–20.

Correspondence, James L. Yarnall and Abigail Booth Gerdts, January 1987-September 1988.

James L. Yarnall, "New Discoveries in American Art," *American Art Journal* 20 (no. 3, 1988): 84–85.

Henry A. La Farge, James L. Yarnall, Mary A. La Farge, with the assistance of Amy B. Werbel, *Catalogue Raisonné of the Works of John La Farge* (New Haven: Yale University Press, in press).

MAGNOLIA BLOSSOM, n.d.
Oil on composition board, 11 × 8⅞
NA diploma presentation, June 7, 1869

James Yarnall believes this work is a study for La Farge's larger representation of a single magnolia in a bowl, reliably assigned a dating of 1863 (Berkshire Museum, Pittsfield, Massachusetts), which it closely resembles. The Academy's painting has long been accepted as dated 1869, because that year-date was written on the reverse of the original support (now obscured by modern attachment of a reinforcing panel). The recent recognition of past Academy practice of noting the year of acceptance of paintings on their reverses has eliminated that inscription from serious consideration.

La Farge was elected an Academician on May 12, 1869, and made his diploma presentation within a month, which suggests he decided to confirm the election promptly, giving a work he had in hand, rather than repeat the experience of a year's anxiety over meeting the Academy's deadline for qualification. Although the study of the single magnolia was probably six years "out of date" by the time of his election to Academician, it would have had credence as a representative example of his work, as La Farge had first gained favorable recognition with his elegant studies of flowers.

REFERENCES
Kathleen A. Foster, "The Still-Life Painting of John La Farge," *American Art Journal* 11 (Summer 1979): 4-37, 83–84.

Correspondence, James L. Yarnall and Abigail Booth Gerdts, January 1987–September 1988.

Henry A. La Farge, et al., *Catalogue Raisonné.*

WINSLOW HOMER

ANA 1864; NA 1865
Boston, Massachusetts 1836–1910 Prout's Neck, Maine

Homer's father was a well-to-do importer of hardware; his mother, a devoted amateur watercolorist. The family moved across the Charles River from Boston to the then country town of Cambridge when Homer was six years old. He showed both talent and interest in art from childhood and was encouraged in its pursuit by his parents. Given financial reverses suffered by his father and his own predilection to an artistic career, the idea of entering Harvard, as had his brother, was bypassed. Instead, in 1855, at the age of nineteen he was apprenticed to John H. Bufford, head of the leading Boston lithography firm. There he was occupied for two years in designing sheet music covers and other popular illustrations. He hated the work, and on his twenty-first birthday, February 24, 1857, when the apprenticeship contract expired, he left Bufford's, vowing never again to be anyone's employee. He immediately set up a studio and began working as a freelance illustrator. Over the next two years his designs, rendered into wood-engravings by technicians, were seen in Boston's *Ballou's Pictorial Drawing-Room Companion* and the newly established New York periodical *Harper's Weekly*. In the autumn of 1859, having attained some little success and some standing with *Harper's*, Homer moved to New York.

Although offered a staff position at *Harper's*, Homer remained a freelance illustrator. *Harper's* was his principal employer, but his work was to be seen in a number of popular periodicals. Homer, ever practical about financial matters, continued to assure his living through illustration work to 1875; however, his overriding intention was to become a painter. He registered in the Academy school for the season of 1859–60—being allowed the unusual privilege of entering the life class directly, without first proving his attainments in the antique class; he was again registered in the Academy's life class for 1860–61 and 1863–64. In 1861 he also had some private instruction in painting from Frederic Rondel.

Harper's sent Homer to Virginia in the spring of 1862 to record General George B. McClellan's campaign to take Richmond. He had visited the Civil War camps briefly the year before and would again, but this was his most sustained experience of military life, and it formed the subject of his first serious work in oil. Homer made his debut as a painter in the Academy's annual exhibition of 1863 with two Civil War subjects; the following year he showed another two scenes related to the war. The annual exhibition of 1865 had special significance as it inaugurated the Academy's impressive new building at Twenty-third Street and Fourth Avenue; Homer showed two scenes of camp life, one being his most ambitious work up to that time, *Pitching Quoits* (Fogg Museum, Harvard University, Cambridge, Massachusetts), and one painting demonstrating his alternate source of subject matter, his summertime activities with his family and friends in New England. Homer was advanced to Academician at the annual meeting held shortly after the opening of the annual exhibition.

Homer's career developed successfully over the next fifteen years. His subjects were genre scenes drawn from his visits to the popular Eastern summer resorts in pursuit of material for his illustrations; and from his summer vacations spent in hunting and fishing in the Adirondacks and visiting friends on their farms in upstate New York. Other than the sporting pictures, his favored themes were children and young people and winsome young country and city women. A visit to France from late 1866 to the autumn of 1867 seemed to have no significant influence on the character of his work. In summer months spent in Gloucester, Massachusetts, in 1873, Homer began to work in watercolor; he would expand the supposed limitations of the medium in increasingly bold, colorful paintings executed throughout his life.

In the spring of 1881 Homer left New York for a two-year stay in England, settling in the small fishing village of Cullercoats on the northeastern coast. Unlike his previous sojourn abroad, this period of intense work, using the stalwart fisherfolk as subjects, brought about a metamorphosis in his art. His figures became monumental, but more significantly, the expressive content of his paintings turned from the transitory moments of day-to-day life to the eternal tension between man and the elements, especially the dominating power of the sea over those who lived and worked in close relationship with it.

Within six months of his return to New York in November 1882 Homer had made the permanent move to the oceanside home and studio at Prout's Neck, Maine, he would occupy for the rest of his life. Over the next twenty-three years, until ill health would diminish his capacity for work, Homer painted ever more monumental images of the sea and the men who earn their livings from it. Winter trips to Florida and the Caribbean, and summer and autumn hunting trips to the Adirondacks and Canada, were the source of a great body of fully matured paintings in watercolors. One of his most powerful images of the sea and of its force, *The Gulf Stream* (Metropolitan Museum of Art, New York), came from his experience of the southern seas.

Homer's work was at once subtle and sophisticated in formal design and expressive content, and accessible to a popular audience. By the end of the century he was arguably the most well-known and highly respected artist in America. Internationally, as an American artist, his reputation was exceeded only by John Singer Sargent and James Abbott McNeill Whistler.

Until his return from England and withdrawal from New York and, thereby, from the accepted career arena of American artists, Homer pursued a fairly active role in the community of his peers. Having maintained a studio in the New York University Building from 1861, in 1871 he moved to the Tenth Street Studio Building, the preeminent artists's address of the period, and retained his studio there to his departure for England.

As the Academy made plans late in 1869 to make a major change in the operation of its school by employing a full-time supervising-instructor, exploratory overtures were made to Homer and George Cochran Lambdin regarding the position. It was reported to the Council that both men were willing to take the job. (Lemuel Wilmarth was hired.) Homer was a member of the Council for the 1873–74 term. He continued to be regularly represented in Academy annuals through 1888, but as the quantity of his oil paintings decreased and opportunities for them to be exhibited increased, his participation in Academy shows became less vital.

Homer died in September 1910. The Academy invited five of his major canvases for its winter exhibition, which opened in December. By the twentieth century, the Academy had given up its practice of reading extensive eulogies on de-

ceased members at annual meetings. However, the Council's expression of respect, while succinct, exactly summarized his achievement:

> Resolved that in the death of Winslow Homer the National Academy of Design has lost one of its most honored members, America a National glory, and the World one of the most powerful and original artists of the Nineteenth Century.

ABG

REFERENCES

NAD minutes, December 20, 1869; November 7, 1910.

William Howe Downes, *The Life and Works of Winslow Homer* (Boston: Houghton Mifflin Company, 1911).

Lloyd Goodrich, *Winslow Homer* (New York: MacMillan Company, 1944).

Philip C. Beam, *Winslow Homer at Prout's Neck* (Boston: Little Brown and Company, 1966).

Gordon Hendricks, *The Life and Works of Winslow Homer* (New York: Harry N. Abrams, Inc., 1979).

M. Knoedler & Co, Inc., New York: Lloyd Goodrich and Abigail Booth Gerdts, *Winslow Homer in Monochrome*, 1986.

CROQUET PLAYER, n.d.

Inscribed reverse, top stretcher crossbar: *Winslow Homer / would like to have the / privilege of painting*; bottom stretcher crossbar: *[illegible] better picture*
Oil on canvas, 8¼ × 12¼
NA diploma presentation, May 7, 1866

Homer spent much of his summer time in the 1860s visiting his family's home near Boston and in the company of a close-knit group of cousins and friends enjoying the usual leisure-time pursuits of the era. The lawn game of croquet had become fashionable in America in the early 1860s, and doubt-less Homer was a player as well as observer. Between 1865 and 1869 he executed five oil paintings representing the sport, using his friends as models. The Academy's painting is accepted as the earliest in series.

REFERENCES

Yale University Art Gallery, New Haven, CT: David Park Curry, *Winslow Homer: The Croquet Game*, 1984.

HENRY PETERS GRAY
ANA 1841; NA 1842; PNAD 1869–71
New York 1819–1877 New York

Gray was encouraged by his father, a wealthy merchant, to pursue his interest in art. His first art study was at Hamilton College, Clinton, New York, shortly after Daniel Huntington had been enrolled there. It is likely that some connection was made with Huntington, for in 1838 Gray became Huntington's student in New York. That same year he had two works accepted into the Academy's annual exhibition. The following year he went to Europe in company with Huntington and Cornelius Ver Bryck. He remained abroad for two years, studying the works of the old masters in Florence and Rome. Upon returning to New York in 1841, Gray established himself as a portrait painter and won instant recognition for his talents. In 1843 he married Susan Clark, also an artist, and in 1845 they went to Italy for a year's stay.

From an early admiration of Washington Allston, it was natural that Gray should strive to emulate the Venetian masters of the Renaissance in compositional models, colorism, and in choice of grand subjects from mythology, history, and occasionally religious and moral themes. (Among his prized possessions was a large copy of Titian's *Venus of Urbino*, which he believed to be a replica. This work was presented to the Academy by his widow and remains in the collection.) Although he continued to receive numerous commissions for portraits, Gray's work in historical painting enjoyed the considerable success that eluded the previous generation of American artists.

Gray's apparent devotion to the Academy as an institution, combined with his attainment of the academic ideal in his art, quickly raised him to a position of leadership among his peers. He served as member of Council in 1845–46, 1848–49, 1854–55 (although absent from the city part of the year), 1855–56, 1857–58 and 1859–1861, when he began nine years of service as was vice president of the Academy under the presidency of Huntington. He then succeeded Huntington and himself served two terms as president. He was chairman of the committee that instituted the Academy's Fellowship Fund in 1863. Through his and others' diligence in securing subscribers to the fund, capital was raised to build the Venetian Gothic edifice at Twenty-third Street and Fourth Avenue that served as the Academy's home from 1865 to 1900.

During what were critical years for the Academy school, 1867–1870, and 1875–76, Gray was appointed a Visitor.

In 1871, being in poor health, Gray returned to Florence. The change of climate was reported to have been quickly restorative, and—always a prolific artist—he was actively engaged on numerous compositions in the four years he remained there. The last two years of his life were spent in New York. The eulogy read into Council minutes, while recognizing the fine qualities of the man, dwelt to an exceptional degree on Gray's adherence to model of the Venetian colorist painters:

> We recall with satisfaction the many noble portraits and compositions of rare beauty with which he has enriched American art, and dwell with a sad pleasure on the years when his courage, enthusiasm, and warm affections gave tone to Society. His philanthropic mind, combining with a passionate love of color and reverence for the great masters of the past, led him to a profound study and mastery of the principles of Venetian painters.
>
> His principle works worthily illustrate the theories which gave such luminous depth, warmth, and harmony to the productions of the school and should be treated not only for their own intrinsic force and beauty, but as reflecting the technical method of a great group of colorists whose practice established the principles on which all good coloring depends.

JPH

REFERENCES

Henry T. Tuckerman, *Book of the Artists. American Artist Life* (New York: G. P. Putnam & Son, 1867), 42–46.

Daniel O'C. Townley, "Living American Artists. No. II. Henry Peters Gray, President of the National Academy of Design," *Scribner's Monthly* 2 (August 1871): 401–402.

NAD minutes, November 19, 1877.

Charles P. Daly, *In Memory of Henry Peters Gray* (New York: Century Association, 1878).

HENRY PETERS GRAY. *The Birth of Our Flag*, 1874 (detail).

Henry Peters Gray

The Birth of Our Flag (or) Origin of the
American Flag, 1874
Inscribed lower left: *Henry Peters Gray Firenze 1874*
Oil on canvas, 72×48
Gift of Mrs. Susan Clark Gray, 1914

The first version of this painting (unlocated) was exhibited in
the Academy annual of 1863, a time when its patriotic allu-
sion to the Union was evident. The immediate source for both
versions was the first stanza of Joseph Rodman Drake's five
stanza poem, *The American Flag*:

> When Freedom from her mountain height,
> Unfurl'd her standard to the air,
> She tore the azure robe of night,
>   And set stars of glory there.
> She mingled with its gorgeous dyes
> The milky baldric of the skys,
> And striped it pure, celestial white,
> With streakings of the morning light;
> Then, from his mansion in the sun
> She call'd her eagle bearer down,
> And gave into his mighty hand
>   The symbol of her chosen land.

Gray's famed use of the coloring and textural techniques
of Titian and proper reuse of classical and old master proto-
types—in this instance a figure reminiscent of one in Raphael's *Galatea*—are put in service of the most expicitly
American painting of his known oeuvre. Although the earlier
(and by all reports, quite small) version did not attract great
notice from the critics, the later was much reported upon by
press visitors to his Florence studio. One such writer, after describing the work in detail, went on to note:

> Pictures of this kind are of course subject to the imputation
> of sensationalism, but where they are really well treated, as
> in this case, precedents of the old masters make it seem suit-
> able that American history and traditions should have their
> own symbolical representations in art, as much as those of
> other and older countries; and in this point of view Mr.
> Gray's choice of a subject appears perfectly legitimate, even
> if it be not in perfect accord with the realistic spirit of the
> age. The painting, in size and in importance, is the most
> considerable composition we have ever seen on Mr. Gray's
> easel; and as one of the best works of one of the best Amer-
> ican artists, it appears to us entitled to a good position in
> some public or national building.

The year following Gray's death, Chief Justice Daly in
his memorial address would again single out this painting for
praise, recall that Gray considered it his masterpiece, and urge
that it be acquired by some national institution.

References
Rufus Willmot Griswold, *The Poets and Poetry of America* (Philadelphia: Carey and Hart, 1843), 147.

"Notes from American Studios in Italy," *Appleton's* 12 (August 8,
1874): 188–89.

Daly, 21.

OLIN LEVI WARNER
ANA 1888; NA 1889
Suffield, Connecticut 1844–1896 New York

During his youth, which was passed in New York State and Vermont, Warner showed an interest in carving and exhibited some of his earliest works, in chalk and plaster, at various county fairs. He was unable to pursue sculpting professionally, however, until 1869, when he had finally saved enough money to go to Europe to study. He was admitted to the École des Beaux-Arts in Paris, studied with François Jouffroy, Jean Falguière, and Michel Mercier, and apprenticed himself to Jean Baptist Carpeaux. On his return to the United States in 1872, he established a studio in New York, but was at first discouraged by the lack of commissions. The first exhibition of one of his works, an ideal piece, in an Academy annual in 1873 does not seem to have helped.

The patronage of Daniel Cottier, among others, brought an end to this period of stuggle in about 1876, when Warner began to receive a number of portrait commissions. His busts of Julian Alden Weir and Charles DeKay both date from 1880 (both, Century Association, New York). In 1877 Warner participated with other young painters and sculptors in the founding of the Society of American Artists, and his work was to appear in the annual exhibitions of that organization for many years. His participation in this rebellious organization did not discourage his exhibiting works, mostly portrait busts, at the Academy; in only five of the years between 1873 and 1891 did he fail to be represented. In 1888 he was engaged by the Academy to teach sculptural modeling in its school. By the end of the year, however, lack of student interest led the Council to take sculpture out of the curriculum. In 1893 the subject was reintroduced, again with Warner as instructor; he continued in this post to his death.

In addition to portrait works, Warner also designed several well-known ideal or allegorical pieces. Possibly the most famous of these is his *Diana* (Metropolitan Museum of Art, New York), which had the distinction of being chosen to illustrate the jacket of Lorado Taft's seminal *History of American Sculpture*, published in 1903. In 1888 Warner was commissioned by Stephen Skidmore to design a bronze and granite public fountain with caryatids for Portland, Oregon. Between 1889 and 1891 he visited the Pacific Northwest and modeled portrait medallions of American Indians representing various tribes of the region. These included *Chief Joseph of the Nez Perce* (Metropolitan Museum of Art), which was shown at the Academy in 1890.

At his early death as the result of a bicycle accident, Warner was working on a commission for two huge bronze doors for the Library of Congress, a project later finished by Herbert Adams. He had just completed his second one-year term on the Academy Council at the time of his death, and his colleagues entered the following tribute to him in the minutes:

> It is hard to become reconciled to the untimely death of Olin L. Warner N.A. who had endeared himself to us all by his great talents, his sturdy integrity, his conscientious performance of duty. As a member of the Council he was rarely absent, and his sound judgment, directly and fearlessly expressed, was of great value in our deliberations. . . . [T]o be so cut off almost at the beginning of the real work of his life, is a serious misfortune to American Art.

DBD

REFERENCES
NAD minutes, October 29, 1888; May 12, 1897.

DANIEL COTTIER, 1878
Inscribed right side: *New York 1878*
Bronze, 11×6×6
NA diploma presentation, May 5, 1890

In May 1890, when Warner submitted an unnamed bust as his Academician diploma presentation, he did so with the reservation that he intended to replace it at a later date with "something of more importance." This demur was frequently attached to diploma works by electees—but rarely remembered. As there is no further mention in the Academy's records of any replacement, it must be assumed that this bust of Cottier was Warner's initial presentation. His implication that the work was somehow unimportant may have referred to its being less than life size, or that it was a portrait and not an ideal conception, or simply may have been a device to ward off a harsh judgment by the Council.

Cottier was born in 1838 in Glasgow, Scotland. He was trained as a glass-stainer and, in 1869, established in London his own decorating firm, Cottier and Company, Art Furniture Makers, Glass and Tile Painters. He soon expanded his interests to buying and selling French and Dutch paintings in England and America. A branch of his business opened in New York in 1873, and Cottier soon became known in America as a patron of artists, especially those that were having difficulties. His gallery on Fifth Avenue was the site in 1875 of an exhibition of works by John La Farge, William Morris Hunt, and others that had been rejected by the Academy jury for its annual exhibition. In the annals of American art history it is with Albert Pinkham Ryder that Cottier is most associated, having been his friend and dealer until Cottier's early death in 1891.

Warner probably met Cottier in 1877; the dealer gave him a room in his offices to use as a studio. Warner began his bust of Cottier in the latter part of that year, probably on commission from the dealer himself. As George Gurney has pointed out, the bust was well received by the critics when it appeared in the Academy annual of 1878, and their published comments represented what must have been the first important critical attention Warner received. The wit and wisdom for which the subject was known are apparent in the expression given to the piece by the sculptor. Indeed, the bust is imbued with a sense of Warner's affection for Cottier, his earliest and most generous patron.

Nine examples of this piece are recorded in Gurney's catalogue raisonné. One of these was lent for exhibition at the Panama-Pacific Exposition in San Francisco in 1915 by Charles E.S. Wood of Portland, Oregon.

REFERENCES
George Gurney, *Olin Levi Warner: A Catalogue Raisonné of His Sculpture and Graphic Works*, 3 vols. (Ann Arbor, MI: University Microfilms, 1978), 2:359–67.

Metropolitan Museum of Art, New York: Catherine Hoover Voorsanger, in *In Pursuit of Beauty: Americans and the Aesthetic Movement*, 1986, 414–16.

WILLIAM STANLEY HASELTINE
ANA 1860; NA 1861
Philadelphia 1835–1900 Rome

Haseltine was born into a family that produced much artistic talent. His mother, Elizabeth Stanley Shinn Haseltine (1811–82), was a painter, and both his brothers were active in the art world: James Henry Haseltine (1833–81) was a sculptor, and Charles Field Haseltine (1840-?) owned Haseltine Art Galleries in Philadelphia. This tradition was carried into the next generation by William's son, Herbert Haseltine, a sculptor and also an Academician.

William Haseltine first studied art in 1850 and 1851 in Philadelphia under the German expatriate artist Paul Weber. After attending the University of Pennsylvania in Philadelphia and Harvard College, Cambridge, Massachusettts, from which he graduated in 1854, he accompanied Weber to Düsseldorf where he continued his artistic training under Andreas Achenbach, an artist with whom Weber himself had studied. In 1856 Haseltine traveled through Germany and the Alps with Emanuel Leutze, Albert Bierstadt, and Worthington Whittredge, eventually coming to Rome, where he remained for two years. He was back in Philadelphia in 1859—when he first had a work included in an Academy annual exhibition—and 1860, but then settled in New York for a time, taking rooms in the Tenth Street Studio Building. He evidently made a number of sketching trips to the New England coast and in the Delaware River valley, for among his submissions to Academy annuals were scenes from these areas shown in the years 1861 through 1865.

Haseltine and his family spent the latter part of the 1860s in France, where he painted in Paris and at Barbizon, and where he showed a number of works at the Salon. In the autumn of 1869 they moved to Rome and eventually found permanent accommodations in the Palazzo Altieri, which they established as a social center for American expatriates and tourists in the city. Haseltine took sketching trips throughout Italy, to Sicily, or to Venice every spring and autumn, and often went to Bavaria or the Tyrol in summers. He was an inveterate traveler all his life and visited most of the countries of Europe at one time or another.

Although a confirmed expatriate, Haseltine always kept close ties with his native land and returned to America several times during the last three decades of his life. He had a studio in New York for a time in 1873–74; worked in Boston for the winter of 1896; and traveled to the American West and Alaska with his son, Herbert, in 1899. Haseltine was a member of New York's Century Association and Salmagundi Club, a trustee of the American Academy in Rome, and a member of the Art Committee for the 1893 World's Columbian Exposition in Chicago.

At his death about 1,500 paintings, drawings, and watercolors were in Haseltine's Palazzo Altieri studio; there they remained for twenty years, eventually passing to his daughter, Helen Haseltine Plowden of London. A selection of these works formed a memorial exhibition presented by the Academy in 1958 and toured to a number of other institutions. In 1961, wanting the residue of her father's oeuvre to return to his native land, Mrs. Plowden asked the Academy to assist her in its distribution to American public collections.

DBD

REFERENCES

Josiah H. Shinn, *The History of the Shinn Family in Europe and America* (Chicago: Genealogical and Historical Publishing Company, 1903), 224–25.

Helen Haseltine Plowden, *William Stanley Haseltine* (London: Frederick Muller, Ltd., 1947).

NAD: *Memorial Exhibition. William Stanley Haseltine, N. A., 1835–1900*, 1958.

NAD minutes, October 6, 1958; December 5, 1966.

Davis and Landgale, New York: John Wilmerding, *William Stanley Haseltine (1835–1900): Drawings of a Painter*, 1983.

SUNRISE AT CAPRI, n.d.
Inscribed lower right: W. S. H.
Oil on canvas, 32 × 56
Gift of Helen Haseltine Plowden, 1953

According to his daughter and biographer, Haseltine first visited Capri in the spring of 1858 and was inspired by the site for the rest of his life. While there he often lodged in a local monastery, following in the tradition of the Nazerene paint-

ers, a number of whom he had met, or at least knew of through Oswald Achenbach, the younger brother of his teacher in Düsseldorf.

Although it is difficult to date this painting, based on its light palette, it has been suggested that it is a late work. It may be this painting that is described in a May 1896 article in the Boston *Standard*:

> A striking painting of large size represents the island of Capri; jagged and picturesque rocks break into the air from the blue waters of the bay and tower to a height of many hundred feet, their rough outlines almost startling by their bold contour. Upon the summit of the highest point of Capri, a monastery was erected long ago to which pilgrims flock every year; the walls of the monastery are still standing and in fair preservation. Never have we seen man's handiwork, in its relation to Nature, more faithfully delineated than by Mr. Haseltine, in this picture.

Sunrise at Capri was selected for the Academy's permanent collection from the Haseltine estate at the invitation of Helen Plowden in 1952. Mrs. Plowden also made a gift to the Academy of a drawing by Haseltine, titled *Capri* and dated 1858, which is related to this painting only in subject matter.

REFERENCES
"Haseltine's Studio," *Boston Standard*, 1 May 1896.

Plowden, 62–65.

NAD minutes, March 17, 1862; October 6, 1952; October 6, 1963; October 3, 1955.

Cheryl Cibulka, in NAD: *Next to Nature*, 91–93.

Augustus Saint-Gaudens

ANA 1888; NA 1889

Dublin, Ireland 1848–1907 Cornish, New Hampshire

Saint-Gaudens was not a year old when his parents emigrated to America. He was raised and educated in New York. He was first apprenticed to Louis Avet, a cameo cutter, in 1861, but several years later he changed apprentice masters but not his chosen craft, joining Jules Le Brethon. He attended the Academy school antique class from 1863 to 1867 and its life class in 1866 and 1867. He recalled these years in his reminiscences:

> Shortly after beginning with Le Brethon, I also entered the National Academy of Design, the picturesque Italian Doge's palace on the corner of Fourth Avenue and Twenty-third Street. . . . This studying in the Academy at nights was very dream-like and in the surrounding quiet, broken only by the little shrill whistle of an ill-burning gas jet, I first felt my God-like indifference and scorn of all other would-be artists. Here too, came my appreciation of the antique and my earliest attempts to draw from the nude with the advice of Mr. Huntington and Mr. Leutze.

The young sculptor went to Paris in 1867 and studied at the Petit École and in the atelier of François Jouffroy. In 1870 he went to Rome where he began to work independently. With the exception of about a year bridging 1872–73 spent in New York, Saint-Gaudens remained in Rome until 1875. It was in Rome that he received his first commissions from Americans. On his return to New York in the early spring of 1875 he met John La Farge, the painter, and architects Stanford White and Charles McKim. The careers of the four would be linked for a number of years in friendship as well as in jointly conceived and executed projects, among which were: Trinity Church, Boston; the Boston Public Library; and creation of the Columbian Exposition's "White City" in Chicago. In 1875 Saint-Gaudens worked for Tiffany Studios and showed for the first time in an Academy annual exhibition. The next year he received his first major public commission, the monument to Admiral David Farragut for Madison Square in New York, which established his reputation when unveiled in 1881. Over the remaining twenty-five years of his life the importance of his commissions, as well as the creativity, grace, and power with which he fulfilled them, would steadily increase; his fame and honors grew in proportion.

In 1877, when he next submitted for the Academy annual, the jury rejected his work. As an exemplar of the new generation of French-trained artists he was not alone in finding less than a warm welcome at America's preeminent, but conservative, exhibition event. The most conspicuous response to the situation was the founding, with Saint-Gaudens's active participation, of the Society of American Artists. Past experience, and his active role in the Society's operation—he was its president in 1881—may have had some bearing on his absence from Academy exhibitions; however, it could just as well have reflected the difficulty of an especially well-employed artist like Saint-Gaudens in finding the time to prepare new and unique work for both the Academy's and the Society's annual shows. The only further instances of Saint-Gaudens exhibiting in Academy annuals were 1888 and 1889; that is, the years coinciding with his elections to membership. Considering the Academy rule limiting nominations to membership to current exhibitors, this suggests some unofficial maneuvering and a desire held mutually by artist and Academy that he be counted in their number.

Saint-Gaudens was arguably America's most significant and most celebrated sculptor of the last quarter of the nineteenth century. From medals to monumental works he set the American standard. Among his most well-known pieces are the relief *Robert Gould Shaw Memorial* for the Boston Common, 1884–97; the allegorical figure on the grave of Marion Hooper, wife of Henry Adams, in Rock Creek Cemetery, Washington, 1886–91; *Diana*, 1892–94 (Philadelphia Museum of Art), which once graced the top of the old Madison Square Garden, New York; and the *William Tecumseh Sherman* monument in Grand Army Plaza, New York, 1892–

1903. Saint-Gaudens's influence on contemporary art and artists was tremendous, primarily by the example of his works, but also as a teacher at the Art Students League, 1888–97, and as a founder of the National Sculpture Society in 1893, and of the American Academy in Rome, in 1897.

In 1885 Saint-Gaudens began summering in Cornish, New Hampshire, the center of an especially sophisticated summer colony of artists, writers, and intellectuals. He purchased a substantial home there in 1891 and in 1900 established his studio on his extensive grounds.

Despite his early rebellion against the Academy, Saint-Gaudens's death brought a warm tribute from the Academy's president, Frederick Dielman, to be recorded in minutes:

> His death, at an age when it might reasonably have been thought that he had many years before him to add to the noble sequence of works, by which he had won a position at the head of his profession in this country, and a notable place among the sculptors of the world and of all time, creates a void in the ranks of the National Academy of Design which the future alone may hope to repair. . . . The loss of the man, who in all his personal relations with his fellow-artists, was as modest and fraternal as his art was unusual and distinguished, is peculiarly our own and its sorrow can only be lightened by the memory of the privilege of his presence, and the pride of association with the maker of his noble work.
>
> During his long and courageous struggle against relentless physical ills in the last decade, his artistic fire has never burned less brightly and, working to the last, his example is one by which all artists may profit.

DBD

REFERENCES

NAD minutes, November 8, 1907.

Homer Saint-Gaudens, "The Reminiscences of Augustus St.-Gaudens," *Century Illustrated Monthly Magazine* 77 (January 1909): 395–413.

John H. Dryfhout, *The Work of Augustus Saint-Gaudens* (Hanover, NH, and London: University Press of New England, 1982).

Burke Wilkinson, *Uncommon Clay: The Life and Works of Augustus Saint-Gaudens* (San Diego, New York, London: Harcourt Brace Jovanovich, 1985).

JULES BASTIEN-LEPAGE, 1880

Inscribed across top: *Jules Bastien-LePage Aetatis XXXI Paris MDCCCLXXX Augustus / Saint-Gaudens Fecit*
Bronze relief, 14⁷⁄₁₆ × 10³⁄₁₆ × ¼
NA diploma presentation, February 3, 1890

Saint-Gaudens and the French painter Bastien-Lepage met in Paris in 1879 and, according to Saint-Gaudens's *Reminiscences*, agreed to exchange portraits. (Bastien's full-length sketch of Saint-Gaudens was destroyed in a fire at the sculptor's studio in 1904.) Bastien had only recently completed his most famous work, his painting *Joan of Arc*, a picture that Saint-Gaudens encouraged its owner, Irwin Davis, to give to the Metropolitan Museum of Art, New York, in which collection it remains today. The sculptor's portrait of Bastien was one of five works he showed at the Paris Salon in 1880. In 1881 the Museum of Fine Arts, Boston, bought a bronze cast of the work, Saint-Gaudens's first sale to a museum. This and another version were shown at the Society of American Artists in 1881, and another was shown at the Society's exhibition of 1892.

This is an example of the low-relief portraits for which Saint-Gaudens became famous in the early years of his career. His work in this form was to have an important influence on both contemporary and later artists. It was Bastien himself, according to Wilkinson, who had encouraged Saint-Gaudens to thus "paint in clay." Art critic Royal Cortissoz believed that this portrait of Bastien showed the sculptor's touch to be "at once caressing and bold; nothing essential is slurred, but neither is anything unduly emphasized. . . .[T]he sculptor makes us feel that in the manipulation of surface he can be as subtle as anybody. . . . It is portraiture for the sake of truth and beauty, not for the sake of technique."

Dryfhout lists twenty-one extant plaster and bronze versions of the work, as well as three reductions. Saint-Gaudens had many of these made as gifts to friends and fellow artists and several were cast in bronze after the sculptor's death. But beyond this fact that an example of the work was probably readily available, it was a singularly appropriate piece for presentation to the Academy. Bastien, who had died in 1884 at the early age of thirty-six, was immensely admired by American artists for his exemplary academic form and technique put in service of highly progressive compositional and conceptual ideas.

REFERENCES

AAA, Gorham Company, Bronze Division, Papers, "Identification Assigned to Statuary & Bronzes, 1906–1930," 3680, p. 209.

Royal Cortissoz, *Augustus Saint-Gaudens* (Boston and New York: Houghton Mifflin and Company, 1907), 12.

Homer Saint-Gaudens, *The Reminiscences of Augustus Saint-Gaudens*, 2 vols, (London: Andrew Melrose, 1913), 1: 215.

National Portrait Gallery, Smithsonian Institution, Washington, D.C.: John Dryfhout and Beverly Cox, *Augustus Saint-Gaudens: The Portrait Reliefs*, 1969, no. 18.

Dryfhout, 107–108.

Wilkinson, 114, 191–92.

71

DWIGHT WILLIAM TRYON
ANA 1890; NA 1891
Hartford, Connecticut 1849–1925 South Dartmouth, Massachusetts

Following the death of his father in a hunting accident, Tryon was raised in the East Hartford home of his maternal grandparents. At the age of fourteen he and his mother moved back to Hartford where he worked for a short time in a gun factory before becoming a clerk and bookkeeper in a bookstore. He worked in this capacity for ten years, sketching and doing ornamental calligraphy on the side. After his marriage to Alice H. Belden in 1873, Tryon opened a studio in Hartford and took on several pupils. Three years later he held a large sale of his work to finance a period of study abroad.

Tryon settled in Paris, where he worked for three winter seasons under drawing teacher Louis Jacquesson de la Chevreuse. In addition, he sought criticism from Henri Joseph Harpignies and Charles François Daubigny. He remained in Europe for five years, spending time with Americans Abbott Thayer, Robert Brandegee, and William B. Faxon. Returning to New York in spring 1881, Tryon took a studio in the Rembrandt Building and was elected to the Society of American Artists the following year. After two summers in Eastchester, New York, he chose South Dartmouth as his off-season residence, spending half of each year sailing and fishing there.

In 1885 Tryon took the position of professor of art at Smith College, Northampton, Massachusetts; he traveled to the campus to teach every three weeks until 1923. His work soon passed from a brief Barbizon-inspired period into his better-known tonalist phase. One such landscape won an Academy Julius Hallgarten Prize in 1887, although the award was rescinded when it was realized that the artist was over thirty-five years of age and thus ineligible.

An important event occurred in 1889 when Tryon met the collector of American and Oriental art Charles Lang Freer. Over the next two decades Freer amassed a large collection of Tryon's work, which passed to the nation with the bequest that established the Freer Gallery, Washington, D.C. Another significant group of Tryon's landscapes is located at Smith College in the art gallery that Tryon endowed shortly before his death.

JD

REFERENCES
Henry C. White, *The Life and Art of Dwight William Tryon* (Boston: Houghton Mifflin, 1930).

Museum of Art, University of Connecticut, Storrs: *Dwight W. Tryon: A Retrospective Exhibition*, 1971.

Mary Ellen Hayward Yehia, *Dwight W. Tryon: An American Landscape Painter* (Ann Arbor, MI: University Microfilms, 1977).

HAYMAKING, n.d.
Inscribed lower left: *D. W. Tryon / East-Chester NY*
Oil on canvas, 24 × 36
NA diploma presentation, January 8, 1892

The farm and peasant scenes that Tryon executed in France under the influence of Barbizon painters preoccupied him during his first two summers back in the United States. The works painted in 1881 and 1882 at Eastchester are generally seen as early attempts of the artist to "find himself" in a remote New York village that never wholly appealed to him. By 1883 he had left Eastchester for his beloved Massachusetts shore.

With the exceptions of the brushy trees and scratchy foreground, *Haymaking* is firmly structured by slick, squared-off brushstrokes. Although the anecdotal figural element would soon disappear from Tryon's work, other aspects of the composition look forward to his better-known tonalist landscapes. The foreground, for example, is left deep and open and the flat forms of the middleground are composed of interlocking geometric shapes kept parallel to the picture plane.

Tryon showed three landscapes in the Society of American Artists exhibition of 1883; one, shown under the title *Haymaking, East Chester, N.Y.* is probably the painting now in the Academy collection. The reviewer for the *New York Daily Tribune* commented on the group of Tryon's works in the 1883 Society exhibition, noting that they looked a bit like the landscapes of Abbott Thayer. He concluded with the insightful comment, "There is a quality which appears to be indecision in this work, as though the artist were groping for a way and not yet quite sure of his path." Buyers were apparently equally ambivalent, for *Haymaking* remained in Tryon's hands until he offered it as his diploma work nearly a decade later.

This painting had been known simply as *Landscape* in Academy records until an old label on its stretcher giving the painting's title as *Haymaking* was noticed in the course of conservation work done in 1980.

REFERENCES
"The Society of American Artists, Second Notice," *New York Daily Tribune*, April 15, 1883.

White, 58.

Yehia, 81–86.

Susan M. Sivard, in NAD: *Next to Nature*, 158–60.

FREDERICK ARTHUR BRIDGMAN
ANA 1874; NA 1881
Tuskeegee, Alabama 1847–1928 Rouen, France

Although Bridgman lived most of his life as a Parisian expatriate, he always remained a devoted and active member of the Academy. Born into the family of an itinerant Massachusetts physician, Bridgman lost his father at age three. The family remained in Alabama, and at age ten Bridgman was already studying art at the Tuskeegee Seminary. His family home was burned to the ground during the Civil War; two years later, Bridgman moved to New York to pursue a living as engraver.

In New York he studied in Brooklyn and at the Academy, where he registered for the antique class for two years beginning in 1863. He obtained work at the American Banknote Company, but broke his contract there in 1866 in order to go to study in Paris. After a brief period at the Atelier Suisse, he entered the class of Jean-Léon Gérôme with the help of Thomas Eakins Bridgman stayed with Gérôme for four years, spending his summers in Brittany with the American artists at Pont-Aven. He showed in the Salon for the first time in 1868 and made his debut in an Academy annual in 1871.

Bridgman traveled a great deal, and in 1871 he left Paris to spend time in the Pyrénées Mountains. There he painted peasant scenes and met the Spanish artist Mariano Fortuny. His first trip to North Africa occurred in 1872 and lasted into the following year. With fellow artist Charles S. Pearce he visited Algeria and Egypt, making some 300 sketches. Bridgman was thus introduced to the Orientalist themes that became his mainstay for most of the rest of his career. He returned to Paris, where he met Bostonian Florence Mott Baker. They were married in 1877.

Bridgman's made several trips to North Africa in later years. He wrote a series of articles on his travels that appeared in *Harper's* in 1888 and were published in book form two years later as *Winters in Algeria*. In Paris he transformed a stable behind his house at 144 rue Malesherbes into a sumptuous Oriental-style palace that he used as a studio. He collected exotic bric-a-brac and was photographed in costumes from his collection of Oriental garb.

In the United States Bridgman's work was fairly well known in the 1870s, but it was not until his major one-man show in 1881 that he achieved real fame. More than 300 works were displayed at the American Art Gallery in New York, and sales made it a financial success. Bridgman, visiting in New York for the occasion, was fêted at a dinner attended by 123 artists. A similar retrospective exhibition occurred in 1887 at the Fine Arts Society in London; he was also a regular contributor to the Royal Academy exhibitions.

The Academy enjoyed the services of its celebrated member as its unofficial representative in Paris. During the 1890s he accepted its assignment to purchase casts for the school, to supervise scholarship students, and to attend to the Academy's financial interests in the French capital.

In these later years Bridgman's art broke a bit from the Orientalist mold; he painted classical figures, landscape, and decorative murals. He also wrote poetry, played the violin, composed music, and published an anti-Impressionist tract entitled *L'Anarchie dans l'art*. In 1901 his wife died. He married Marthe Jaeger four years later. His last years were spent at Lyon-la-Forêt.

JD

REFERENCES

"Frederick A. Bridgman," *Harper's New Monthly Magazine* 63 (October 1881): 694–705.

Frederick Arthur Bridgman, *Winters in Algeria* (New York: Harper & Bros., 1890).

Frederick Arthur Bridgman, *L'Anarchie dans l'art* (Paris: Société Française d'Editions d'Art, 1898).

Obituary, *New York Times*, January 17, 1928.

Ilene Susan Fort, "The Oriental Genre Paintings of Frederick Arthur Bridgman," graduate paper, Graduate Center, City University of New York, 1979.

Jill Newhouse, New York: Ilene Susan Fort, *The Drawings of Frederick A. Bridgman*, 1983.

ORIENTAL INTERIOR, 1882
Inscribed center left: *To The National Academy of Design / F. A. Bridgman / 1882*
Oil on canvas, 18 × 24
NA diploma presentation, October 23, 1882

Bridgman's election as a full Academician followed his highly successful New York exhibition in 1881. On May 1, 1882, an interim study was accepted by the Council as his diploma contribution pending the arrival of a more important work. *Oriental Interior* is a simpler, quieter variant of Bridgman's usual café type. *An Interesting Game*, 1881 (Brooklyn Museum, Brooklyn, New York) and another work also entitled *Oriental Interior*, n.d. (unlocated; reproduced in Sheldon, opposite p. 1) show more complicated arrangements of six or seven figures engaged in some kind of communal activity. The interior here conforms well to the general description of Arab cafés offered in Bridgman's *Winters in Algeria*: "mud floors and walls, with soot-stained palm-tree ceilings and doors, with nooks and corners of the most curious possible conception."

REFERENCES

Bridgman, *Winters in Algeria*, 202–3.

George William Sheldon, *Recent Ideals of American Art* (New York: D. Appleton & Co., 1890).

James W. Lane, "The Heritage of the National Academy," *Art News* 40 (January 15–30, 1942): 16.

Stephen Edidin, in NAD: *From All Walks*, 29.

Fort, "Oriental Genre Paintings of Frederic Arthur Bridgman," 30–31.

WILLIAM MERRITT CHASE
ANA 1888; NA 1890
Williamsburg, Indiana 1849–1916 New York

Chase spent his adolescence in Indianapolis, where in 1867 he received his first professional artistic instruction from portrait painter Barton S. Hays. His study was interrupted that year by a three-month period of service in the United States Navy, but finding himself unsuited for nautical life, he returned to Indianapolis. Chase went to New York in 1869 and took over Joseph O. Eaton's temporarily empty studio, near the Academy building, and registered for the Academy's antique class. Two years later, he joined his family in their new home in Saint Louis, where he opened a studio and executed portraits and still lifes.

Financed by local businessmen, Chase left in 1872 for an important six years of study abroad. He enrolled in the Munich Royal Academy, where his teachers included Karl von Piloty and Alexander von Wagner. In addition, he fell under the influence of Wilhelm Leibl, the most radical painter in Munich, whose bold, bravura manner was drawn from the art of Gustave Courbet and the Dutch old master Frans Hals. Fellow Americans studying in Munich at the time included J. Frank Currier, Frederick Dielman, Frank Duveneck, Walter Shirlaw, and John Twachtman. Chase, Duveneck, and Twachtman spent nine months of 1877 together in Venice.

Soon after, Chase returned to New York where he accepted a teaching position at the Art Students League, thus beginning almost four decades of educating American art students. He became legendary as a tolerant, insightful, and direct instructor, not only at the Art Students League, but also at the Brooklyn (New York) Art Association, the Pennsylvania Academy of the Fine Arts, Philadelphia, and his own schools, the Shinnecock Summer School of Art on Long Island, 1891–1902, and the Chase School of Art in New York, 1896–1907.

After arriving in New York, Chase found ready society in the circle of young, European-trained artists who formed the Tile Club, a bohemian social organization that took a yearly trip or artistic retreat. Gregarious by nature, he joined other artistic social clubs and became active in the Society of American Artists, serving as its president in 1880 and again from 1885 to 1895. With such friends as J. Carroll Beckwith, Robert Blum, and H. Siddons Mowbray, Chase remained quite busy in the early 1880s, taking summer trips to Europe, helping found the Society of Painters in Pastel, and working to organize the Statue of Liberty Pedestal Fund Art Loan Exhibition. By the time he married Alice Gerson in 1886, he had become a fixture in cosmopolitan New York, occupying a lavishly and exotically appointed studio in the celebrated Tenth Street Studio Building.

The bold brushwork that Chase had learned in Munich always stayed with him, but shortly after arriving in New York, he abandoned the bituminous dark tones that had also characterized his early style. Instead, he explored the high color and light of plein-air park scenes, sparkling figure and costume studies, and from the 1890s, the open landscapes of Long Island dunes. Never a painter of probing psychological depth, Chase concentrated on purely formal concerns. His seemingly easy technical virtuosity was made possible by a sure paint application, an avoidance of overly detailed preliminary drawing, and constant attention to value relationships. Despite their facility and attractive subjects, Chase's paintings did not enjoy a brisk market; large sales held 1887, 1891, and 1896 proved financial disasters. He fortunately also had his teaching and a successful practice as a portrait painter.

Chase enjoyed considerable prominence in the American art world late in life. It was Chase who was invited to fill the vacancy among The Ten upon the death of John Twachtman in 1902. During the summers between 1902 and 1914, he took groups of students abroad for leisurely painting classes. In 1907 he was able to purchase a villa in Florence.

Chase was a faithful contributor to the annual exhibitions of the Academy and received its Thomas R. Proctor Prize in 1912, but considering his multifarious activities and teaching agenda, it is not surprising that he was not otherwise active in Academy affairs.

JD

REFERENCES

Katherine Metcalf Roof, *The Life and Art of William Merritt Chase* (New York: Charles Scribner's Sons, 1917).

Kenyon Cox, *Commemorative Tribute to William Merritt Chase* (New York: American Academy of Arts and Letters, 1922).

Art Gallery, University of California, Santa Barbara: *William Merritt Chase*, 1964.

Henry Art Gallery, University of Washington, Seattle: Ronald G. Pisano, *A Leading Spirit in American Art: William Merritt Chase, 1849–1916*, 1983.

ROBERT BLUM [1888]
Inscribed reverse: 1889
Oil on canvas, 21⅛ × 17⅛
ANA diploma presentation, March 18, 1889

Chase and Blum were intimate friends and depicted one another a number of times. Frequent traveling companions, they spent time in Europe together in 1881, 1882, and 1884, the latter trip resulting in Chase's painting of Blum in his Zandvoort Holland garden, *A Summer Afternoon in Holland (Sunlight and Shadow)* (Joslyn Art Museum, Omaha, Nebraska). They shared many interests, including Japanese and Spanish art and the pastel medium; in 1884 they helped found the Society of Painters in Pastel and worked together to organize its first exhibition. Both were elected Associate members of the Academy on April 19, 1888, but Chase did not paint Blum's diploma portrait until September (Weber, 311).

Chase was often criticized for his emotional disengagement from his subjects. Commenting on his portrait work, Samuel Isham saw "no more attachment to [his sitters'] personalities than if they were brass pots or Kennebec salmon." Yet perhaps because of his personal bond with Blum, Chase has here created an affecting, penetrating likeness that emotionally transcends much of his oeuvre.

The date inscribed on the reverse of the painting would refer to its point of acquisition by the Academy and was applied by a hand other than Chase's.

REFERENCES

Samuel Isham, *The History of American Painting* (New York: Macmillan, 1927), 384.

Parrish Art Museum, Southampton, NY: Ronald G. Pisano, *William Merritt Chase in the Company of Friends*, 1979, 18–19.

Michael Quick, in NAD: *Artists by Themselves*, 20, 25.

Bruce Weber, *Robert Frederick Blum (1857–1903) and His Milieu*, (Ann Arbor, MI: University Microfilms, 1985), 311.

STUDY OF A YOUNG GIRL (or) AN IDLE MOMENT (or) AT HER EASE, n.d.

Inscribed upper left: *W. M. Chase*
Oil on canvas, 44×42
NA diploma presentation, November 24, 1890

Although Chase did not meet James Abbott McNeill Whistler until after he painted *Study of a Young Girl*, the influence on him of Whistler's flat, tonal aestheticism is unmistakable in this painting. Chase allows the coarse weave of the canvas to remain prominent, but despite the thin application of paint, his color is rich and resonant. The asymetrical composition is structured mainly by broad masses of matte color; however, detail and modeling in the girl's face are less restrictive. Her slightly plaintive yet largely unreadable expression injects an element of unease, particularly in the oddly listless manner in which she turns to the viewer, unable or unwilling to raise her head in acknowledgement. In the opposite corner of the canvas, the colors of her hair and flesh are picked up by the two floating ovals of pigment, a calculated device for formal balancing (mimicking Oriental colophon stamps), which, by the single overlapping of the ovals, adds the illusion of depth to an otherwise flat area.

The importance that Chase attached to the painting may be gauged by the fact that in 1884 he sent it to the first Brussels exhibition of Les Vingt, a progressive artists group supportive of Impressionism and Neo-Impressionism. Other Americans invited to send pictures were Whistler and John Singer Sargent. *Study of a Young Girl* was evidently a success; critic Emile Verhaeren of *La Libre Revue* described it as "exquisite." When it was exhibited in Chicago five years later, the painting was no less impressive. The critic of the Chicago *Tribune* called it one of Chase's best portraits, while acknowledging that in its emphasis on formal values over personality and likeness, it might not be properly termed a portrait.

Chase occasionally changed the titles of his works for different exhibitions, and in various exhibition catalogues and references in Academy records after its acquisition, the painting has been known as *Portrait*, *Study of a Young Girl*, *An Idle Moment*, and *At Her Ease*. Its identification is further complicated by the fact that a pastel work by Chase was also entitled *At Her Ease* and was shown with the present painting (then known as *An Idle Moment*) at the same exhibition in Chicago in 1889.

REFERENCES
Emile Verhaeren, "Exposition des Vingtistes à Bruxelles," *La Libre Revue* 16 (1884): 233.

"Mr. Chase's Pictures," Chicago *Tribune*, September 15, 1889.

Laurene Banks, in NAD: *From All Walks*, p. 32.

Information conveyed by Mary Anne Goley and Ronald J. Pisano.

ROBERT FREDERICK BLUM

ANA 1888; NA 1893
Cincinnati 1857–1903 New York

Robert F. Blum was born to immigrant German parents who discouraged him from pursuing a career in art. At sixteen, however, Blum quit high school to work as an apprentice lithographer at the Cincinnati firm of Gibson and Co. He began night classes at the McMicken School and, soon after, at the Ohio Mechanics' Institute, where he studied from life under Frank Duveneck. His fellow students included Alfred Brennan, Kenyon Cox, and John Twachtman. Blum developed an early fascination with the work of Spanish artist Mariano J. M. B. Fortuny, whose sparkling, iridescent paint surfaces long remained an influence.

In 1876, Blum, Brennan, and Cox moved to Philadelphia for a short time. They studied at the Pennsylvania Academy of the Fine Arts under the conservative but tolerant Christian C. Schussele. A far greater influence, however, was the Japanese exhibit at the centennial fair, which Blum visited. His lifelong interest in Japanese art and life ultimately led him to undertake a pioneering two-year visit to that country in 1890.

After nine months in Philadelphia, Blum returned to Cincinnati to experiment with the medium of etching. Disenchanted with what he perceived as philistinism in his hometown, he left for New York in 1878 and obtained work as an illustrator for *St. Nicholas* and *Scribner's Monthly* magazines. Always an experimenter in media, Blum received critical acclaim for "impressionistic" watercolors he showed in the 1879 exhibition of the American Society of Painters in Water Colors. In 1880 he again had an opportunity to develop his etching technique when he met James Abbott McNeill Whistler in Venice during his first trip to Europe. He also spent time with Duveneck in Venice, as well as with the other American artists assembled there around Duveneck.

On his return to New York that year, Blum moved into the Sherwood Studio Building, but the next two summers were again spent in Europe. He and his traveling companions, J. Carroll Beckwith, William Merritt Chase, and William J. Baer, spent months in Venice, Spain, and Holland. Blum again wished to see Venice in 1884, but an outbreak of cholera kept him temporarily in Zandvoort, Holland, with Chase and Charles Ulrich. He returned to Venice, however, in 1886, 1887, and 1889.

Blum's paintings of Venetian subjects were well received for their flickering light and brightly patterned surfaces. Although membership in the Academy is not predicated on individual works, his *Venetian Bead Stringers* (Cincinnati Art Museum, Cincinnati, Ohio), shown in the 1888 Academy annual, was generally thought to have been the spur to his election as an Associate.

When he was not abroad, Blum was an active participant in the New York art world. He was elected to the Society of American Artists in 1882, and a year later he helped found the Society of Painters in Pastel and served as its first president. He served on the Academy's Council from 1895 to 1898. From 1896 to 1900 Blum taught morning classes at the Art Students League.

Blum's long-awaited trip to Japan came in 1890. He was commissioned for a series of drawings to illustrate articles on Japan by Sir Edwin Arnold that appeared in *Scribner's*. While there, he also worked in oil and pastel.

Upon his return, he established a fruitful relationship with patron Alfred Corning Clark, who bought over thirty pictures by him. In 1893 Clark completed building Mendelssohn Hall on West 40th Street, the home of the Mendelssohn Glee Club. He commissioned Blum to paint two murals for the hall. These large works, *Moods to Music* and *The Vintage Festival* (both now in the collection of the Brooklyn Museum, Brooklyn, New York), occupied him from 1893 to 1898.

When Blum died of pneumonia, he was at work on murals for the New Amsterdam Theatre. The Academy's memorial to him entered into the minutes, May 11, 1904, describes his last years: "never of a robust constitution the life of his later years was a constant fight against a malady that, he himself thought, made him incapable of doing his best work for long periods and certainly took from him the joy of living."

JD

REFERENCES

AAA, 1654.

Robert Blum, "An Artist in Japan," *Scribner's Magazine* 13 (April 1893): 399–414.

Charles H. Caffin, "Robert Frederick Blum," *American Studio Talk* (December 1903): clxxvii–cxcii.

Martin Birnbaum, *Robert Frederick Blum: An Appreciation* (New York: Berlin Photographic Co., 1913).

Cincinnati (Ohio) Art Museum: Richard J. Boyle, *Robert F. Blum, 1857–1903*, 1966.

Bruce Weber, *Robert Frederick Blum (1857–1903) and His Milieu*, (Ann Arbor, MI: University Microfilms) 1985.

TWO IDLERS

Inscribed lower right: *Blum 1888–9*
Oil on canvas, 29 × 40
NA diploma presentation, March 26, 1894

In September following his 1888 election as an Associate, Blum began *Two Idlers*, his submission to the Academy's 1889 annual exhibition. It was painted near the Brick Church, New Jersey, home of Blum's friends, William and Laura Baer, who have also been identified as the sitters (Weber, 312). Miniaturist William Baer grew up blocks from Blum in Cincinnati, and the two remained lifelong friends—Baer traveled with Blum, shared his studio, and ultimately served as executor of his estate. Baer's German wife, Laura Schenk, was an accomplished musician. Each day Blum traveled from New York by train, bringing props from his Manhattan studio. Rainy, increasingly cold weather forced Blum to hurry to work up the painting to a point where it could be finished in the studio.

Two Idlers was generally well received at the Academy exhibition, with the critic of the *Nation* commenting on the "delightful bits of painting which for technical quality could not be surpassed by Boldini himself." There was some speculation that the painting would be given a prize, but no award was forthcoming. The high-keyed color and effect of glare that several reviewers criticized might have led to Blum being passed over for honors.

It has often been pointed out that *Two Idlers* bears a similarity to William Merritt Chase's *A Summer Afternoon in Holland (Sunlight and Shadow)* of 1884 (Joslyn Art Museum, Omaha, NE), a work depicting Blum in his Zandvoort garden and featuring the same tasseled hammock.

REFERENCES

Charles M. Kurtz, *Academy Notes* (New York: Cassell & Company, 1889), 28.

"Fine Arts. The Academy Exhibition," *Nation* 48 (April 11, 1889): 312–13.

"The Academy Exhibition," *Art Age* 9 (April 1889): 77.

Exhibition review, *Art Interchange* 22 (April 13, 1889): 1.

Parrish Art Museum, Southampton, NY: Ronald J. Pisano, *William Merritt Chase in the Company of Friends*, 1979, 18-19, 47.

Laurene Banks, in NAD: *From All Walks*, 13, 25–26.

Weber, 311–15.

WILLIAM JAMES WHITTEMORE
ANA 1897
New York 1860–1955 East Hampton, New York

After an education in New York private schools, Whittemore spent three months in the winter of 1877 in the studio of the landscapist William Hart. For the next few years he worked in his father's business, where he learned gilding, and then spent several years between 1882 and 1886 attending the Academy's antique and life classes and also working at the Art Students League. In the late 1880s he went abroad, entering the Académie Julian in Paris for study under Jules Lefebvre and Jean-Joseph Benjamin-Constant.

Whittemore married artist Alice V. Whitmore in 1895; they built a home in East Hampton and made frequent trips to Europe. Proficient in landscape, genre, and still life, he gradually adopted portraiture (with ivory miniatures a speciality) as his main emphasis around the turn of the century. In the Academy's winter exhibition of 1917 he won the Thomas R. Proctor Prize for portraiture. Whittemore was a steady contributor to Academy exhibitions, his work appearing in annuals over a span of sixty years.

JD

REFERENCES
AAA, De Witt McClellan Lockman interview, 504.

CHARLES C. CURRAN, 1888–89
Inscribed upper right: *Wm. J. Whittemore 1889/Paris*
Oil on canvas, 17 × 21
ANA diploma exchange presentation, May 7, 1934

Whittemore and Curran met in New York while studying under Walter Satterlee. The two friends shared a studio in the Sherwood Building and in autumn 1888, left for Paris together. This unusual portrait of Curran shows him painting from the Venus de Milo in the Louvre galleries. According to a story told by Whittemore in an interview with De Witt McClellan Lockman, he had difficulty leaving the Louvre with the painting because of a guard's strict interpretation of a rule prohibiting the painting of portraits in the museum.

The painting encountered further problems when it was sent to New York as Curran's Associate diploma presentation. Whittemore claimed that William Hart had told him to make it "unusual," so while keeping to the seventeen by twenty-one inches regulation size, he made his canvas horizontal rather than the expected vertical. A portrait of Curran was accepted by the Council on May 6, 1889. Five months later, it was replaced by a self-portrait. It is not known whether the portrait accepted initially was the present work or a third canvas. In any case, the Council made known its view that Whittemore's painting had too many genre features to be a proper diploma portrait. Curran apparently took back the work, and waited forty-five years before broaching the subject again. In 1934, he petitioned the Council (of which he was then a member) to allow the substitution of Whittemore's painting for his self-portrait. This time, his request was granted.

The painting's former frame bore Curran's inscription memorializing the saga of its entrance into the collection: "painted in Paris 1888 [illegible] offered to Council of the Academy as Diploma portrait [illegible] refused by council who said they wanted a portrait [illegible] a genre presented to the Academy in 1936 [sic] by Charles C. Curran"

REFERENCES
NAD minutes, May 6 and October 14, 1889; May 7, 1934.
AAA, De Witt McClellan Lockman interview, 504.

THOMAS ALEXANDER HARRISON
ANA 1898; NA 1901
Philadelphia 1853–1930 Paris

Alexander Harrison was educated in the Philadelphia suburb of Germantown, Pennsylvania, where his family lived for a number of years. After working for his father, a civil engineer and merchant, for a short period he briefly studied art in Philadelphia before taking a job with the U.S. Coast and Geodetic Survey at age nineteen. For several years he worked along the New England and Florida shores as well as on the Pacific Northwest coast. Leaving his job in Seattle in 1877, he spent a year and a half at the San Francisco School of Design before embarking for Paris in spring 1879.

Harrison studied with Jean-Léon Gérôme at the École des Beaux-Arts, but he also spent time in Brittany at the artists colony at Pont-Aven. Soon he became the acknowledged leader of the Americans at the rugged seaside resort. In 1881 he met and became a close friend of Jules Bastien-Lepage, who encouraged him to experiment with plein-air painting. After the Salon exhibition of Harrison's celebrated *In Arcadia*, 1885, which was purchased by the French government, he moved to the forefront of international investigations of bright outdoor light and the relationship of figures to landscape. At the same time he began his long series of marines, predominately nocturnal beach scenes.

Despite his international reputation and election to the Society of American Artists in 1885, the Academy seems to have been slow to invite him to join their ranks, probably because of his residence in France and infrequent submissions to Academy annuals. The year of his election to Associate, 1898, he also made a lengthy stay in America.

In later years he taught winter classes in Paris and spent time in New Hope, Pennsylvania. He also traveled to North Africa. A joint exhibition of Harrison's and his brother Birge's work was organized in the United States in 1913.

JD

REFERENCES

Anna Seaton-Schmidt, "Some American Marine Painters," *Art and Progress* 2 (November 1910): 3–8.

City Art Museum of Saint Louis, MO: Arthur Hoeber, *A Retrospective Collection of Paintings of Alexander Harrison, N.A., and Birge Harrison, N.A.*, 1913.

Dayton (Ohio) Art Institute: Michael Quick, *American Expatriate Painters of the Late Nineteenth Century*, 1976.

Doreen Bolger Burke, *American Paintings in the Metropolitan Museum of Art. Volume III: A Catalogue of Works by Artists Born between 1846 and 1864* (Princeton, NJ: Princeton University Press, 1980), 159–60.

MOONRISE, n.d.
Inscribed lower left: A. *Harrison*
Oil on canvas, 20¼ × 60¼
NA diploma presentation, April 7, 1902

Harrison's early work on the U.S. Coastal Survey may have left him predisposed to the charms of his most celebrated pictorial type, nocturnal beach scenes. He began the long series of expansive horizontal "wave" paintings in the early 1880s. The most famous example was his 1885 *The Wave* (Pennsylvania Academy of the Fine Arts, Philadelphia), a sunlit depiction of the complexities of advancing and receding sheets of water on glistening sand.

Harrison's diploma contribution depicts a slightly more volatile night sea. The breaking wave is situated in the center of the painting; however, the moon is placed to the left, creating a slight asymmetrical tension by appearing to draw the right edge of the foaming line of water up the picture plane, as if by some powerful gravitational pull. As always, Harrison

is particularly sensitive to the play of light, darkening the undersides of crests not penetrated by the soft moonlight, and heightening the values of the translucent water as it spreads itself, frothing, onto the flat beach.

The painting was long known simply as *Marine* until the recent discovery of a label fragment on its stretcher bearing its title and suggesting the likelihood the Academy's painting was that shown by Harrison at the Chicago Inter-State Industrial Exposition in 1889.

In 1910 the Council agreed to lend *Moonrise* to Henry Wolf so he might make an engraved reproduction of it; however, no engraving has been located.

REFERENCES
NAD minutes, April 18, 1910.

Norton Gallery of Art, West Palm Beach, FL: Bruce Weber, *In Nature's Ways: American Landscape Painting of the Late Nineteenth Century*, 1987, 12.

Kenyon Cox

ANA 1900; NA 1903

Warren, Ohio 1856–1919 New York

Born into a family of intellectuals, Kenyon Cox spent much of his early career convincing his parents that painting was an advantageous and profitable profession. Between the ages of nine and thirteen he spent most of his time in bed, the result of a serious tumorous growth on his chin. It was at this time that he took up drawing. After a series of successful operations, he continued his studies in 1869. Cox spent four years at the McMicken School, Cincinnati, and supplemented his studies with night work at the University of Cincinnati. In 1874 Frank Duveneck returned to Cincinnati and began a life class at the Ohio Mechanics Institute, which Cox attended. His fellow students included Robert Blum and John Twachtman.

In company with Blum, Cox passed part of 1876 studying at the Pennsylvania Academy of the Fine Arts, Philadelphia, under Christian C. Schussele. Blum and Cox disliked their teacher and dreamed of traveling to Europe to study the work of their idols, Mariano Fortuny and Giovanni Boldini. Japan was also of great interest to the two students, particularly after visiting the exhibits at the 1876 Centennial Exposition.

Cox left for France in 1877, visiting Rouen before arriving in Paris. That winter he entered the atelier of Emile Carolus-Duran, and he made his first visit to the town of Grez, near Fontainebleau, which would become his favorite vacation spot. Cox must have impressed his teacher, for by 1878 he was assisting him with his painting *Apotheosis of Marie de Medici* in the Luxembourg Palace. Cox, however, grew disenchanted with Carolus-Duran's lax methods, especially after he failed to be admitted to the École des Beaux-Arts in March 1878. To add academic rigor to his training, he began a class with Alexandre Cabanel. After a summer in Rouen, Grez, and Italy, he also began attending the Académie Julian, where he excelled. In March 1879 he finally was admitted to the

École to work under Jean-Léon Gérôme, with whom he remained until 1882. During these years he was also painting portraits and spending time in Grez, London, and Brussels, where he worked briefly on a large war panorama before quitting because of his employers' refusal to provide costumed models.

Returning first to Cincinnati in 1882, and then to New York in 1883, Cox was almost immediately elected to the Society of American Artists. Permanently marked by his academic training abroad, he began exhibiting "academies," or large-scale nude studies, which caused considerable controversy in the art world. His work was not well received, and for fifteen years he had to struggle to live on his portrait and landscape work. Cox had begun to write criticism while still abroad; now, to supplement his income, he turned seriously to writing, launching a long career as a critic, author, and lecturer. His initial job was with *The Nation*, but he was soon writing for other periodicals as well. He also did illustration work for *Century* and other magazines, and in 1886, after Will Low and Thomas Dewing had declined the job offer and recommended Cox, Dodd, Mead, and Company engaged him to illustrate Dante Gabriel Rossetti's *Blessed Damozel*, for a fee of $1,500. Another source of income for Cox was teaching at the Art Students League; there he met the student, Louise Howland King, who became his wife in 1892.

In the 1890s Cox's career was on the upswing thanks to his experimentation in decorative mural work. Over the years he executed important works in the Iowa and Minnesota Capitols; the Library of Congress in Washington; the Appellate

Court Building, New York; the Essex County Courthouse, Newark, New Jersey; the Citizens Bank, Cleveland, Ohio; and the Walker Art Building at Bowdoin College, Brunswick, Maine. He was active in the Society of Mural Painters, serving as its first vice president.

The Academy first honored Cox in 1889 with a Julius Hallgarten Prize, but perhaps because of his conflicting work as a critic, eleven years passed before he was elected Associate. Advancement to Academician came more promptly, and at the earliest constitutionally permitted opportunity thereafter he was elected to the Council, beginning a period of thirteen years active involvement in management of Academy affairs. Cox served as a Council member from 1904 to 1907; he was then elected recording secretary, a post he held to 1910, when he returned to the Council for a three-year term. Following the obligatory year off Council, he was elected to another three-year term in 1914, and again reelected in 1918, but served only one year. He was a frequent lecturer in the Academy school from 1900 to 1917, and gave a class in composition in 1917–18. The second and final award given Cox for work in Academy exhibitions was a Joseph S. Isidor Gold Medal presented in the winter exhibition of 1910.

Still plagued with money problems late in life, he continued writing and lecturing. In 1905 he began publishing a series of volumes of his essays, the most enduring of which was *The Classic Point of View*, 1911. Ironically, although Cox's own career had been hindered by his progressive views of the 1880s, he became ultraconservative at the end of his life, vehemently attacking such exhibitions as the 1913 Armory Show.

JD

REFERENCES

Avery Architectual and Fine Arts Library, Columbia University, Kenyon Cox Papers.

Minna C. Smith, "The Work of Kenyon Cox," *International Studio* 32 (July 1907): III–XII.

Richard Murray, "Kenyon Cox and the Art of Drawing," *Drawing* 3 (May-June 1981): 1–6.

Marianne Doezema, "Kenyon Cox and American Figure Painting," [Georgia Museum of Art] *Bulletin* 10 (Spring 1985).

H. Wayne Morgan, ed., *An American Art Student in Paris: The Letters of Kenyon Cox, 1877–1882* (Kent, OH: Kent State University Press, 1986).

A BLONDE, 1891

Inscribed lower left: *Kenyon Cox 1891*
Oil on canvas, 41 × 36
NA diploma presentation, June 1, 1903

Few of Cox's large-scale "academies" drew as much criticism as *A Blonde* when it was shown in the 1892 Society of American Artists exhibition. Viewers failed to find a rationale for this type of pure, unabashed study without a trace of allegory. In retrospect, Samuel Isham, in his *History of American Paintings*, 1905, defended Cox's lonely campaign for the nude: "Almost the only man to paint the nude as it is understood in Europe, except as part of decorations, was Kenyon Cox. In the years following his return from Europe he painted repeatedly large life-size studies of the same general type as the Etudes of the Salons, and painted them well and learnedly."

Others, however, could not easily dismiss the "clinical" tone of works like *A Blonde*. One critic wrote, "Mr. Cox's 'Blonde' should never, we think, have left the class-room. In its way an admirable study of the nude, it is most disagreeable in color and almost vulgar in pose" (*Art Amateur*, 3). A particular aspect singled out for criticism was the prominent ridge of the model's spine: "Another sinner against the ideal is Mr. Cox, whose study of a backbone and appurtenances in his nude 'Blonde' is not, in any proper sense, a picture at all. It is, no doubt, a good study of anatomy, but as much out of place in a public exhibition as a drawing from a skeleton" (*The Critic*, 280). The most vehement attack on *A Blonde* appeared in *The Studio*, where even its merit as a demonstration study was disputed: "Mr. Cox's . . . 'Blonde' . . . is not even praiseworthy from the class-room demonstrator's point-of-view. The model is curled up most uncomfortably on a sofa, and looks more like an embryo with its too big head and small legs, than a finished human. It is certainly a very ugly figure, and puzzles us to guess why it was painted" (*The Studio*, 234).

A writer himself, Cox had an opportunity to respond to his critics six months later when he published an essay entitled, "The Nude in Art." "[T]he study of the nude," he argued, "is the necessary foundation for all good representation of the human figure . . . . [U]nless some artists occupied themselves almost entirely with the nude, the standard of construction and draughtsmanship would soon be lowered for all" (Cox, 747). His personal and sustained study was thus seen as a means of preserving and advancing the state of American figural drawing and painting in general.

REFERENCES
"The Society of American Artists of New York. Fourteenth Exhibition," *The Studio* 7 (May 28, 1892): 234.

"The Society of American Artists," *Art Amateur* 27 (June 1892): 3.

"The Fine Arts: The Society of American Artists' Exhibition—Second Notice," *The Critic* 17 (1892): 280.

Kenyon Cox, "The Nude in Art," *Scribner's Magazine* 12 (December 1892): 747–49.

Samuel Isham, *History of American Painting* (New York: Macmillan, 1905), 480.

CASS GILBERT, 1907

Inscribed upper left: *Cass Gilbert* A. N. A. /
By Kenyon Cox, 1907
Oil on canvas, 30 ⅛ × 25 ⅛
ANA diploma presentation, March 4, 1907

Gilbert was born in Zanesville, Ohio in 1859. He attended school in Saint Paul, Minnesota, before taking his degree at the Massachusetts Institute of Technology, Cambridge. In 1880, following a tour of Europe and Egypt, he began his professional career by becoming the personal assistant of Stanford White. Three years later he went to Saint Paul and with James Knox Taylor established his own office.

In the 1890s Gilbert began moving toward a more formal style of neoclassicism than that associated with McKim, Mead, and White. Beginning with the Minnesota State Capitol Building, 1895, his commissions became increasingly more important. By 1899 he had moved his headquarters to New York, where in 1912 he erected perhaps his most celebrated accomplishment, the Woolworth Building.

As his fame grew, Gilbert assumed important positions in national artistic and architectural circles. At various times he served as president of the American Institute of Architects, the Architectural League, and the National Institute of Arts and Letters. He was elected an Associate of the Academy in 1906, and an Academician in 1908. He was a member of the Council from 1909 to 1912 and was president from 1926 to 1933, the first architect to hold an Academy officership.

Cox was a natural choice to execute Gilbert's Associate portrait, for they had collaborated on several occasions, with Cox murals embellishing Gilbert's Minnesota State Capitol Building, Essex County (New Jersey) Courthouse, and Citizens Bank, Cleveland, Ohio. In writing in 1910 to a colleague he was trying to persuade not to decline election to the Academy because of the difficulty of fulfilling the portrait requirement, Gilbert said Cox had painted his portrait "on two Sundays." Some exaggeration in this statement must be allowed in the circumstances; it is more likely that the portrait was based on two sittings. Cox thought it one of his best portraits, as he wrote to his friend, Leonard Opdycke, in 1914.

REFERENCES

NAD archives, Gilbert to Wilson Eyre, May 11, 1910.

Avery Architectural and Fine Arts Library, Columbia University, Kenyon Cox to Leonard Opdycke, May 18, 1914.

Minna Smith, "The Work of Kenyon Cox," *International Studio* 32 (July 1907): XIII.

Steven Bedford in NAD: *Between Traditions and Modernism*, 1980, 12.

CASS GILBERT·A·N·A·
BY KENYON COX, 1907·

Thomas Cowperthwait Eakins
ANA 1902; NA 1902
Philadelphia 1844–1916 Philadelphia

Eakins attended Philadelphia's rigorous Central High School from 1857 to graduation in 1861; at the school he excelled in mathematics, sciences, French, and, most significantly, drawing, which he studied all four years. For the next several years he worked with his father, a writing master and teacher of penmanship, while studying at the Pennsylvania Academy of the Fine Arts from 1862 to 1866. For about the year 1864–65 he supplemented the Pennsylvania Academy's anatomy lectures with attendence at anatomy classes and demonstrations at Philadelphia's Jefferson Medical College.

In the autumn of 1866, with that solid grounding in art study, Eakins went to Paris, where he was admitted to the École des Beaux-Arts to study under Jean-Léon Gérôme. The relationship between the highly distinguished French artist and his aspiring American student would remain warm. Excepting a Christmas visit home to Philadelphia in 1868, Eakins remained abroad studying and traveling into the summer of 1870.

Besides his primary work with Gérôme, he also spent several months in the spring of 1868 studying clay modeling with Augustin Alexandre Dumont and a year later worked briefly in the atelier of Léon Bonnat. Having felt he had attained all he could from formal instruction, Eakins passed the final six month of his European experience in Spain, chiefly in Seville, where he produced his first serious work.

Resettled permanently in the family home in Philadelphia—where he would reside all his life except for two years following his marriage in 1884 to Susan Macdowell—Eakins embarked on his career. That career would be marked in near-equal parts by rejection of his paintings and teaching methods by the majority of the artistic establishment and the affection and respect of his students and a limited number of perceptive, progressive colleagues and patrons. He was uncompromising in the vision he transcribed in his art, and in his expectation that students exercise their full vision, in an era that valued idealization in its imagry and extreme modesty of conduct—even in artists' study of the figure. Eakins passed a lifetime of controversy with, and near-isolation from, his peers and public.

While Eakins came to rely on work as an instructor and lecturer as his principal source of income, he was a dedicated teacher. He first taught—without salary—evening drawing classes at the Philadelphia Sketch Club from 1874 to 1876. When the Pennsylvania Academy of the Fine Arts reopened in the autumn of 1876, after five years of building construction, he became the unpaid assistant to Christian Schussele, its professor of drawing and painting. In 1877, when dissident Pennyslvania Academy students formed the Philadelphia Art Student's Union, Eakins accompanied them as instructor. A year later, in the autumn of 1878, he returned to the Pennsylvania Academy as assistant professor of painting and chief demonstrator of anatomy. At Schussele's death in August 1879 Eakins assumed his postion and title and at last received a salary. In 1882 he was appointed director of the Pennsylvania Academy school, the position from which he was forced to resign in February 1886, ostensibly because of his use of the entirely nude male model in life classes. His students promptly bolted the Pennsylvania Academy to form the Art Students League of Philadelphia, with Eakins as instructor; the League, with Eakins's leadership, survived to 1893.

Simultaneously with his teaching in Philadelphia, Eakins had begun commuting to New York for appointments as lecturer on anatomy at several of the city's art schools. From 1881 through the school year 1884–85 he taught at the Students' Art Guild of the Brooklyn Art Association; in November 1885 he became the regular lecturer in anatomy at the Art Students League of New York and continued through the 1888–89 season; that same 1888–89 year was his first as the National Academy's lecturer in anatomy; 1891–92 was the beginning of seven seasons as the lecturer in anatomy for the Women's Art School of the Cooper Union.

Eakins gave his annual series of ten lectures at the National Academy beginning in 1888, and remained the Academy's lecturer on anatomy through 1894–95. During the 1893–94 season Eakins united the previously separated male and female classes, with some repercussions from students and press. Within the 1894–95 school year the chairman of the Council's school committee, and former fellow-student, Edwin Blashfield, had an informal and apparently amicable discussion with Eakins concerning some reservations the Academy had about his teaching methods. At the artist-managed Academy reaction was not so aggressive as it had been in Philadelphia; Eakins's contract was not renewed the next year, whether by mutual agreement or one-sided decision is not recorded.

Eakins painted in watercolor in the earlier years of his career. He executed his first sculptures in 1883 and continued to work occasionally in sculpture through the mid-1890s; and from 1884 he was one of the most committed artist-photographers of the nineteenth century. Painting in oil was his primary medium, however. He executed major subject pictures, such as scenes of scullers on the Schuylkill River, professional boxers, and sport hunters (where the central figures were generally specific persons), but it was in portraiture that his expressive gift was most consistently and powerfully demonstrated.

For nearly twenty years from his first major opportunity to be introduced to a public at the Philadelphia Centennial Exposition, when arguably his greatest work, *The Gross Clinic, Portrait of Professor Gross,* was rejected for display within the fair's art exhibition, Eakins was regularly thwarted in his efforts to have his work included in prestigious exhibitions. For much of that time his response was to withdraw from the conventional professional arena, concentrating on his work and on teaching. His paintings were fairly regularly seen in Pennsylvania Academy exhibitions to 1884, but only rarely over the next decade. Eakins was surprised and angered at the rejection of his first submission in 1875 for the National Academy annual, yet he tried again. His work was shown in the annuals of 1877 through 1879, 1881, and 1882. He exhibited with the progressive Society of American Artists from the year of its founding, 1878, into the mid-1880s; however, in 1892 he resigned from the Society, stating that its consistent rejection of his work for the exhibitions of the three previous years demonstrated an intolerable difference in standards.

Eleven Eakins paintings were included in the art exhibition of the 1893 World's Columbian Exposition in Chicago. He received a medal, the first since several of his watercolors had received an award in the 1878 Massachusetts Charitable Mechanics' Association exhibition in Boston. While the years following the Columbian Exposition hardly saw a blossoming of general enthusiasm for Eakins art, they were more receptive to the uncompromising realism and psychological penetration of his vision. Beginning in 1894 he again became a regular exhibitor at the Pennsylvania Academy. He participated in National Academy annuals in 1895, 1896, 1902, and yearly from 1904 throughout his life, and in 1905 received the Academy's Thomas R. Proctor Prize for portraiture. His work was accepted for the first Carnegie Institute International, Pittsburgh, in 1896, and was seen regularly in Carnegie shows from 1899 through 1912; in addition, he was frequently a member of the Carnegie jury. Among the awards he now received were medals in the Saint Louis world fair of 1904 and the Pennsylvania Academy's Temple Gold Medal the same year. Ill health, including failing eyesight, curtailed his capacity to work for the last five years of his life.

ABG

REFERENCES
Lloyd Goodrich, *Thomas Eakins* 2 vols. (Cambridge, MA: Harvard University Press, 1982).

Self-Portrait [1902]

Oil on canvas, 30×25
ANA diploma presentation, May 5, 1902

The only other known Eakins *Self-Portrait* is now in the collection of the Hirshhorn Museum and Sculpture Garden, Smithsonian Institution, Washington, D.C. It carries an inscription on its reverse written by Charles Bregler, Eakins's student, stating it was executed in 1902 as a study for the Academy's portrait. The study differs somewhat from the finished work in pose and feeling, and no details of clothing are articulated; however, Eakins does appear to be the same age in both works.

If, as seems likely, Eakins painted his own portrait explictly to fulfill the requirement of his March 12, 1902, election to Associate, he did so with dispatch. The portrait's acceptance and confirmation of Eakins's membership in the Academy coming within two months of his election, and before the annual meeting of that year, allowed the Academy to take the unprecedented action of advancing an Associate of only nine days standing to full Academican.

ABBOTT HANDERSON THAYER

ANA 1898; NA 1901
Boston, Massachusetts 1849–1921 Dublin, New Hampshire

Thayer spent his boyhood in Vermont and New Hampshire, where he developed an early interest in wildlife. While at the Chauncy Hall School in Boston from 1864 to 1867, he received some instruction in art from Henry Morse. He executed animal portraits on the side. His move to Brooklyn, New York, in 1867 enabled him to study with J. B. Whittaker at the Brooklyn Academy of Design and at the Academy school, where he was enrolled in the antique class from 1870 to 1874 and the life class from 1871 to 1873. He married Kate Bloede in 1875, and the two left for Paris where Thayer worked for four years at the École des Beaux-Arts under Henri Lehmann and Jean–Léon Gérôme.

After his return to Brooklyn in 1879, Thayer spent the next two decades living in New York, Massachusetts, Connecticut, and New Hampshire. He was active in the Society of American Artists, serving as its vice president and president in 1883 and 1884. Election to the Academy followed his receipt of the Thomas B. Clarke Prize in its annual exhibition of 1898. By then he had long since given up his earlier mode of cattle scenes and landscapes, opting instead for idealized figural works that often depicted his family and friends. (He remarried in 1891 shortly after the death of his first wife.)

Thayer had designed and built a summer home on property given him in Dublin in 1888. As of 1901 he lived there year-round, adopting an insular and eccentric lifestyle defined by phobias and an intense devotion to his natural surroundings. Much of the next few years were dedicated to advancing his theories on protective coloration, published in 1909 in his book, *Concealing Coloration in the Animal Kingdom*. He did continue to exhibit with the Academy, and in the 1915 annual received the Saltus Gold Medal. Late in life he was supported by two wealthy patrons, Charles Lang Freer and John Gellatly.

JD

REFERENCES
Homer Saint-Gaudens, "Abbott H. Thayer," *International Studio* 33 (January 1908): LXXXI–LXXXVII.

Royal Cortissoz, *American Painters* (New York: Charles Scribner's Sons, 1923), 25–43.

Nelson C. White, *Abbott H. Thayer, Painter and Naturalist* (Hartford: Connecticut Printers, 1951).

Everson Art Museum, Syracuse, New York: Ross Anderson, *Abbott Handerson Thayer*, 1982.

WINTER LANDSCAPE, 1902

Inscribed lower right: *Abbott H. Thayer / Jan. 1902*
Oil on canvas, 29⅜ × 34⅞
NA diploma presentation, May 5, 1902

Thayer returned to the landscape genre in earnest near the turn of the century. The painting of the scenery around his Dublin home is said to have been a therapeutic distraction for the artist when he was faced with unsolved problems in his figural works. He revered the New Hampshire landscape, particularly nearby Mount Monadnock, which he painted many times. Taking his cue from his favorite philosopher, Ralph Waldo Emerson, he looked to the study of landscape for the moral truth it would yield, a rationale also used by the artist to explain his allegorical pictures of women.

Winter Landscape was painted during the first year that Thayer's family remained in Dublin through the cold months. Pristine blankets of snow obviously appealed to him; most of the landscapes of this period are winter scenes. Through them, he was able to demonstrate repeatedly how the light turquoise winter sky creates blue shadows on the snow, an important principle in his theories of the protective coloration of blue jays.

REFERENCES
Kate Nearpass, in NAD: *Next to Nature*, 164–67.

Susan Hobbs, "Nature into Art: The Landscapes of Abbott Handerson Thayer," *American Art Journal* 14 (Summer 1982): 30.

Anderson, 103.

HERMON ATKINS MACNEIL

ANA 1905; NA 1906

Everett, Massachusetts 1866–1947 Queens, New York

MacNeil's early artistic education was accomplished at Massachusetts Normal Art School, Boston, which had been established in 1873 to train drawing teachers. In Boston in the late 1870s he also had some contact with William Rimmer, either as a student or by attending his anatomical lectures. The extent or exact nature of this study is unclear. Frank Jewett Mather recalled that "To the end of his life MacNeil mentioned Rimmer with admiration and gratitude."

Following his 1886 graduation from the Normal Art School, MacNeil taught drawing and modeling at Cornell University, Ithaca, New York, before leaving in 1888 for Paris to pursue academic training as a sculptor. He entered the Académie Julian under Henri Chapu, and studied with Jean Falguière at the École des Beaux-Arts.

Returning to America in 1892, he worked with sculptor Philip Martiny, on figures for various buildings at the Columbian Exposition in Chicago; for this work he was awarded the Designers Medal. He remained in Chicago and taught at the Art Institute school for three years. It was during this period that he became interested in depicting the American Indian, several of whom he met at the Exposition. He spent several months traveling throughout the West making portrait and anthropological studies of Native Americans.

Shortly after his 1895 marriage to fellow sculptor Carol Brooks, MacNeil won the Rinehart Scholarship, established by the estate of American sculptor William Henry Rinehart. This permitted him to pass the next four years in Rome, where he produced many of his most well-known Indian subject pieces. In 1900 he worked on decorations for the U.S. Government Building at the International Exposition in Paris. His *The Sun Vow* (Metropolitan Museum of Art, New York) won a silver medal in the Exposition; it remained one of his most popular Indian studies. The following years brought more honors for work exhibited at the 1901 Pan-American Exposition, Buffalo, New York; the 1902 Charleston (South Carolina) Exposition; the 1904 Louisiana Purchase Exposition, in Saint Louis, Missouri; the 1910 Buenos Aires Exposition; and the 1915 Panama-Pacific International Exposition, in San Francisco.

On his return to New York from Rome, MacNeil set up a studio at College Point, Long Island. A sequence of important commissions quickly established him as a major American sculptor. His work of 1905, *The Coming of the White Man*, modeled for the city of Portland, Oregon, was followed by the McKinley Memorial for Columbus, Ohio, of about 1907, and a figure of Ezra Cornell executed for the campus of Cornell University.

After World War I major commissions included the equestrian *Pony Express Rider* in Saint Joseph, Missouri; the figure *Washington as Commander-in-Chief of the Army* for the Washington Square Arch, New York; and the pedimental group for the east wing of the U.S. Supreme Court Building, Washington, D.C. Many portrait figures and busts, several of which are in the collection of New York University, date from these years as well. His design for the U.S. Liberty quarter was minted between 1916 and 1932.

MacNeil was a member of the Academy school faculty from 1906 into 1919. He then was visiting professor at the American Academy in Rome in 1919 and 1920 and later taught at the Pratt Institute and the Art Students League in New York. He was president of the National Sculpture Society from 1910 to 1912 and again from 1922 to 1924, and his design, *Into the Unknown*, was adopted as the Society's seal.

By the late 1920s, however, MacNeil's style, basically formed in the Beaux-Arts aesthetic, was considered old fashioned; the modern trend toward abstraction was gaining ground. His last major work, the *Fort Sumter Memorial*, was executed in 1932, fifteen years before his death. The wide geographical distribution of his work, especially his monumental pieces, as well as his designs for medals and coins has made his oeuvre more familiar to today's public than his name. As his student, Adolph Block, wrote: "The public . . . often enjoys a sculpture by MacNeil without being aware of the man who created it."

DBD

REFERENCES

"Some Recent Work by H. A. MacNeil," *Brush and Pencil* 5 (November 1899): 68.

Hermon A. MacNeil, "Sculpture—A Report of Progress," *The American Magazine of Art* 8 (August 1917): 411–14.

Frank Jewett Mather, Jr., "Hermon Atkins MacNeil," in American Academy of Arts and Letters, *Commemorative Tributes*, n.d., 74–80.

Adolph Block, "Hermon A. MacNeil," *National Sculpture Review*, (1963–64): 17.

Wayne Craven, "Hermon Atkins MacNeil," in *Dictionary of American Biography*, supplement 4, 1974, 533–34.

A Chief of the Multnomah Tribe, 1905

Inscribed front: *Multnomah*; back: *H. A. MacNeil '05 / Roman Bronze Works, New York*
Bronze, 37½ × 12 × 10
NA diploma presentation, March 4, 1907

This figure is half of a full-sized bronze group originally called *Peace Signal*, but eventually titled *The Coming of the White Man*, executed by MacNeil on a commission from David P. Thompson, a pioneer businessman of Portland, Oregon. The design for the group was finished by 1903 and was unveiled in 1907 in Washington Park, Portland, a gift of the heirs of the recently deceased Thompson to fulfill his desire to leave a fitting memorial to the city. The work represents the first confrontation of an unspecified chief of the Multnomah tribe of Oregon with the white man, or men, whose existence is suggested but not depicted. In the original composition the chief is accompanied by a medicine man, who displays the emotions of fear and suspicion not obvious in his erect and defiant companion. As Jean Holden wrote in 1903:

> Superstitious, without experience, and without a common language, Multonomah [sic] meets the stranger like a brave man who feels the inviolability of the human soul and dares the rest. From the crown of his proud head to the sole of his well-planted foot, he shows no excitement. All trace of emotion is left to the tribesman at his side, who signals to the invader with the freshly-plucked branch of an oak.

In its rich modeling and exploitation of a varied surface texturing, the group reveals MacNeil's years of Paris training. The work was prefigured compositionally by *The Sun Vow*, which is also a two-figure Indian group.

By 1905 MacNeil had authorized the Roman Bronze Works to produce casts of a reduced version of the chief, alone. As many as twelve of these were made; the Metropolitan Museum of Art and the American Academy of Arts and Letters, in New York, have casts. No comparable castings of the subsidiary figure or of the original composition as a whole are known. Not all of the castings of *Multnomah* are dated as is the Academy's, suggesting this example may have been cast specifically for presentation to the Academy.

REFERENCES

NAD minutes, December 3, 1906.

AAA, Hermon Atkins MacNeil Papers, 2726.

Jean Stansbury Holden, "The Sculptors MacNeil," *World's Work* 14 (October 1903): 9403–19.

FREDERICK CHILDE HASSAM
ANA 1902; NA 1906
Dorchester, Massachusetts 1859–1935 East Hampton, New York

As a boy Childe Hassam studied drawing with Walter Smith in Boston. While attending high school he worked as a book-keeper for the publishing firm of Little, Brown and Company, and on finishing school in 1876, was apprenticed to George E. Johnson, a Boston wood engraver. Between 1877 and 1879 he studied drawing and painting in evening classes at the Boston Art Club, the Lowell Institute, and also with Ignaz Gaugengigl.

By the early 1880s Hassam was working independently as an illustrator, as well as painting, at first primarily in water-color. His earliest one-man exhibition occurred in 1882. In the following year his work was first included in an Academy annual, and he made his first trip abroad, visiting Spain, Italy, France, and Holland. On his return to Boston that year Hassam turned his attention more fully to oil painting and began producing scenes of the city's more elegant streets, highly de-tailed genre scenes, but already showing an interest in repre-senting effects of light and atmosphere. In 1886 Hassam went to Paris for a stay of three years; there he studied at the Aca-démie Julian with Lucien Doucet, Gustave Boulanger, and Jules Joseph Lefebvre. He continued to depict the rainy or twilight atmosphere he had favored and to execute large urban scenes, the marked influence of the work of the French Impressionists rapidly became apparent in his freer brushing style, textural application of paint, and preference for sunlit scenes. Richly colored garden scenes shown in strong sunlight predominate in the work executed during summers spent at Villiers-le-Bel.

When Hassam returned to America in October 1889, it was to settle in New York, which remained his essential home throughout his life. He became one of the most well-known practitioners of American Impressionism. His work grew in-creasingly sensitive to changes in light, atmosphere, and the seasons. These developments as well as his use of rich tex-tures, broken strokes, and high palette reflect the influence of urban scenes by Monet and Pissarro. But it was, perhaps, in the joyous spirit of Hassam's work that it was most closely al-lied to French Impressionism.

Hassam had first shown his work in an Academy annual in 1883; his next appearance was in 1886, the same year he first showed with the Society of American Artists. He re-mained a consistent exhibitor in Academy exhibitions throughout his life. In 1890, the second time he was repre-sented in a Society exhibition, he was elected to its member-ship and continued to show with the Society—usually a quan-tity of works—yearly through 1897. The following year he was among the group that detached itself from the Society to form The Ten American Painters. Hassam's conspicuous alignment with what some construed as the Academy's opposition may well have been the reason for his relatively late induction into membership. It is interesting to note that of the several prizes established for Academy annuals in 1884, Hassam was the first artist of the Impressionist school to receive one, when the Thomas B. Clarke Prize was awarded him in 1905. He would also receive Benjamin Altman prizes in the winter exhibitions of 1922 and 1924, and annual of 1926; and the Saltus Medal in the annual of 1935.

Hassam was a great and convivial traveler. In addition to return visits to Europe, over the years he summered at most of the Eastern art colony resorts popular with artists. Before the turn of the century he was inspired by the lush wild flower garden and light at Appledore, an island off the coast of New Hampshire, painting floral scenes there *en plein air*. During the 1900s and 1910s, he spent time at Cos Cob and Old Lyme, Connecticut; Newport, Rhode Island; and Provincetown and Gloucester, Massachusetts. All these locales provided subjects for his paintings in watercolor as well as oil, and for etchings, a medium that grew to a major interest in the later years of his life. He also worked at East Hampton, New York, on Long Island, where he purchased a home in 1919.

After the turn of the century, Hassam gave increasing prominence in his work to the figure: women both clothed and nude in interior settings, and nudes among rocks at the edge of the sea. His style altered from an Impressionist technique in service of developing the features of the subject, to a greater emphasis on surface patterning of color and texture. The longest-lived of the first generation of American Impression-ists, Hassam's late work, although well-regarded, became something of an anachronism in the 1930s; however, his "Flag Series," near-expressionistic representations of the parades along New York's Fifth Avenue during and after the end of World War I, are considered among his greatest works.

ABG and MAL

REFERENCES
New-York Historical Society, DeWitt McClellan Lockman Papers, Childe Hassam interview, 1927.

Doreen Bolger Burke, *American Paintings in the Metropolitan Mu-seum of Art. Volume III: A Catalogue of Works by Artists Born be-tween 1846 and 1864* (Princeton, NJ: Princeton University Press, 1980), 351–54.

William H. Gerdts, *American Impressionism* (New York: Abbeville Press, 1984).

THE JEWEL BOX, OLD LYME, 1906
Inscribed lower left: *Childe Hassam 1906*
Oil on canvas, 24×20
NA diploma presentation, January 7, 1907

When Hassam's NA diploma work was accepted, it was re-corded in Council minutes as titled *The Pines*, and that is the title given it in the checklist of the collection published in 1911. On February 7, 1921, Hassam's request to remove his painting for "restoration" was granted by the Council. There is no documentation of the work being returned, which is not unusual in Academy record keeping. Subsequent registrations of the collection record the Hassam as titled *The Jewel Box, Old Lyme*, prompting doubt as to whether the artist returned a different painting. It would have been highly unlikely for an exchange of diploma works to occur without formal permis-sion of the Council and consequent record in minutes; no such records exist, but neither is there any documentation of the source, time, or reason for the change in title. According to Kathleen Burnside, however, who with Stuart Feld is pres-ently preparing the catalogue raisonné of Hassam's works, it was not out of character for the artist to change the title of a painting in favor of a more poetic reference.

REFERENCES
Kevin Avery, in NAD: *Next to Nature*, 172–74.

Telephone interview with Kathleen Burnside, 1987.

CHARLES WEBSTER HAWTHORNE
ANA 1908; NA 1911
Lodi, Illinois 1872–1930 Baltimore, Maryland

Hawthorne grew up in the port town of Richmond, Maine, where he developed an attachment to the sea. In the autumn of 1890, after graduation from high school, he moved with his family to New York, where his father, a ship's captain, worked for a shipping firm; Hawthorne went to work with a dry goods company and later in a stained glass factory.

He had early showed an artistic talent, and with the opportunities available in New York, began studies in illustration and design at the Cooper Union. He moved on to study at the 16th Street Trade School and then to the Art Students League, where he took evenings classes with Frank Vincent DuMond in 1893. He received a scholarship for the 1894–95 school year, which allowed him to give up work and attend day classes with George de Forest Brush, Henry Siddons Mowbray, and William Merritt Chase. In March 1895 Hawthorne entered the antique class at the Academy school and in October 1895, the life class. The following summer he attended Chase's school at Shinnecock on the Long Island shore. There he met Ethel Marion Campbell, also a painter, whom he married in 1903. In 1897 Hawthorne helped Chase organize his New York School and worked as his assistant there that year.

Hawthorne spent the summer of 1898 in Holland at the fishing village of Zandvoort. Letters written during this period to his future wife reveal his interest in the Dutch masters, particularly Hals. Here he began to experiment in painting exclusively with the palette knife. Upon his return from Europe he began painting and exhibiting with the Country Sketch Group, organized by Van Dearing Perrine; and exhibited with the Group in their 1899 New York show and had fifteen canvases in their 1901 Chicago exhibition.

In the summer of 1899 Hawthorne founded the Cape Cod School of Art in Provincetown, Massachusetts, although it was 1903 before he completed building his studio. He would spend the summer months painting and teaching there for the rest of his life. Hawthorne was the central figure around which the artists colony developed; he was seminal in the founding of the Provincetown Art Association and the Beachcombers Club. It was his monumental images of the native residents of Provincetown, rendered in stark, but sympathetic realism, that initially established Hawthorne's standing as an artist.

In his teaching he exerted a major influence on the character of American painting in the earlier twentieth century. His teaching methods are described by his students in *Hawthorne on Painting* (1938, 1960). Among future Academy members active in Provincetown were: William Auerbach-Levy, Gifford and Reynolds Beal, Max Bohm, George Elmer Browne, Edwin Dickinson, Jerry Farnsworth, Childe Hassam, Ernest Lawson, Leon Kroll, Richard E. Miller, Ross Moffett, John Noble, William Paxton, Robert Philipp, Henry Varnum Poor, Helen Sawyer, Maurice Sterne, Frederick Judd Waugh, and John Whorf.

Hawthorne exhibited with the Society of American Artists from 1897, made his debut in an Academy annual exhibition in 1900, and was given his first one-man show at the Clausen Gallery, New York, in 1902, but it was through the exhibitions of the Salmagundi Club in New York that he got his real start. He received the Club's Adolf Obrig Prize in 1902, and in 1904 won both the Shaw and the Evans prizes.

At the Club's 1905 awards dinner, the collector John Gellatly suggested that Hawthorne be sent to Italy. Gellatly, along with Messrs. Harrison, Rhodes, and Humphreys, financed his trip. Hawthorne taught at the Art Students League from 1904 into 1906, but the remainder of 1906 and 1907 he was in Italy. There he and Ettore Caser experimented with a recipe for Tintoretto's medium, which had been discovered in the Venice archives. It was later manufactured in the United States as Hawthorne Medium.

In 1908 he taught at the New York School of Art; in 1909 he wintered in Nutley, New Jersey; and the winters of 1910–11 and 1915–16 were spent in Bermuda, where Hawthorne had purchased a house. The three winters from 1911 to 1914 were spent in Paris, where he exhibited in the Salons and in 1912 was elected associate in the Société Nationale des Beaux Arts; he became a full member in 1913. In Paris he associated with Richard E. Miller, Max Bohm, and John Noble, all of whom later settled in Provincetown.

Hawthorne established his New York winter studio in Macdougal Alley in 1917 and in 1919 purchased a house on West Fourth Street. He taught a life class at the Academy school for two seasons, 1922–24, taught at the Art Students League 1924–25, and then returned to the Academy for another year of teaching, 1925–26. He also taught at the Art Institute of Chicago, the John Herron Art Institute in Indianapolis, Indiana, and at the Carnegie Institute, Pittsburgh, Pennsylvania.

After a successful exhibition at Schaus Gallery, New York, in 1908, William Macbeth represented his work and negotiated his first sale to a museum, *The Venetian Girl* to the Worcester (Massachusetts) Art Museum in 1909. After Macbeth's death in 1917, Hawthorne exhibited with the Babcock Gallery and Grand Central Art Galleries.

The Academy also recognized Hawthorne early, awarding him Julius Hallgarten prizes in 1904 and 1906. In the annual exhibition of 1911 he received the Thomas B. Clarke Prize for *The Trousseau* on the jury's first ballot, without a dissenting vote, an unprecedented honor in the history of the Academy. The Academy would also award him its Joseph Isidor Gold Medal in the winter exhibition of 1914; the Joseph Isidor Gold Medal and a Benjamin Altman Prize in the winter exhibition of 1915; Andrew Carnegie Prize, winter exhibition, 1924; and Thomas R. Proctor Prize, winter exhibition, 1926.

RP

REFERENCES
AAA, Hawthorne correspondence with William Macbeth and Ethel Marion Campbell; DeWitt McClellan Lockman Papers, biographical sketch.

Marion Campbell Hawthorne, *Hawthorne on Painting* (New York: Pitman Publishing Corporation, 1938).

Elizabeth McCausland, *Charles W. Hawthorne, An American Figure Painter*, (New York: American Artists Group, Inc., 1947).

Edwin Dickinson, introduction, and an appreciation by Hans Hofmann: *Hawthorne on Painting: From Students' Notes Collected by Mrs. Charles W. Hawthorne* (New York: Dover Publications, Inc., 1960).

Chrysler Art Museum of Provincetown, MA: *Hawthorne Retrospective*, 1961.

CHARLES WEBSTER HAWTHORNE. *La Gigia*, n.d. (detail).

LA GIGIA, n.d.

Inscribed lower right: *C. W. Hawthorne*
Oil on canvas, 55 × 37½
NA diploma presentation, March 4, 1912

When William Macbeth, on Hawthorne's behalf, offered this painting to the Academy, he referred to it by its present title in his accompanying letter, and it was so designated in Council minutes. In her 1947 book on Hawthorne Elizabeth McCausland mistakenly assumed that *The Offering*, the work that had received the Academy's Benjamin Altman Prize in the winter exhibition of 1915, to be Hawthorne's subject painting in the Academy's collection. Ms. McCausland's error may be excused, as the action of the old woman—pouring onto the ground what may be presumed to be wine from the carafe in her other hand—could well be interpreted as the old world custom of making an "offering" of respect and thanks to nature by returning to earth a sampling of the wine it has yielded.

The title, a feminine nickname common to northern Italy, and the apparent action depicted, suggest dating the painting to Hawthorne's 1906–07 stay in Italy or, possibly, to sometime shortly after his return.

REFERENCES
Chad Mandeles, in NAD: *From All Walks*, 50.

ROBERT INGERSOLL AITKEN
ANA 1909; NA 1914
San Francisco 1878–1949 New York

Aitken attended San Francisco's Mark Hopkins Institute of Art, where he studied sculpture with Douglas Tilden and drawing with Arthur Mathews. He opened his own studio in the city at the age of eighteen. He went to Paris in 1895, but deciding that the influence of the French was not beneficial for American artists, returned to the United States having stayed only three months. Aitken's first major commissions included a bronze monument to Bret Harte, which the young sculptor executed for San Francisco's Bohemian Club, an organization that was to give him encouragement and patronage for the rest of his life. His first public exhibition was held at the Club's headquarters in 1896. In 1901 he won the competition for a memorial to Admiral Dewey to be placed in San Francisco's Union Square; his conception of *Victory* for the monument received much critical acclaim.

Between 1901 and 1904 Aitken was head of the department of sculpture at the Hopkins Institute. In 1905 fifty-three of his sculptural models were featured in an exhibition at the Bohemian Club. Despite his earlier derision of French artists, he returned to Paris in 1904; this time he remained for three years, even having a work accepted in the Salon of 1907. He came back to the United States in the latter year and settled in New York, where he opened a studio and began teaching at the Art Students League. His artistic career was interrupted by World War I, when he served in Europe, achieving the rank of captain in the infantry.

Aitken first exhibited at the Academy in 1907, received the Helen Foster Barnett Prize in the winter exhibition of the following year, and continued to be a consistent exhibitor in NAD exhibitions. Particular critical attention was given his *Michelangelo*, which he showed at the Academy in 1912. He designed the Academy's Elizabeth N. Watrous Gold Medal, an award he won himself in the winter exhibition of 1921 for a model of his monument *George Rogers Clark*. He was first elected to the Academy's Council for a three-year term beginning in 1915, although active participation was interrupted by his military service. He was returned to the Council for three-year terms in 1921 and 1926; at the conclusion of the latter term he was elected a vice-president of the Academy, a position to which he was annually relected through 1933. Aitken also taught in the Academy school for the three seasons from 1919 into 1922, and after a year's absence returned to the faculty in 1923, remaining the Academy's instructor in sculpture for a decade. He was also chair of the Council's School Committee for some years. Aitken was president of the National Sculpture Society, 1920–22, and vice-president of the National Institute of Arts and Letters, 1921–24.

DBD

REFERENCES

AAA, Robert Aitken Papers, 1027.

Elizabeth Anna Semple, "Art of Robert Aitken," *Overland Magazine* 61 (March 1913): 218–25.

Arthur Hoeber, "Robert I. Aitken, A. N. A., An American Sculptor," *The International Studio*, 50 (July 1913): 3–7.

Gene Hailey, ed., *California Art Research*, first series, vol. 6. WPA Project 2874 (San Francisco, 1937), 60–94.

Obituary, *New York Times*, January 4, 1949.

MEDITATION, 1907
Inscribed base rear: *R. I. Aitken Paris 1907*
Bronze, 16×13×10
NA diploma presentation, October 5, 1914

Academy minutes recorded the acceptance of Aitken's diploma work, which was titled *Meditation*. Over the years the present work came to be designated in registration records simply as *Head—Girl*. There can be no doubt, however, that it is the piece received from the artist in 1914 to confirm his election to Academician.

A version owned at the time by the National Sculpture Society was exhibited at the Buffalo Fine Arts Academy and Albright Art Gallery in 1909 and 1910.

REFERENCES

Buffalo (New York) Fine Arts Academy and Albright Art Gallery: *A Collection of Small Bronzes Lent by the National Sculpture Society*, 1910.

WALTER AUGUSTUS COLE
Indian Pond, New York 1881–1913 Summit, New Jersey

The third of Timothy Cole's four sons, Walter Cole spent virtually his entire life in Europe, where his father was engaged in executing engravings of old master paintings. He was a child of two when the family took up residence in Italy; by his adolescent years, they were living in Holland and then England. Encouraged by his father, he studied engraving and became Timothy Cole's prize pupil. He also spent several years as a student in Paris. In 1909, while in Paris, Cole became ill and relocated to Brussels for rest. He had developed tuberculosis and was soon sent to Switzerland for a year to regain his strength. His health did not significantly improve over several years however; he returned to America to enter a sanatorium and there died. While in Belgium, Cole had invented a process for color etching that was lost at his death.

JD

REFERENCES

Alphaeus P. Cole and Margaret Ward Cole, *Timothy Cole, Engraver* (New York: Pioneer Associates, 1935).

NAD archives, letter from Orlando Cole, June 11, 1987.

JD telephone interview with Percy Cole, July 10, 1987.

TIMOTHY COLE, 1907
Inscribed left: *Timothy Cole / Painted by / Walter Cole / Paris / 1907*
Oil on canvas, 33×25
ANA diploma presentation, February 3, 1908

Timothy Cole was born in London, England, in 1852. Following the death of his mother, he was brought at the age of five to Chicago. In 1868 he began a two-year apprenticeship as an engraver at the firm of Bond & Chandler. His prospects for launching a career, as well as his possessions were destroyed by the great Chicago fire of 1871. Cole moved to New York where he could get freelance engraving work.

In spring 1875, he met Alexander W. Drake, the art superintendent for Scribner's. Drake liked Cole's work, and the artist began to engrave for the publishing company. Over the next several years Cole did engravings after works by such artists as Winslow Homer, Robert Blum, Abbott Thayer, Elihu Vedder, George Inness, John La Farge, and James Abbott McNeill Whistler. The turning point in his career came in 1883 when he was asked to travel to Europe to execute a series of engravings after the old masters for *Century* magazine. Cole stayed abroad for almost twenty-eight years to complete the project, spending approximately ten years in Italy, four in Holland, four in England, six in Spain, and four in France.

In 1910 he returned to the United States for the first time since his 1883 departure. As he grew older, this most celebrated American wood engraver became known as the last master of a dying art form. His "revolution" in wood engraving had been the move toward a truer, more exact reproduction, but the development of illustration by photographic reproduction made even his painstaking efforts obsolete.

Cole was elected an Associate in 1906. Walter Cole's portrait of his father was painted during the month of January 1907, while the family was in France. He shows his father at work, with the beginnings of a beard he was growing at the time (Cole, 136). Cole was advanced to Academician in 1908. He died in 1931.

REFERENCES

NAD archives, Ralph C. Smith, manuscript biography of Timothy Cole.

Alphaeas P. Cole and Margaret Ward Cole, *Timothy Cole, Wood Engraver* (New York: Pioneer Associates, 1935).

LOVELL BIRGE HARRISON
ANA 1902; NA 1910
Philadelphia 1854–1929 Woodstock, New York

Birge Harrison, a younger brother of the marine painter Alexander Harrison, received his first formal art education at the Pennsylvania Academy of the Fine Arts, Philadelphia, which he began attending in 1874. On the advice of John Singer Sargent he went to Paris in 1876, where he entered the atelier of Charles Émile Auguste Carolus-Duran. In 1878 he began four years of attendence at the École des Beaux-Arts, where he studied under Alexander Cabanal.

Harrison began painting *en plein air*, spending the summers in the town of Grez-sur-Loing, near the Forest of Fontainebleau, and in Brittany at Pont-Aven and Concarneau. Rustic peasant subjects in atmospherically rendered pastoral settings were typical of his work of the early 1880s. He first exhibited in an Academy annual exhibition in 1881, and his work was seen there again in 1882 and 1883, the same year he became a member of the Society of American Artists. His first major painting, *November*, drawn from his Pont-Aven experience, was accepted into the 1882 Paris Salon and immediately purchased by the French government. Within a year of this auspicious launch of his career Harrison's health failed. He spent the next several years traveling around the world. In this period he wrote and illustrated travel articles for *Harper's*, *Scribner's* and *Atlantic Monthly* from such exotic sites as India, Australia, the South Seas, California, and the American Southwest. Harrison did little painting in these years; he did not show at the Academy again until 1889.

He finally came to rest in 1890 or 1891 in Santa Barbara, California, although over the five or six years he lived there, he made several trips to Paris. In 1896 Harrison returned to the East Coast, establishing residence in Plymouth, Massachusetts, where he began executing the paintings of the New England landscape, frequently in snow, for which he became best known. He would also find subject themes in the city streets of Quebec and New York, notably *The Flat Iron Building After Rain* (Saint Louis Art Museum, Missouri).

Harrison was a leader among the landscape painters known as Tonalists, to whom, as Harrison stated "The effect under which a subject is painted has come to mean more . . . than the subject itself—the 'mood' more than the motive." In contrast to artists working in the Impressionist mode, whose subjects were presented in full sunlight, the Tonalist sought out the subdued, poetic effects to be obtained from presenting scenes at twilight, in gray and rainy weather, and especially for Harrison, in moonlight.

In 1903 Harrison moved to Woodstock, New York, which remained his base for the rest of his life, although there were extended trips to Quebec, Canada, the Arctic Circle, and Charlestown, South Carolina. It was also in 1903 that Harrison's work was again seen in Academy exhibitions; his paintings continued a constant presence in Academy shows through 1927.

Harrison was a founder of the New York Art Students League Summer School in Woodstock and its chief instructor from 1906 to 1911. A prolific contributor of articles to the journals, his book *Landscape Painting*, based on his Woodstock lectures, was published in 1909. It was especially noted among his accomplishments as "a standard work for students" in the Academy's eulogy.

MAL

REFERENCES
Birge Harrison "The 'Mood' in Modern Painting," *Art and Progress* 4 (July 1913): 1015

Charles Louis Borgmeyer, "Birge Harrison—Poet Painter," *Fine Arts Journal* 29 (October 1913): 582–606.

NAD minutes, April 23, 1930.

National Cyclopaedia of American Biography, vol. 26, (New York: James T. White & Co., 1940), 162–63.

THE HIDDEN MOON, n.d.
Inscribed lower left: *Birge Harrison*
Oil on canvas, 25¼ x 30⅛
NA diploma presentation, October 3, 1910

This painting represents perhaps Harrison's favorite subject, the night sky and the effects of the moonlight on the broad masses of clouds. Moonlight produced what he called a "lost-edge" effect, a "general diffusion of tone," which subordinated the details of a scene to an enveloping, mysterious light.

REFERENCES
Birge Harrison, *Landscape Painting* (New York: Charles Scribner's Sons, 1909), 48.

Susan M. Sivard, in NAD: *Next to Nature*, 155–57.

ROBERT HENRI

ANA 1905; NA 1906

Cincinnati, Ohio 1865–1929 New York

Born Robert Henry Cozad, Henri grew up in towns established by his father: first Cozaddale, Ohio, where he attended the Chickering Classical and Scientific Institute in Cincinnati, from 1875 to 1879, then Cozad, Nebraska. In 1881 the family moved to Denver, where his father continued in the real estate business; however, a year later his father shot and killed one of his employees. With the senior Cozad under indictment for murder, the family fled to Atlantic City, New Jersey, and assumed the Henri surname.

After finishing his basic education in private school in New York, Henri enrolled at the Pennsylvania Academy of the Fine Arts, Philadelphia, in 1886, studying with Thomas Anshutz, James B. Kelly, and Thomas Hovenden. He demonstrated his outstanding leadership abilities early in his career. By 1887 Henri had organized a portrait class and sketch classes at the Pennsylvania Academy and had became the center of a group that included Charles Grafly, Alexander Stirling Calder, and Edward Redfield.

From the autumn of 1888 to 1891, Henri, along with Grafly among others, was in Paris, where his principal studies were at the Académie Julian under William Adolphe Bouguereau, Tony Robert-Fleury, and Gabriel Ferrier. In the two years Henri remained abroad, he traveled in France, visiting Corcarneau, Brittany, Pont-Aven, Brolles, and Barbizon; and with Redfield, visited Venice. In the autumn of 1891 he returned to Philadelphia.

At the beginning of 1892 Henri again enrolled at the Pennylvania Academy, again for study with Anshutz and Kelly, but also with Robert Vonnoh. In the fall he began teaching at the School of Design for Women, Philadelphia, a position he retained into 1895. Just at the close of the year he met John Sloan; through Sloan he would come to know William Glackens, Everett Shinn, and George Luks, all of whom were to become members of The Eight. In 1893 he opened his own summer school at Darby Creek, Pennsylvania, and had two of his mural studies included in the Columbian Exposition in Chicago.

Henri's second extended European residence began in the summer of 1895 and lasted through the summer of 1897. This time he maintained his base in Paris, but made trips to London, Germany, Italy, Belgium, and Holland; he also taught his own privately organized art classes. On his return to Philadelphia his first one-man shows occurred at the Pennsylvania Academy of the Fine Arts, October 1897, and the next month at William Merritt Chase's school in New York. The National Academy's 1898 Annual Exhibition was the first in which Henri was represented. He married in June that year, and the wedding trip to Paris extended to another two-year residence, again passed in painting, teaching, and traveling.

On his return in 1900, Henri settled in New York. He taught at the Veltin School until 1902 and then began a six-year tenure as an instructor at Chase's New York School of Art. During this period Henri's work was increasingly exhibited in one-man shows and several times in group shows with—in various combinations—Sloan, Glackens, Luks, Shinn, Arthur B. Davies, Maurice Prendergast, and Ernest Lawson. He won his first award in the 1901 Pan-American Exposition held in Buffalo, New York, and saw the first purchase of one of his paintings by a major museum, the Carnegie Institute, Pittsburgh.

Henri was elected to the Society of American Artists in 1903. In 1906, as a member of both the Society and the Academy, he was a member of the committee that brought about the fusion of the two organization that spring, which was ratified by the Academy at the same annual meeting at which Henri was elected an Academician. He served on the jury for the Academy's winter exhibition that year and on the jury for the Academy's annual the next spring. It was during the jurying for that 1907 annual that Henri took the first step toward making an overt gesture of protest against the selection and hanging practices of the Academy by removing two of his own paintings from consideration. Over the next year he met several times with his closest friends and fellow artists, out of which came Henri's May 1907 announcement of the formation of The Eight. Besides himself the group was Sloan, Glackens, Luks, Davies, Lawson, Shinn, and Prendergast. The now-famous exhibition by this group opened at the Macbeth Gallery in New York in the winter of 1908 and then toured to the Pennsylvania Academy of the Fine Arts, the Art Institute of Chicago, and seven more cities. (Of the group Glackens had become an Associate of the Academy in 1906; Lawson was elected an Associate in 1908, and his qualifying portrait by Glackens was accepted by the Council in January 1911; Shinn was elected to membership in 1935.)

Henri is perhaps best known as the leader of The Eight and for his subsequent leading position in advancing the artistic avant garde. The Eight's exhibition was followed by a number of significant independent exhibitions Henri was instrumental in organizing. Others include the Exhibition of Independent Artists, 1910; the MacDowell Club series, 1911–19; the Armory Show, 1913; and the Forum Exhibition, 1916. It was probably as a teacher that Henri made the greater impact on American art of the twentieth century. He opened his Henri School of Art in New York in 1909, remaining with it into 1911. He was then associated with the Modern School of the Ferrer Society to 1916, while from 1915 to 1927 he taught at the Art Students League, New York. *The Art Spirit*, a compilation of his philosophy and ideas about art assembled by Margery Ryerson, was published in 1923.

In his later years Henri traveled extensively, spending time in Woodstock, New York; Monhegan Island, Maine; Santa Fe, New Mexico. He often summered in Europe, principally at the home he established on Achill Island, Ireland, in 1913. At his death the Academy noted "his vividness, versality and cosmopolitanism" in its eulogy. In 1931 the Metropolitan Museum of Art, New York, presented a memorial exhibition of his work.

MAL

REFERENCES

Robert Henri, Margery Ryerson, comp., *The Art Spirit* (Philadelphia: J. B. Lippicott Company, 1923; with introduction by Forbes Watson, 1930).

NAD minutes, April 23, 1930.

William Innes Homer, with the assistance of Violet Organ, *Robert Henri and His Circle* (Ithaca, NY: Cornell University Press, 1969).

Chapellier Galleries, New York: Donelson F. Hoopes, *Robert Henri 1865–1929*, 1976.

Robert Henri: Painter, Delaware Art Museum, 1984.

GEORGE W. BELLOWS, 1911
Inscribed lower right: *George W. Bellows* ANA/*Robert Henri* NA
Oil on canvas, 32 × 25⅞
ANA diploma presentation, December 4, 1911

George Wesley Bellows

ANA 1909; NA 1913
Columbus, Ohio 1882–1925 New York

The son of an architect and builder, Bellows was a descendant of the founder of Bellows Falls, Vermont. He attended Ohio State University in Columbus from 1901 to 1904, leaving school after his junior year. With money earned from selling cartoons and playing semiprofessional baseball, he moved to New York, where in September 1904 he entered William Merritt Chase's New York School of Art, studying with Robert Henri and Kenneth Hayes Miller until 1906. Henri became a lifelong mentor and friend; Bellows once referred to Henri as "my father" (Bellows, *Arts and Decoration*).

It was at the New York School that Bellows met Emma Story of Montclair, New Jersey, whom he married in 1910. The couple purchased a house at 146 East 19th Street in New York, where the majority of Bellows's work was executed. That year Bellows took over F. Luis Mora's life class at the Art Students League, teaching there again from 1917 to 1919. In the summer of 1911 he spent one month with Henri on Monhegan Island, Maine, returning to Maine on summer sketching trips often during throughout the teens.

Bellows never traveled to Europe, a fact usually cited in discussions of his creation of American Realism, a style of painting considered indigenous, straightforward, and masculine. Yet as a member of the executive committee of the 1913 Armory show, he was instrumental in presenting European modernism to the American public.

Bellows contributed illustrations to *The Masses*, whose art editor was John Sloan, from 1912 until the magazine ceased publication in 1917. In 1916 the artist began experimenting with lithography. In the summer and fall of 1917 Bellows traveled to California and New Mexico.

In 1919 Bellows, with Henri, Sloan, and Walt Kuhn, was a founder of the New Society of Artists, an attempt to reform academic practices. In the fall of 1919 he taught at the Art Institute of Chicago. During this period Bellows was influenced by Dynamic Symmetry, a theory developed by the artist-illustrator Jay Hambidge that approached artistic composition through geometric ratios. In 1920 Bellows purchased property in Woodstock, New York, eventually designing and building a house there.

Bellows quickly received artistic recognition from the Academy. His work first appeared in its exhibition in 1907, just a year after he had completed his formal training. He was awarded a Julius Hallgarten Prize in the annual of 1908, and was elected to membership just a year later. Bellows continued to exhibit regularly in Academy exhibitions through 1918, and continued to be well rewarded there: a Julius Hallgarten Prize, 1913; Isaac N. Maynard Prize, 1914; and Joseph S. Isidor Gold Medal in the winter exhibition of 1916. Despite his absence from its exhibitions for the preceding several years, upon his unexpected death following an appendectomy, the Academy eulogized him as "an experimentor, interested in every new thing and every new medium . . . He was a leader, perhaps *the* leader of the younger group of men."

MAL

REFERENCES

George Bellows, review of *The Art Spirit* by Robert Henri, *Arts and Decoration* 20 (December 1923); 26.

Mary Fanton Roberts, "George Bellows—An Appreciation," *Arts and Decoration* 23 (October 1925): 38–40.

NAD minutes, April 22, 1925.

The Paintings of George Bellows (New York: Alfred A. Knopf, 1929).

Charles H. Morgan, *George H. Bellows: Painter of America*, with introduction by Daniel Catton Rich (New York: Reynal & Co., 1965).

Mahonri Sharp Young, *The Paintings of George Bellows* (New York: Watson-Guptill Publications, 1973).

Columbus (Ohio) Museum of Art: Lee Malone, *George Wesley Bellows: Paintings, Drawings, and Prints*, 1979.

Three Rollers [1911]

Inscribed lower right: *Geo. Bellows*
Oil on canvas, 39⅝ × 41¾
NA diploma presentation, December 1, 1913

From late July to late August 1911, Bellows was on a sketching trip to Monhegan Island, Maine, with his friend and mentor, Robert Henri, and Randall Davey, another Henri student. In a letter to his wife, Emma, Bellows described his enthusiasm for the barren coastline:

> I've painted seven little beauts all of which will make beautiful big canvases if I succeed in enlarging the idea in size. The Island is only a mile wide and two miles long, but it looks as large as the Rocky Mountains. It's three times as high as Montauk and all black and gray rock. Beautiful pine forests and wonderful varieties of all kinds. . . . My head is full of millions of great pictures which I will never have time to paint (Letter to Emma, summer 1911, quoted in Morgan).

When Bellows returned, he executed several compositions during a period of concentrated activity that ended in November. *Three Rollers*, a brooding, broadly painted depiction of the promontory Blackhead, completed in October 1911, *Evening Swell*, *The Sea*, and *The Rich Woods*, were all based on small panels done on the spot at Monhegan Island.

REFERENCES

The artist's record book A, 122, no. 151.

George Bellows, "The Big Idea: George Bellows Talks About Patriotism for Beauty," *Touchstone* 1 (July 1917) 269–75.

Morgan, 135–36.

Cheryl Cibulka, in NAD: *Next to Nature*, 198–200.

GEORGE GARDNER SYMONS
ANA 1910; NA 1911
Chicago, Illinois 1861–1930 Hillside, New Jersey

There are few details known of the earlier life and career of Gardner Symons. The son of German immigrants whose surname was Simon, he reported his first artistic training to have been at the Art Institute of Chicago, yet there is no record of his attendance at that institution. Symons lived in Europe for almost a decade, studying in Paris, Munich, and London. In 1896 he was in the United States, for he toured California with the painter William Wendt in that year. In 1899 he exhibited at London's Royal Academy and around that time he began painting at the artists colony at Saint Ives, Cornwall, using a plein airist technique for his landscapes and marines. Walter Elmer Schofield arrived in Saint Ives in 1902, and the two artists' work bore a marked affinity thereafter.

Although contemporary biographical sketches on him repeatedly say he returned to America in 1909, he acquired a studio in Laguna Beach, California, in 1906, which he maintained at least on a part-time basis to 1915. He became identified with the California School, which also included, among others, Edgar Payne, Armin Hansen, and William Wendt. Although he frequently visited Europe, Symons worked primarily on the American East Coast, dividing his time between New York and Colerain, Massachusetts, where the snow scenes that became his speciality were sited.

Symons's first major success was winning the Academy's Andrew Carnegie Prize in the winter exhibition of 1909; the prize-winning painting, *An Opalescent River*, was promptly acquired by the Metropolitan Museum of Art, New York. A number of major awards followed in the next several years; at the Academy he received a Saltus Gold Medal in 1913 and a Benjamin Altman Prize in 1922. His expansive landscape compositions had much in common with those of Schofield and Edward Redfield. Their viewpoint often provided a panoramic sweep of scenery; colors were bright and vigorously brushed, and the resulting effect tend to impose a decorative pattern on descriptive landscape features.

Symons served on the Academy Council from 1923 to 1926. Four years later, when he died after a long illness, the Council remembered him especially as "first and foremost a student of nature. All his canvasses, even those of very large dimensions, were produced in the open." Symons's widow, Zara, later married the painter Louis Betts.

MAL

REFERENCES
NAD minutes, April 23, 1930.

Doreen Bolger Burke, *American Paintings in the Metropolitan Museum of Art. Volume III: A Catalogue of Works by Artists Born between 1846 and 1864* (Princeton, NJ: Princeton University Press, 1983), 406–7.

SWIFT FLOWING RIVER IN WINTER, n.d
Inscribed lower right: *Gardner Symons*
Oil on canvas, 29 × 38⅝
NA diploma presentation, October 7, 1912

Breaking of the River Ice, a near twin to this painting, was awarded a William A. Clark Prize in the Corcoran Gallery of Art Biennial exhibiton of 1912.

REFERENCES
Marie Louise Handley, "Gardner Symons—Optimist," *The Outlook* 105 (December 27, 1913): 881–87.

117

LAWTON SILAS PARKER

ANA 1916
Fairfield, Michigan 1868–1954 Pasadena, California

Parker was raised in Kearney, Nebraska. Although accounts differ on whether he was fourteen or eighteen years old when he won a competition for the best drawing by an amateur, it was the prize, a scholarship at the Chicago Art Institute school, with which his successful but erratic career got its start. He studied under John Vanderpoel at the Institute, probably at two periods in the 1880s, passing the time in between in Kansas City (whether in Kansas or Missouri is also not clear) painting portraits and building decorations. It does seem sure that his last period of study in Chicago was in 1888 and that he went to Paris that year. He was accepted at the École des Beaux-Arts in the spring of 1889 and enrolled at the Académie Julian that autumn. This first stay abroad lasted into 1890. Parker then may have again been in the Midwest, supporting himself with portrait work before another period of study, this time at New York's Art Students League, with William Merritt Chase and H. Siddons Mowbray.

Parker accepted a post as life class instructor at the Saint Louis School of Fine Arts around 1891, but was there only briefly for he became the director of fine arts at Beloit (Wisconsin) College in 1893, remaining there two years. Parker was again in New York by late 1895, when he enrolled in the Academy's antique class for the 1895–96 season, and may also have been attending the Art Students League. In 1896 he won a major scholarship available to students of the several New York art schools, the $4,000 John Armstrong Chaloner Prize for study in Paris. In Paris he returned to the École, where he worked under Jean-Léon Gérôme, and to the Académie Julian, and also became a pupil of James Abbott McNeill Whistler. By 1897 Parker was studying mural painting with Paul Besnard, whom he assisted in the decoration of Cazin Hospital in Berck. Parker was in New York briefly in 1898, when he was appointed president of Chase's New York School of Art, but by 1900 he was back in Paris. He won his first important prize in that year's Salon, established his own school of painting in Montparnasse—and then returned to Chicago to teach at the Institute school in 1901, and in 1902 at the progressive Chicago Fine Arts Academy.

Parker was back in France in 1903 and on this occasion became relatively settled in the Paris suburb most associated with Impressionism, Giverny. With fellow Americans Frederick Frieseke, Richard Emil Miller, Karl Andersen, Guy Rose, and Edmund Greacen he was identified with what the press called the Giverny Group. Parker's work up to this time had been largely portraits and studio-posed figure studies. At Giverny he turned toward a plein airist portrayal of women in intimate settings or sunlit gardens. He nevertheless did not abandon the controlled style of painting thoroughly learned in his years of academic study; it stood him in good stead for his continued work as a portraitist.

In 1913 Parker attained the honor for which he would be best remembered, the gold medal in the Paris Salon, with a figure painting executed in the studio because of bad weather; he was the first American ever to win this traditionally French first prize. He returned to America that year, going first to live in Chicago and then in New York. This was the period of his greatest critical attention and professional success. A one-man show of his work was presented in Chicago in 1912; he received an honorary degree from the University of Nebraska in 1914; in the Academy's winter exhibition of 1916 he received a Benjamin Altman Prize.

Sometime in the 1920s Parker returned to France. He lived in Pailly sur Oise near Paris, where he maintained a studio. In the 1930s, with patronage for his paintings lessening, he worked more in graphic media. With the outbreak of World War II, he sent his family to live in Santa Monica, California, but did not join them until around 1942, when the German occupation became personally oppressive. Parker later purchased a home in Pasadena.

MAL

REFERENCES

Laura McProud, *Souvenir of the Lousiana Purchase: American Students' Census, Paris 1903*, 1903.

Rowland Sheldon, "Two American Artists Distinguished Abroad: Lawton Parker and C. Arnold Slade," *Fine Arts Journal* 30 (May 1914): 240–51.

George Breed Zug, "The Art of Lawton Parker," *International Studio* 57 (December 1915): 37–43.

William H. Gerdts, *American Impressionism* (New York: Abbeville Press, 1984).

May Brawley Hill, in NAD: *Artists by Themselves*, 126.

FREDERICK CARL FRIESEKE, n.d.

Oil on canvas, 25⅝ × 32
ANA diploma presentation, November 3, 1913

The setting for this portrait is probably the porch of Frieseke's home in Giverny. This work was first mentioned in Academy Council minutes for April 21, 1913, when Frieseke's year to confirm his election as an Associate by presentation of a portrait had nearly expired. The Council accepted the information that Parker had brought the portrait with him on his return from Europe, although it (or, perhaps, Parker) could not be located at that time. In the circumstance, the Council was patient, and the portrait did turn up later that autumn.

PAUL H. MANSHIP
ANA 1914; NA 1916
Saint Paul, Minnesota 1885–1966 New York

Manship began his career as a painter but, on discovering that he was colorblind, turned to sculpting. He studied both at the Saint Paul Institute School of Art from 1892 to 1903. After a period of work as a designer and illustrator in Saint Paul, he went East in 1905 to continue his training, first at the Art Students League, New York, and then at the Pennsylvania Academy of the Fine Arts, Philadelphia, where he studied under Charles Grafly. According to his son, John, Manship was influenced during these years by the work of Solon Borglum for whom he served as assistant. He also worked with Isidore Konti who encouraged him to apply for a scholarship to the American Academy in Rome, an honor he won in 1909. His going to Rome instead of Paris was responsible for Manship's introduction to classical art which was to have a lasting influence on his art.

Manship returned to New York in 1912 and enjoyed immediate professional success. He was given several important exhibitions, most notably that held at the Architectural League in 1913, and major American museums began to acquire his works. The Metropolitan Museum acquired the *Centaur and Dryad* in 1913 and in 1916 a portrait of Manship's daughter, Pauline Frances. Among important commissions awarded to Manship during these years were several from architects. For Grant La Farge he executed sculptures for the Blessed Sacrament Church, Providence, Rhode Island; for Welles Bosworth, a number of works for the American Telephone and Telegraph Building, New York; and many garden sculptures for Charles Platt.

Following World War I, during which Manship served with the Red Cross in Italy, he and his family lived in London and then in Paris, returning to the United States in 1927. Many of his most well-known works date from these years, such as the *Diana and Actaeon*, 1925, and *Indian Hunter and His Dog*, 1926, both of which reflect the artist's gift for transforming classical motifs into a modernist idiom. Manship also received a large number of major commissions during the years between the wars and kept studios in both New York and Paris to handle all the work. Among the most monumental, as well as widely recognized of Manship's commissions in this period, are the decorative scheme for the western terminus of Rockefeller Center Plaza, centered on the *Prometheus*, 1934, and the sculptures for the 1939 New York World's Fair.

The situation changed, however, following World War II, when critical appreciation of Manship's work lessened. Some important commissions nevertheless continued to come to him: a statue of John Hancock in 1948 and of Theodore Roosevelt in 1967, both for Boston, and an armillary sphere for the 1964 New York World's Fair. His creative powers did not retreat as his age advanced, and he remained an active and interesting artist until his death at the age of eighty.

Manship first exhibited at the Academy in 1907 and continued to do so sporadically into the 1960s. Two of his most successful early works received the Academy's Helen Foster Barnett Prize, *Centaur and Dryad* in the winter exhibition of 1913, and *Dancer and Gazelles* in the winter exhibition of 1917. In the annual exhibition of 1963 he was award the Academy's Saltus Gold Medal.

According to Manship's wishes, at his death the contents of his studio were divided between the National Museum of American Art and the museum of his native city, the Minnesota Museum of Art.

In 1913 when he was vice president of the Academy, Herbert Adams in a letter to Grant La Farge, essentially recommending the technical and aesthetic excellence of the young Manship's work about to be shown in the winter exhibition, aptly predicted his future: "It seems to me that here is a man who, if given a chance to work out his natural bent, may do American art an incalculable good."

DBD

REFERENCES
Herbert Adams, "Paul Manship," *Art and Progress* 6 (November 1914): 20–21.

Edwin Murtha, *Paul Manship* (New York: MacMillan Company, 1957).

Minnesota Museum of Art, Saint Paul: John Manship, "Paul Manship: A Biographical Sketch," in *Paul Manship: Changing Taste in American Art*, 1985, 133–47.

DRYAD, n.d.
Bronze, 12⅝ × 7 × 4
NA diploma presentation, May 7, 1917

Manship created the central figure group of *Centaur and Dryad* in Rome in 1912, his final year at the American Academy, and completed the pedestal after his return to New York late that year. It was perhaps the most admired of the works shown at the Architectural League shortly after his return. Its purchase by the Metropolitan Museum of Art, New York, was a singular accomplishment for so young an artist. Another cast of the work shown at the Academy's winter exhibition late in 1913 further contributed to its becoming one of Manship's most well-known early works.

The Academy's piece is both a marked reduction in scale from the full work, which is just under two and a half feet in height, and an excerpted detail from it, representing the dryad alone. Although her molesting companion's right hand is seen carressing her breast, his figure, most of the swirling drapery that is so much a part of the decorative scheme of the full piece, and the elaborated pedestal are eliminated. The dryad's legs and right arm are also truncated in the Academy's version.

Classical allusions, in form as well as content, predominate in both the original and this reduced version. Manship did not ignore the erotic implications of the subject. Edwin Murtha reported that the sensuality of the dryad herself was responsible for the Postmaster of New York's refusal to allow a magazine carrying illustrations of the *Centaur and Dryad* and others of Manship's early works to be sent through the mails.

At least five casts of the full sculpture were made and are now in public collections, casts of the single figure appear to be rarer and were evidently not exhibited by Manship.

REFERENCES
Edwin Murtha, 150.

Susan Rather, *The Origins of Archaism and the Early Sculpture of Paul Manship* (Ann Arbor, MI: University Microfilms, 1986), 212–17.

DRYAD
PAUL H. MANSHIP, N.A.

HENRY BRYSON BURROUGHS
ANA 1904; NA 1930
Boston 1869–1934 New York

Bryson Burroughs grew up and received his first art instruction in Cincinnati, Ohio, where his mother had moved after the death of his father. As a child he attended public school and studied drawing at the Cincinnati Art Museum. In 1889, after working as a cartoonist for a Cincinnati newspaper, he moved to New York, where he studied at the Art Students League under Kenyon Cox and H. Siddons Mowbray.

Burroughs won the League's Chanler Scholarship in 1890, which provided for five years of study abroad. In Paris he enrolled at the Académie Julian and the École des Beaux Arts. His teachers included Gabriel Ferrier, William-Adolphe Bouguereau, and Luc-Olivier Merson. Of the three, Merson was the most influential; however, several critiques that Burroughs received from another mural painter, Pierre Puvis de Chavannes, proved to be of more lasting value. Burroughs had previously admired the brightly colored detail of the English Pre-Raphaelite painters. The exposure to Puvis de Chavannes awakened a new appreciation for cool, subdued colors and calm, simply conceived figures.

After a trip to Italy in 1895, Burroughs and his wife of two years, sculptor Edith Woodman Burroughs, returned to the United States. The two had met as students at the Art Students League, and Bryson Burroughs soon began teaching at that institution. He also gave instruction at the Cooper Union School and the Norwich (Connecticut) Academy Summer School.

In 1906, realizing that it was too difficult to support his young family with his painting, Burroughs took a part-time curatorial post at the Metropolitan Museum of Art, New York. He was hired to assist curator Roger Fry, but within a year he had replaced the Englishman as head of the paintings department. Burroughs remained at the Metropolitan until 1934, splitting his days between morning work in his studio and afternoon curatorial duties at the museum. In 1926, ten years after the death of Edith Burroughs, he married a member of the paintings department staff, Louise Guerber.

Although it sometimes required great effort to convince reluctant trustees, he managed to make important and forward-looking acquisitions for the museum, including the first Cézanne in an American public collection. He defended current European trends such as Cubism and Fauvism while simultaneously championing such American artists as John Singleton Copley, Thomas Eakins, and Albert P. Ryder.

Among artists he had a reputation for tolerance. He was elected to the Society of American Artists in 1901 and he served on its juries as an advocate for art far more progressive than his own classical compositions. He gained some renown in 1914 when he had a one-man show at the Galeries Levesque in Paris. One painting from the show was purchased by the French government.

In the United States, his private commissions included fresco murals for the entrance hall of the Century Association and decorations for the Harry Harkness Flagler residence. Retrospective exhibitions of his work occurred in 1933 at the Century Association and in the year following his death at the Metropolitan Museum of Art.

JD

REFERENCES

Hamilton Easter Field, "Bryson Burroughs: The Man and His Work," *Arts & Decoration* 12 (December 1919): 82–84.

Edgar Holger Cahill, "Bryson Burroughs," Shadowland 6 (August 1922): 10–11, 66–67.

Forbes Watson, "Bryson Burroughs," *Parnassus* 6 (January 1935): 3.

Metropolitan Museum of Art, New York: *The Bryson Burroughs Memorial Exhibition*, 1935.

Gwendolyn Owens, "Pioneers in American Museums: Bryson Burroughs," *Museum News* 57 (May/June 1979): 46-53, 84.

Hirschl & Adler Galleries, New York: *The Paintings of Bryson Burroughs (1869–1934)*, 1984.

PLUTO AND PROSERPINE, 1914
Inscribed lower center: *Bryson Burroughs / 1914*
Oil on canvas, 24 × 36 ¼
NA diploma presentation, April 22, 1931

In *Pluto and Proserpine*, the flattened, slender figures painted in muted colors are typical of the work of Burroughs and attest to the influence of Puvis de Chavannes. Also characteristic is the plateau landscape with its low-lying, expansive valley. Burroughs made landscape studies for his mythological paintings during the summer at his vacation homes at West Haven Island, Maine, and near Peconic, Long Island (William M. Ivins, Jr., in *Memorial Exhibition*, xv).

Pluto and Proserpine is one of a group of at least six paintings dealing with the story of the god of the underworld, his wife, and her mother Ceres. Contemporary critics often noted the "humor" in Burroughs's interpretations of myths; they saw an element of modern life in his sometimes odd figural arrangements and naive facial expressions. Here Proserpine is formally isolated with an uncertain look on her face, perhaps preparing to be taken back to Hades on her husband's chariot.

There is some confusion surrounding this painting and another of the subject by Burroughs that uses an alternative name for the goddess in the title, *Pluto and Persephone*, 1916–20, (in the artist's estate at the time of the memorial exhibition at the Metropolitan Museum of Art). The Academy's *Pluto and Proserpine* may have been exhibited several times at the Montross Gallery in New York and at the Buffalo Fine Arts Academy between 1918 and 1921.

REFERENCES

Andre Dezarrois, "Paris Discovers a New Painter in Bryson Burroughs," *New York Times*, July 19, 1914.

"What Paris Thinks of Mr. Bryson Burroughs," *Town and Country* 69 (5 December 1914): 23.

Metropolitan Museum of Art, *The Memorial Exhibition*, XV.

Hirschl & Adler Galleries.

Letter from Gwendolyn Owens, September 11, 1986.

FREDERICK CARL FRIESEKE
ANA 1912; NA 1914
Owosso, Michigan 1874–1939 Mesnil-sur-Blangly, France

Frieseke was the son of the owner of a brick manufactury. Although the artist maintained his contacts with Michigan throughout his life, in about 1881 his widowed father took the family to Florida. In the fall of 1893 he entered the school of the Art Institute of Chicago, where he studied with John Vanderpoel and Frederick Warren Freer for three years. The next year he passed in study at the Art Students League in New York; he then moved on to Paris, where he enrolled at the Académie Julian under Jean-Joseph Benjamin-Constant and Jean Paul Laurens while also working with James Abbott McNeill Whistler at the Académie Carmen. From this time of taking up his studies in France, Frieseke would become a lifelong expatriate.

From 1898 to as late as 1907 Frieseke enjoyed the financial assistance of Rodman Wanamaker, the president of the American Art Association of Paris. Wanamaker also gave him the commission for a large mural decoration for his New York store, as well as for decorations for the breakfast room in his home; when installed in 1904 these decorations brought Frieseke his first favorable public attention. Murals executed for the Shelbourne Hotel, Atlantic City, New Jersey, installed in 1906, added to his fame.

From 1900, the year he first exhibited in a Paris Salon, Frieseke had been summering in Giverny. In 1906 he acquired the house next door to Monet's that had formerly been Theodore Robinson's, and retained it to 1919. It was in this period of his residence in Giverny that he attained the heights of international fame and admiration for his consumately Impressionist canvases. Despite his proximity to Monet, it was Renoir among the French Impressionist painters with whom his work had greatest affinity. Frieseke's favored subject matter were ladies in varying states of dress seen in their boudoirs; woman standing amidst lush flower gardens, and especially the play of outdoor light on the nude female form.

In 1904 he won a silver medal at the Saint Louis Exposition, a gold medal at the Munich Exhibition, and had a painting purchased by the Musée Luxembourg. He received the William A. Clark Prize in the Corcoran Gallery, Washington, D.C., Biennial exhibition of 1908. Seventeen of his paintings were shown at the Venice Biennale of 1909, and again a work was purchased by the local museum for its permanent collection. His first major exhibition in America was presented by the Macbeth Gallery in New York in 1912. The Pennsylvania Academy of the Fine Arts awarded him its Temple Gold Medal in its annual exhibition of 1913, and in 1915 Frieseke attained his highest honor, the grand prize of San Francisco's Panama-Pacific Exposition.

William Macbeth remained Frieseke's dealer and close associate throughout his life. Sales were ample and prestigious: a work was even acquired by the modern art gallery of Odessa, Russia. Frieseke's emphasis on langorous nudes heedlessly sunning themselves meant American patronage was not as enthusiastic as European.

Frieseke was made a Chevalier of the French Legion of Honor in 1920. In the same year he purchased a summer home at Mesnil-sur-Blangly in Normandy, giving up his association with Giverny. Although he continued exhibiting widely—including regular participation in Academy annual exhibition—receiving admiring reviews, and garnering significant awards, his popularity and patronage gradually diminished. Although he did not change his essentially Impressionist manner of painting, nor his favored subject matter, his palette darkened somewhat; as the years passed these factors combined to put his art increasingly out of touch with contemporary trends and tastes.

ABG

REFERENCES
Clara T. MacCheseney, Frieseke interview *New York Times*, 7 June 1914, 1.

Telfair Academy of Arts and Sciences, Savannah, GA: Moussa Domit, *Frederick Frieseke, 1874–1939*, 1974.

Muskegon (Michigan) Museum of Art: Arleen Pancza, "Frederick Carl Frieseke," in *Artists of Michigan from the Nineteenth Century*, 1987, 168–73.

HOLLYHOCKS, n.d.
Inscribed lower left: F. C. Frieseke
Oil on canvas, 25½ × 32
NA diploma presentation, November 2, 1914

Frieseke succinctly explained to Clara MacChesney his method so clearly exemplified by this painting: "If you are looking at a mass of flowers in the sunlight out of doors you see a sparkle of spots of different colors—then paint them that way."

It was Frieseke's dealer and friend, Robert Macbeth, who at the artist's request, made the selection of this painting to be presented to the Academy.

REFERENCES
Clara MacChesney, "Frederick Carl Frieseke, His Work and Suggestions for Painting From Nature," *Arts and Decorations* 3 (November 1912): 13–15.

Janet Rosenthal, in NAD: *Next to Nature*, 179–81.

ROBERT C. SPENCER

ANA 1914; NA 1920
Harvard, Nebraska 1879–1931 New Hope, Pennsylvania

As the son of a Swedenborgian clergyman without a permanent parish, Robert Spencer led a restless life throughout his youth, living in Illinois, Missouri, Virginia, and Yonkers, New York. In 1899 he was admitted to the New York College of Physicians and Surgeons, but decided instead to study art. That year he began three years of study in the schools of the Academy; it was at the Academy school he formed what was to be a lifelong friendship with fellow student Charles Rosen. From 1903 to 1905 Spencer worked with William Merritt Chase, and probably Robert Henri, at the New York School of Art. He also spent about one year as a draftsman and surveyor in a civil engineering firm sometime before 1906, the first of four years that he lived in Frenchtown, New Jersey, and Point Pleasant, Pennsylvania. It is likely in this period that Spencer met Edward Redfield and also William Lathrop, who, although his senior by twenty years, became a good friend. For the summer of 1909 Spencer lived at Daniel Garber's Lumberville, Pennsylvania, home and studio and studied with the rising young Impressionist, a short but influential experience. In 1910 Spencer settled in New Hope, in Pennsylvania's Bucks County, sharing a house with the painter Charles Frederic Ramsey. Lathrop introduced Spencer to Margaret Alexina Harrison Fulton, architect, painter, and niece of Alexander and Birge Harrison, whom he married in 1914.

It was in this period that Spencer painted the series of pictures of Pennsylvania mills, and the women who worked in them, by which he is best remembered today. Spencer, with Rosen, Lathrop, Garber, Rae Sloan Bredin, and Morgan Colt, formed the New Hope Group in 1916 for the purpose of presenting exhibitions of their work. By the 1910s Spencer was well known for his scenes of working-class life, which combined an Impressionist palette and short, tight, aggressive brushstroke, with Ash Can School subjects. His factories and tenement houses served as a backdrop for his figures, for it was "the human side, . . . the intimate contact with man" that was essential to him. In the 1920s, however, Spencer turned to the Delaware River for subject matter, and, after two trips to Europe in the later twenties, he concentrated on imaginary European scenes.

Spencer's awards received in Academy exhibitions reflect the course of his career. He received a Julius Hallgarten Prize in 1913, an Inness Gold Medal the next year, a Benjamin Altman Prize in 1921, and Joseph S. Isidor Gold Medal in 1928.

Spencer had suffered several nervous breakdowns and he took his own life with a pistol shot.

MAL

REFERENCES

New-York Historical Society, DeWitt McClellan Lockman interview with Robert Spencer, 1926.

New Jersey State Museum, Trenton: Thomas Folk, *Robert Spencer (1879–1931): Impressionist of Working Class Life*, 1983.

ACROSS THE RIVER, n.d.

Inscribed lower right: *Robert Spencer*
Oil on canvas, 25 × 30
NA diploma presentation, October 4, 1920

This village is probably being seen across the Delaware River, which was becoming one of Spencer's favorite motifs at about the time he was elected an Academician. The mill and tenement buildings that had been featured in his earlier paintings were literally being distanced by his increased attention to landscape.

126

HARRIET WHITNEY FRISHMUTH
ANA 1925; NA 1929
Philadelphia, Pennsylvania 1880–1980 Southbury, Connecticut

Frishmuth spent much of her youth traveling in Europe with her mother and sisters, attending school in Paris and summering in Switzerland. Her artistic development began in Switzerland when she took lessons in modeling from a Mrs. Hinton, possibly Lucy Brownson Hinton, an American painter and sculptor. In Paris she worked under Rodin, Jean-Antoine Injalbert, and Henri-Desiré Gauquie; in Berlin under Professor Cuno von Euchtritz; and in New York under Hermon MacNeil and Solon Borglum at the Art Students League. After an apprenticeship with Borglum and then with Karl Bitter, she opened her own studio in New York. In 1913 she moved into No. 6 Sniffen Court in Manhattan, where she was to live and work until 1937. Her most important sculptures were executed in this location.

Her first important commission was a relief of Dr. Abraham Jacobi, which she executed for the New York County Medical Society in 1910 and exhibited at the Academy in that year. Frishmuth specialized, however, in small, figural bronzes, especially allegorical works. Rhythmic and decorative qualities are the most apparent aspects of these works. *Saki Sundial*, modeled in Paris in 1913, began the series and perhaps the most famous of these are *The Vine* (Metropolitan Museum of Art) and *Joy of the Waters*, the latter work being representative of Frishmuth's several fountain conceptions. Beginning in the 1930s, she turned more and more to introspective, quieter works such as *Reflections*, which she exhibited at the Academy in 1930, and *Daydreams*, a work of 1939. Among her portraits is a bust of Woodrow Wilson done for the Virginia State Capitol in Richmond.

Frishmuth began exhibiting at the Academy in 1908 and showed her work regularly at the Academy through the 1930s. She won the Elizabeth N. Watrous Gold Medal at the Academy's winter exhibition of 1922, and the Julia A. Shaw Memorial Prize in the winter exhibition the following year.

In addition to her membership in the Academy, Frishmuth was a member of the National Sculpture Society and the Architectural League of New York.

DBD

REFERENCES
Ruth Talcott, "Harriet Whitney Frishmuth, American Sculptor," *Courier* (Syracuse University Library) 9 (October 1971): 21–35.

Beatrice Gilman Proske, "Harriet Whitney Frishmuth, Lyric Sculptor," *Aristos, The Journal of Esthetics* 2 (June 1984): 1.

THE JOY OF THE WATERS, 1920
Inscribed rear right side of base: *Harriet Frishmuth Sc / D 1920*; foundry mark stamped back of base: *Gorham Co. Founders / QBKX*
Bronze, 44½ × 9 × 11½
NA diploma presentation, October 7, 1929

This figure was first modeled in 1917 and cast in bronze in 1920. It is fitted around the base, which itself suggests spraying water, with small pipes for the work's functioning as a fountain. The vertical movement of water would repeat the vertical movement of the figure. The sculpture was first conceived in a life-size version and cast in an edition of sixty-five. The Academy's piece is from an edition of forty-five casts of a smaller version and was cast on July 2, 1920, by the Gorham Company in New York.

Charles Aronson, a major collector of Frishmuth's work, has written that the first life-size version was posed for by model Janette Ransome in 1917 and remodeled in 1920 with the model Desha posing. But Frishmuth herself, in her taped memoirs edited and printed by her friend and assistant, Ruth Talcott, did not mention Ransome, but stated about the piece: "This bronze was the result of a lull in commissions. 'Desha, what would you do if you were standing barefoot on a rock and a little cold ripple hit your foot?' 'Ooh, this,' and the Joy was on its way." Desha had been sent to Frishmuth by Frances Grimes in 1916 and soon became her most popular model, according to Frishmuth, posing for ninety percent of the sculptor's decorative figures.

Joy of the Waters was Frishmuth's choice to represent her at the Woman's World's Fair in Chicago in 1925; she also included it in her one-artist show at the Grand Central Galleries, New York, in 1928, and in a number of other exhibitions; it quickly became one of her most well-known works.

Other casts of the smaller version may be found in the collections of the Dayton, Ohio, Museum of Fine Arts and Indianapolis Museum of Art, Indiana; examples of the life-size version are held by the Chrysler Museum of Art, Norfolk, Virginia, and by the Saint Paul, Minnesota, Botanical Gardens.

REFERENCES
AAA, Gorham Company, Bronze Division, Papers, "Identification Assigned to Statuary & Bronzes, 1906–1930," 3680, f. 213.

Charles N. Aronson, *Sculptured Hyacinths* (New York, Washington, Hollywood: Vantage Press, 1973), 107–109.

Talcott, 23, 32.

Newark Museum: Gary A. Reynolds, *American Bronze Sculpture*, 1984, 40.

CARL CLEMENS MORTIZ RUNGIUS
ANA 1913; NA 1920
Britz bei Rixdorf, Germany 1869–1959 New York

The son of a Lutheran minister interested in natural history, Rungius began to draw the animal world at an early age. In 1889 he enrolled in the Berlin Art School, and entered the Berlin Academy of Fine Arts and the Berlin School of Applied Arts the following year. Among his teachers were Max Koch and Paul Meierheim, a noted wildlife painter. Rungius spent 1891 in the Prussian cavalry, which developed his skills as a marksman.

Rungius first visited the United States in 1894, joining an uncle on a hunting expedition in Maine. He also spent time in Wyoming before briefly returning to Germany in 1896. By 1897 he was settled in Brooklyn, New York, doing illustrations for sports periodicals while trying to establish himself as a painter. He made frequent trips to Wyoming and to New Brunswick, Maine, in the turn-of-the-century years; 1904 was passed in the Yukon with the naturalist Charles G. Sheldon. In the year following this extensive trip, Rungius became a U.S. citizen.

In 1910 he acquired a studio in Manhattan, which led to his widening acquaintance in the New York art world, and visited the Canadian Rockies for the first time. Thereafter he used his summers to gather material for his paintings of animals in the wild in Wyoming or in Alberta, Canada. As Wyoming became more settled, he increasingly sought his favored subject matter further north, finally building a studio in Banff in 1921, which he visited annually until the year before his death. Prior to 1914, when he devoted himself completely to painting, he was an avid hunter and a companion to Theodore Roosevelt on several hunting expeditions. From 1912 to 1936 Rungius was much occupied in painting the collection of the New York Zoological Society.

Rungius's reputation was based on his portrayal of big game animals of the American West in their natural surroundings; yet around 1912 he began to give primary attention to landscape alone as the subject of his paintings. By the mid-1920s he had returned to his and his public's first love, the caribou, antelope, bighorn sheep, and bear of the Canadian Rockies.

Rungius was active in many arts organizations, including the Society of Animal Painters and Sculptors, the Painters of the Far West, and the National Arts Club. He was also a charter member of the Camp Fire Club of America and an honorary member of the Boy Scouts of America. Rungius served one three-year term on the Academy's Council, 1927–30. For contributions to Academy annual exhibitions he received an Ellin P. Speyer Memorial Prize in 1925, an Andrew Carnegie Prize in 1926, and a Saltus Gold Medal in 1929. In the early 1950s his studio in Banff was made into a museum.

MAL

REFERENCES
New-York Historical Society, De Witt McClellan Lockman Papers, interview with Carl Rungius.

National Cyclopaedia of American Biography, 45, 56–57.

Lorne E. Render, *An Artist's View of Nature: Carl Rungius*, (Edmonton, Alberta: Provincial Museum and Archives of Alberta, 1969).

ON THE RANGE, 1920
Inscribed lower left: *Rungius*; reverse:
On the Range—C. Rungius/1920
Oil on canvas, 30¼ × 36¼
NA diploma presentation, May 16, 1920

The artist believed the Academy would not have considered him for membership on the strength of his paintings of wild animals: "At one time I gave up painting animals and took to landscape painting instead, and it was on the latter I was made A.N.A. and N.A. I had only painted three landscapes when I was made A.N.A." His choice of a representative example of his work to present to the Academy, a painting that somewhat untypically concentrates on landscape and a domestic animal familiar as an artistic subject, bears out his reading of Academy psychology.

Rungius only occasionally represented the native human denizen of the west, the working rancher; his interests were those of a naturalist-artist rather than those of such artists as Frederic Remington and Charles Russell, for whom the color and drama of cowboy genre was a central interest.

REFERENCES
New-York Historical Society, De Witt McClellan Lockman Papers, interview with Carl Rungius, 28.

LILIAN WESTCOTT HALE
ANA 1927; NA 1931
Hartford, Connnecticut 1881–1963 Saint Paul, Minnesota

The daughter of Edward Westcott, an executive in one of Hartford's arms manufacturing businesses, Lilian Wescott first studied painting with Miss Elizabeth Stevens and at the Hartford Art School. In about 1897 she spent a summer at William Merritt Chase's art school at Shinnecock, New York, on Long Island. It has been suggested that it was on Chase's advice that Hale sought to continue study at the Museum of Fine Arts School, Boston; however, it is more likely her award of the school's Hartford Paige Scholarship was the deciding factor. She began her five years of study at the Boston school in 1899, entering Edmund Tarbell's painting class directly, without being required to take the preliminary classes.

It was at the Hartford home of a friend that she met Phillip Leslie Hale, a drawing instructor at the Boston Museum School, whom she married in 1901. The following year her work was first included in a major exhibition, the Pennsylvania Academy of the Fine Arts annual. Her first solo exhibition was a group of drawings presented at the Rowlands Galleries, Boston, 1908. She was a regular participant in the exhibitions held in Boston by the Guild of Boston Artists, the Boston Art Club, the Saint Botolph Club, and the Copley Society, but she by no means limited showing her work to that city. In New York she showed at the Arlington Galleries and the Grand Central Gallery; from 1924 through 1949 her work was frequently seen in Academy exhibitions. Among her many awards was a gold medal at the Panama-Pacific Exposition, San Francisco, in 1915, the Julia A. Shaw Memorial Prize in the Academy winter exhibition of 1924, and a Benjamin Altman Prize in the Academy's winter exhibition of 1927.

Shortly before the birth of their daughter, Nancy, in 1908, the Hales settled in Dedham, Massachusetts, a suburb of Boston. Hale often chose scenes from within her home and of the landscape surrounding it—especially under snow—for her delicate charcoal studies. She was known primarily as a portraitist, however. It was in the years between the first and second world wars that she received her greatest recognition for her freely brushed, and often unconventionally posed, depictions of her subjects. Stylistically Hale's work showed her training at the Boston museum school and its particular blend of carefully delineated form and impressionist concentration on the action of light.

Philip Hale died in 1931. Lilian Hale had always maintained her studio at home, and remained in Dedham until 1955, when she moved to her daughter's home in Charlottesville, Virginia, and there she continued to execute portraits.

ABG and MAL

REFERENCES
Rose V. S. Berry, "Lilian Westcott Hale—Her Art," *The American Magazine of Art* 18 (February 1927): 59–70.

Nancy Hale, *The Life in the Studio* (Boston: Little Brown and Company, 1957).

Museum of Fine Arts, Boston: Trevor Fairbrother, *The Bostonians: Paintings of an Elegant Age, 1870–1930,* 1986.

Dedham (Massachusetts) Historical Society: Greer Hardwicke and Rob Leith, *Two Dedham Artists: Philip and Lilian Hale,* 1987.

Telephone interview with Erica E. Hirshler, May 11, 1989.

AN OLD CHERRY TREE, n.d.
Inscribed lower left: *Lilian Westcott Hale*
Oil on canvas, 30 × 25
NA diploma presentation, Februrary 1, 1932

Although a noted portraitist, Hale also produced landscapes that concentrate on the problems of rendering light and color in the natural environment. She was an active gardener and many of her landscapes were depictions of her garden outside her Dedham home.

REFERENCES
Janet Rosenthal, in NAD: *Next to Nature,* 185–87.

133

GERTUDE HORSFORD FISKE
ANA 1922; NA 1930
Boston, Massachusetts 1878–1961 Weston, Massachusetts

Fiske was born into a wealthy and socially prominent family that traced its ancestry to Massachusetts's Governor William Bradford. After attaining her general education in private schools and making her formal debut, she entered the Boston Museum of Fine Arts School in about 1904, where she passed six years in study with Edmund Tarbell, Frank Benson, and Philip Hale and took Tarbell's Advanced Painting Masters Class (1912–13). She also spent summers in Ogunquit, Maine, in classes with Charles H. Woodbury, the teacher who perhaps had the strongest influence on the character of her work. She would continue to make Ogunquit her favored summer resort throughout her life.

Fiske's first major success was the award of a silver medal at the San Francisco Panama-Pacific Exposition of 1915 and the purchase of the prize-winning painting by Mrs. E. H. Harriman. The following year the first solo exhibition of her work was presented by the Guild of Boston Artist (of which she was a founding member). In 1917 both the Cleveland Ohio Museum of Art and the Rhode Island School of Design, Providence, presented exhibitions of her work. Her career was well-established by the mid-1920s.

Commissioned portraits were the mainstay of Fiske's practice; however, her subject interests ranged broadly: figure studies in both indoor and outdoor settings; landscapes; beach scenes; amusement parks; and occasional still lifes. All were painted in vibrantly colored, simplified forms and powerful, free brushstroke that attested to her affiliation with the Boston School and Woodbury. She also worked in etching and was a member of both the Chicago and the Boston Society of Etchers.

She was regularly represented in Academy exhibitions and was awarded the Academy's Shaw Prize in the winter exhibition of 1922; Thomas B. Clarke Prize in the annuals of 1922 and 1925; the Thomas R. Proctor Prize in the winter exhibitions of 1929 and 1930; and the Julia A. Shaw Prize again in the 1935 annual. Among her other distinctions was appointment to the Massachusetts Art Commission in 1929, the first woman to serve on that body.

RP

REFERENCES

Patricia Jobe Pierce, *Edmund C. Tarbell and the Boston School of Painting, 1889–1980* (Boston: Pierce Galleries, 1980), 163.

Museum of Fine Arts, Boston: Trevor Fairbrother, *The Bostonians: Paintings of an Elegant Age, 1870–1930*, 1986, 207.

Vose Galleries, Boston: Carol Walker Aten, *Gertrude Fiske*, 1987.

SELF-PORTRAIT, 1922
Inscribed lower right: *Gertrude Fiske 1922*
Oil on canvas, 30¼ × 25⅛
ANA diploma presentation, May 7, 1923

Richard Henry Recchia
ANA 1941; NA 1944
Quincy, Massachusetts 1885–1983 Rockport, Massachusetts

Recchia's father, a native of Verona, Italy, was a marble carver who had worked for Bela Pratt and Daniel Chester French, and it was in his father's studio that the younger Recchia had his earliest training. He studied with Pratt at the school of the Museum of Fine Arts, Boston, from 1904 to 1907, and then worked as his assistant until 1912, when under the patronage of Pratt and French he went to Paris. On his return to Boston early the next year he rejoined Pratt in his Boston studio and continued to serve as his apprentice an additional five years.

Recchia's first major commission, the *Architecture* panels for the exterior of the Museum of Fine Arts, was executed during this period, and he soon became known as a competent carver in relief. His success was further assured when, in 1915, he won medals for several of his works exhibited at San Francisco's Panama-Pacific Exposition. He specialized in portraiture and figural pieces for gardens. Examples of these are his relief, *Robert Brown*, at Brown University, Providence, Rhode Island, and a bronze cast of his garden sculpture, *Baby and Frog*, 1923, in Brookgreen Gardens, South Carolina. On a monumental scale he created the equestrian *General John Stark* for the city of Manchester, New Hampshire, winning the commission in competition with eighty-three other sculptors. On a more whimsical note, he sculpted a *Mother Goose* for the Rockport (Massachusetts) Carnegie Library, and illustrated a number of children's books written by his wife, Kitty Parsons.

In 1928, Recchia established his home and studio in Rockport, Massachusetts, where he lived and worked for the rest of his life. He remained an active participant in Boston art life, was a founder of the Boston Society of Sculptors, a charter member of the Guild of Boston Artists, and a member of the Rockport Art Association, the North Shore Arts Association, and the National Sculpture Society.

Recchia was a frequent exhibitor at the Academy from his first appearance in an annual in 1909. Among his numerous awards was the Academy's Elizabeth N. Watrous Gold Medal, conveyed in the annual exhibition of 1944.

DBD

REFERENCES
"Richard Recchia Creates a Heroic Statue of General John Stark," *American Artist* 15 (June 1951): 53–55.

Michael Lantz and Theodora Morgan, "Richard H. Recchia of Rockport," *National Sculpture Review* 27 (Summer 1978): 20–22.

Beatrice Gilman Proske, *Brookgreen Gardens Sculpture* (Brookgreen, SC: Trustees of Brookgreen Gardens, 1968), 216–18.

Paula M. Kozol, "Richard H. Recchia (1888–1983)," in *American Figurative Sculpture in the Museum of Fine Arts, Boston* (Boston: Museum of Fine Arts, 1986), 416–26.

The Dreamer, n.d.
Inscribed on back: *R. H. Recchia*, with the foundry stamp of the Seal [Beal?] Casting Company, Providence, RI
Bronze, 19¾ × 5¾ × 5½
NA diploma presentation, October 2, 1944

Recchia showed a version of this work—possibly the cast presented to the Academy—in the National Sculpture Society's exhibition of 1923, suggesting the work dates from that year or slightly earlier. Another cast of the work is in a private collection, Drexel, Massachusetts.

REFERENCES
AAA, National Sculpture Society, "Exhibition of American Sculpture Guide," May 3, 1923, N134.

137

WALTER UFER

ANA 1920, NA 1926

Louisville, Kentucky 1876–1936 Albuquerque, New Mexico

Ufer's father, a master engraver of gunstocks and a political radical, emigrated from Cologne, Germany, in 1875. The younger Ufer was also always given to strong convictions—beginning as a child when he was sure he wanted to be an artist. Having showed much promise in his early drawings he took an offered chance to work in a lithography firm in Louisville rather than enter high school. It proved a severe disappointment as he was employed only as an errand boy. Two significant events occurred in his life in 1893: he made his way to Chicago to see the art exhibitions of the Columbian Exposition and he was given an opportunity to go to Hamburg, Germany, to become a real apprenticed lithographer and study at the Hamburg's Royal Applied Art School. After a year in Hamburg and another two traveling the country as a journeyman lithographer, he settled in Dresden, where he continued to support himself working as a lithographer and took up the study of painting at the Dresden Royal Academy.

He returned home in 1898 and worked for two years on the staff of the *Louisville Courier*. He then went to Chicago where he worked with an engraving firm days and studied at the J. Francis Smith School in the evenings. In 1904 he accepted a post teaching at the Smith School and married Mary Monrad Frederiksen, a fellow art student. The next year he took a job he would hold for six years in the advertising department of Armour & Company. In 1911 he had enough money saved to return to Europe, where over the ensuing two years he traveled and painted in France, Italy, Germany, Denmark, Sweden, and North Africa. He studied in Munich under Walter Thor.

Upon Ufer's return to Chicago in 1913, he exhibited a selection of his paintings from the European stay and attracted the attention of Carter H. Harrison, a former mayor of Chicago, art collector, and lover of the landscape of the Southwest. Carter was primarily responsible for encouraging a number of artists to migrate to the Southwest and for subsidizing the expenses of the trip; in 1914 Ufer arrived in Taos, New Mexico, under Carter's sponsorship. In 1917 he was invited to join the Taos Society of Artists and he exhibited in their group shows until they disbanded in 1927. Although Ufer thought of himself as part of the Taos community from the time he arrived there, his growing public considered him a Chicago artist. Until 1920 he spent part of each winter in Chicago; thereafter he was in New York a few months of each year. His first successes were awards won in Chicago exhibitions, the Cahn Prize in 1916 and Logan Prize in 1917. This was followed by his receiving the Academy's Thomas B. Clarke Prize in 1918. (He would receive Benjamin Altman prizes in Acad-

emy annual exhibitions of 1921 and 1926 and a Joseph S. Isidor Gold Medal in the winter exhibition of 1926.)

Most of his time was spent in Taos, however, and there he abandoned the academic painting procedures he had studied so thoroughly and began to paint directly from nature. His long classical training remained evident in his stongly formed figures and dashing paint application, but the intense light and color of his canvases was a direct response to the New Mexico scene.

Ufer was a political radical, a member of the IWW, and a follower of Trotsky. He served on the national executive committee of the American Artists Congress, wrote articles for its magazines, and regularly joined strikers' picket lines around the state of New Mexico. Unlike many of the Taos School painters, he did not represent the natives of the Southwest as picturesque elements of a colorful but timeless region. Ufer showed the Indians as individuals; he portrayed them realistically as part of a contemporary world in which they faced a bleak future.

Ufer was immensely successful in the 1920s, his paintings selling frequently and at high prices; he also was a prodigious spender. The stock market crash of 1929 not only severely curtailed the market in his paintings, but wiped out much of his personal funds, which were invested in securities. His final years were beset by money problems and illness related to his prolonged alchoholism.

RP

REFERENCES

Denver Art Museum: *Picturesque Images from Taos and Santa Fe*, 1974, 194–200.

Patricia Janis Broder. *Taos: A Painter's Dream* (Boston: New York Graphic Society, 1980), 21–39.

JIM, n.d.

Inscribed lower right: *W. Ufer*; reverse: *Jim / Dipl. N. A. / Walter Ufer*

Oil on canvas, 40⅛ × 36¼

NA diploma presentation, October 4, 1926

Jim Mirabel, the Pueblo Indian depicted in this picture, was Ufer's friend and favorite model. It was he, with another of the artist's close friends, who, in accordance with Ufer's last wishes, scattered his ashes to the wind over the Taos Valley.

HENRY OSSAWA TANNER
ANA 1909; NA 1927
Pittsburgh, Pennsylvania 1859–1937 Paris

Tanner passed his early childhood in Washington, D.C., where his father, a minister of the African Methodist Episcopal Church, worked in several churches and schools. In 1866 the family moved to Philadelphia, where Tanner attended the public schools. By 1872 the young man had decided to become an artist. He worked in a family friend's flour business until his fragile health broke down. While he recuperated in the Adirondack mountain area of New York and then in Florida, he sketched and painted.

Tanner entered the Pennsylvania Academy of the Fine Arts, Philadelpia, in 1880, and remained two years as a student under Thomas Eakins. Some stronger than usual bond must have been established between them, for twenty years later Eakins would paint, and keep, a portrait of Tanner (Hyde Collection, Glens Falls, New York). Tanner remained in Philadelphia for another six years, trying unsuccessfully to establish his career; occasionally he did sell drawings and prints to magazines. His works were exhibited in Pennsylvania Academy shows and in the National Academy annual exhibitions of 1885, 1886, and 1887. In 1888 he moved to Atlanta, Georgia, where he opened a photography studio. Although this venture failed, Tanner remained in Atlanta through 1890, teaching drawing to faculty members and painting portraits at Clark University.

Financed largely by the patronage of Bishop Joseph Crane Hartzell, a trustee of Clark, Tanner went to Paris in 1891. He enrolled in the Académie Julian, where his principal teachers were Jean-Joseph Benjamin-Constant and Jean Paul Laurens. He attended the Julian well into the 1890s.

Tanner's first mature works were genre scenes with rural African-American subjects. It was a work of this type that was, in 1894, his first to be accepted in a Salon. He soon after turned to the biblical themes that would preoccupy him for the rest of his life. Although Tanner's approach to the construction of biblical subjects was aligned with long-standing European traditions, the individual spirituality of his works was recognized and appreciated by contemporaries. Rodman Wanamaker, a wealthy Philadelphia businessman living in Paris, financed the artist's trips to Egypt and Palestine in 1897 and 1898. Tanner had several times had his works accepted for the Salon; his contribution of 1899, *Christ and Nicodemus on a Rooftop*, was shown the same year at the Pennsylvania Academy of the Fine Arts, where it won the Lippincott prize and was purchased for the collection.

By the turn of the century Tanner's work was regularly winning major prizes; its forms were also growing increasingly simplified, largely through the use of a more limited palette and glazing techniques, and content increasingly spiritual. The government of France purchased his *Disciples at Emmaus* in 1906, and he was made a Chevalier of the Legion of Honor in 1923. He received medals at the Pan-American Exposition in Buffalo of 1901, at the Saint Louis Exposition of 1904, and the San Francisco Exposition of 1915. A one-man show of his paintings was mounted at the American Art Galleries, New York, in 1908. He traveled widely, making several trips to England, the Near East, and Africa, but, despite his acclaim in America, Tanner visited infrequently, preferring the more liberal atmosphere of both Paris and Normandy, where he had acquired a farmhouse in 1903.

ABG and MAL

REFERENCES
NAD minutes, April 17, 1938.

Frederick Douglass Institute and National Collection of Fine Arts, Smithsonian Institution, Washington, D.C.: *The Art of Henry O. Tanner*, 1969.

Marcia M. Mathews, *Henry Ossawa Tanner: American Artist*, (University of Chicago Press, 1969).

National Museum of American Art, Smithsonian Institution, Washington, D.C.: Lynda Rosco Hartigan, *Sharing Traditions: Five Black Artists in Nineteenth-Century America*, 1985.

THE MIRACULOUS HAUL OF FISHES, n.d.
Inscribed lower right: *H. O. Tanner*
Oil on canvas, 38 × 47 ½
NA diploma presentation, October 3, 1927

This subject is from the Gospel of Saint Luke, 5: 1-11, which tells of one of Christ's miracles and his calling of Simon Peter, James, and John to follow him. Standing by the Sea of Galilee, Christ sees two boats at the shore and their fishermen washing their nets. He enters Simon's boat and after preaching to a crowd of followers on the shore, tells Simon to go out upon the lake and cast his net. Simon protests that they have taken nothing all the previous night, but at Christ's bidding will try again. Their net fills with so many fish it breaks; they call to the other boat for help, and both boats become so laden with fish they begin to sink. Simon, James and John are amazed and fearful, for they feel unworthy of such a miracle. Christ tells them not to fear, "for henceforth thou shalt catch men. . . . [T]hey forsook all, and followed him."

Tanner was not a literal illustrator of biblical stories. He distilled their spiritual essence by reducing all representative details to a few essentials and rendering these in a nearly abstract expressionist style.

FRANK TENNEY JOHNSON
ANA 1929, NA 1937
Big Grove, Iowa 1874-1939 Los Angeles, California

Johnson's English forebears arrived in America in the mid-seventeenth century. Following the pattern of Western migration, his grandfather settled in Wisconsin in 1842, and following the Civil War his father moved on to Iowa. When Johnson was fourteen years old, the family returned to Wisconsin, where he began formal schooling. He showed a great aptitude for drawing and in 1891 went to Milwaukee, where he studied under various painters and worked as an engraver and illustrater. In 1895 he was in New York for a brief time and studied at the Art Students League.

Johnson was in New York again in 1902. This time he pursued his artistic studies with Robert Henri at the New York School of Art while working as a newspaper artist, engraving shop foreman, and later as a fashion artist. In 1904, after a successful exhibition of his Western paintings, he went on an extended trip to Colorado where he gained first-hand knowledge of Western life for use in his action-packed paintings. Returning to New York, he illustrated stories by Zane Grey and other writers and continued exhibiting his paintings. In about 1927 he established his home in Alhambra, California, and there he developed an extensive collection of Western hats, boots, saddles, ropes, and weapons, which were useful props for his paintings as well as a personal extension of his fascination with the Western genre.

Johnson received the Salmagundi Club's Shaw prize in 1923 and the Allied Artists of America's Brown and Bigelow Silver Medal in 1929. In that same year he was elected to the National Arts Club as well as to the Academy. Although easel paintings on Western themes were Johnson's primary work, he also worked occasionally on a larger scale; in 1927 he executed the curtain and two flanking murals on historical subjects for the stage of the Carthay Circle Theater in Los Angeles. A memorial exhibition of Johnson's work was held at Grand Central Art Galleries, New York, in 1942.

At about the time Johnson became a member, the Academy instituted the biographical questionnaire form it asks all newly elected members to complete for historical record. Johnson was unusually expansive in his, writing the following:

Born beside The Overland Trail on the prairie in South-Western Iowa, and having been reared in the Cattle Business, with its wild life in the open, it was but natural that I should choose the painting of Western Life as the means of expressing myself. As a boy I saw the long lines of Prairie Schooners and the Stage Coaches on the winding Overland Trail: the Long-horned Texas cattle and the cattlemen.

Since then I have been so busy exploring all parts of the West—associating with and living the life of the Mountain-man, Trapper, Cowboy, Prospector, and depicting on canvas the many phazes [sic] of Western Life which I have witnessed, and are now but a memory, that I haven't had time to visit Europe, but I hope to do so some day.

Although I am a legal resident of California, with a lovely home, spacious grounds, and a fine large studio, where many of my paintings are made, I spend at least three months every winter in my New York City home and studio.

RP

REFERENCES

"A Unique Monument to Old California," *American Magazine of Art* 18 (January 1927): 23–25.

The National Cyclopaedia of American Biography, vol. 28 (New York: James T. White & Co., 1940), 5–6.

Harold McCracken, *The Frank Tenney Johnson Book: A Master Painter of the Old West* (Garden City, NY: Doubleday, 1974).

SOUTHERN NIGHT, 1927
Inscribed lower left: *F. Tenney Johnson A. N. A./1927*
Oil on canvas, 27¾ × 36
NA diploma presentation, December 6, 1937

Ernest Leonard Blumenschein

ANA 1910, NA 1927

Pittsburgh, Pennsylvania 1874–1960 Albuquerque, New Mexico

In 1878 the Blumenschein family moved to Dayton, Ohio, where the elder Blumenschein was appointed director of the Dayton Philharmonic Orchestra. Ernest's professional schooling was began at the Cincinnati College of Music where he studied violin. More interested in art than music, he turned to classes in illustration at the Art Academy of Cincinnati under Fernand Lungren.

In 1892 Blumenschein went to New York, where he studied at the Art Students League, supplementing his income by playing first violin under Anton Dvorak. Blumenschein made his first trip to Paris in 1894, where he met Bert Phillips, Eanger I. Couse, and Joseph Sharp, with whom he would later be associated in Taos, New Mexico.

Returning to New York in 1896 he shared a studio with Bert Phillips and worked on illustration commissions from *McClure's*, *Scribner's*, *Century*, *Harper's*, and *America* magazines. On an assignment for *McClure's* in 1898, Blumenschein and Phillips traveled to the Southwest and first discovered Taos. On this initial visit Blumenschein only stayed for a few months; Phillips, however, remained.

Blumenschein returned to Paris in 1899, again staying two years, before returning to New York for a year. In 1902 he left again for Paris, this time remaining until 1909. He and Mary Greene married in 1905.

Upon the couple's return to New York they took a studio in the Sherwood Building, collaborated on illustration work, and taught at Pratt Institute. Blumenschein taught painting and illustration at the Art Students League from 1912 to 1915. He was also providing illustrations for books by Jack London, Willa Cather, Booth Tarkington, Joseph Conrad, Stephen Crane and Hamlin Garland.

Blumenschein made annual sketching trips to Taos until 1919. After an exhibition of his Southwestern pictures at the Fakir Club in New York, and with the reassurance of an inheritance, the Blumenscheins moved permanently to Taos. Once in Taos, Blumenschein gave up illustration work and concentrated solely on his painting. His subject matter revolved completely around Indian life and customs. His compositions were panoramic and often included large numbers of figures. Their stagelike settings were academically derived, which gave a monumentality and drama to his works. He would often focus on the religious, ritualistic and superstitious elements of Indian culture, which he would emphasize through a surrealistic or symbolic style.

Blumenschein also executed murals including three panels for the Missouri State Capitol, 1926, and *The Spanish Peaks* for the post office at Walsenburg, Colorado, 1937.

Blumenschein's work was early included in major competitive exhibitions, and he received many awards, among them the Philadelphia Watercolor Society's Beck Prize in 1910, and the Art Institute of Chicago Potter Palmer Gold Medal in 1917. The Academy awarded him a Joseph S. Isidor Gold Medal in the winter exhibition of 1912, and Benjamin Altman prizes in 1921 and 1925.

RP

References

Laura M. Bickerstaff, *Pioneer Artists of Taos* (Denver: Old West Publishing Co., revised ed. 1983), 29–50.

Denver Art Museum: *Picturesque Images from Taos and Santa Fe*, 1974.

Colorado Springs (Colorado) Fine Arts Center: William T. Henning, Jr., *Ernest L. Blumenschein Retrospective*, 1978.

Helen Greene Blumenschein, *Recuerdos: Early Days of the Blumenschein Family* (Silver City, NM: Tecolote Press, 1979).

Patricia Janis Broder, *Taos: A Painter's Dream* (Boston: Little Brown & Co., 1980), 64–95.

THE LAKE, n.d.
Inscribed lower right: *E. L. Blumenschein*
Oil on canvas, 24 ⅛ × 27
NA diploma presentation, October 18, 1927

JOHN CLEMENTS GREGORY

ANA 1927; NA 1934
London 1879–1958 New York

Gregory may have begun his art studies in England with his grandfather, the British portrait painter John Crowe Read. It is known that after spending part of his childhood in New Zealand, he arrived in the United States in 1893. He was apprenticed to J. Massey Rhind, in New York, from 1899 to 1902, to learn his true calling, sculpture. He also studied under George Gray Barnard and Hermon MacNeil at the Art Students League in New York between 1900 and 1903. The following year he went to London where he enrolled in the Lambeth Art School. He then went to Paris, entered the École des Beaux-Arts and studied under Antonin Merci for two years. Gregory returned to the United States in 1906 and worked as an assistant to MacNeil, Gutzon Borglum, and Herbert Adams until 1912. In that year he became an American citizen and won a fellowship to the American Academy in Rome where he studied for two years. In 1915 he opened his own studio in New York and remained in the city for the rest of his life. He taught modeling at Columbia University's School of Architecture, and was director of sculpture at the Beaux-Arts Institute of Design in New York.

Gregory was known as a highly traditional sculptor, his work even occasionally being characterized as neoclassical, probably due more to his common use of classical subject matter than to his sculptural technique. His public works include panels for the Folger Shakespeare Library in Washington, D.C., 1929–30; the Huntington Mausoleum in San Marino, California, 1927–29; and *Memories*, 1951, a war memorial for the cemetery at Suresnes near Paris. He was also a noted medalist and designer of decorative architectural sculpture.

Gregory served on the Academy Council from 1935 to 1939, and was president of the National Sculpture Society from 1934 to 1939. He received the Society's medal of honor in 1956, and following his death, the Society established the John Gregory Award in his memory.

DBD

REFERENCES

"John Gregory, 78, Noted Sculptor," *New York World-Telegram and Sun*, 21 Feburary 1958.

Steven Eric Bronson, "John Gregory: The Philadelphia Museum of Art Pediment," M.A. thesis, University of Delaware, 1977, 1–14.

PHILOMELA, 1930

Inscribed at truncation: *1930 J. Gregory*
Marble, 10¼ × 7½ × 8¾
NA diploma presentation, May 22, 1934

This bust is a marble replica of the head of Gregory's life-size, full-length kneeling bronze figure *Philomela*, which he designed in 1919–20 for the garden of the Manhasset, Long Island, home of Mrs. Payne Whitney. The original plaster of the full piece won a medal of honor from the Architectural League of New York in 1921, and was exhibited extensively during the early 1920s. A fourteen-inch reduction of the full piece is in the collection of the Metropolitan Museum of Art, New York.

Kineton Parkes reported in 1933 that the head had been reproduced in marble and wrote of the full-length: "This is now widely and favourably known in America, and in England, too, for it has been extensively illustrated in both countries. It is a remarkably pleasing composition in which the subject provides the detail . . . . it is cunningly modeled."

Philomela, a character from classical mythology, was fooled by Tereus, king of Thrace, into believing that Procne, her sister and his wife, was dead, leaving Philomela free to marry him. When the truth was revealed that Procne was not dead but had only been silenced by having her tongue pulled out, the sisters sought revenge on Tereus by killing his son and serving him to his father as dinner. The gods were not amused by the women's method of vendetta and, as punishment, turned Procne into a swallow and Philomela into a nightingale.

In the full-length version of his sculpture Gregory therefore presented Philomela as a winged creature, still human, only just becoming a bird. Considering the results of her metamorphosis, she made an appropriate subject for garden sculpture. The most well-known interpretation of the mythological lady is in a poem by Matthew Arnold, a work that may well have influenced Gregory. Arnold placed his Philomela on a "fragrant lawn" in "the moonlight on this English grass," evocations that understandably could have acted as nostalgic inspiration for the British-born sculptor.

REFERENCES

Leon V. Solon, "The Garden Sculpture of John Gregory," *The Architectural Record* 55 (April 1924): 401–40.

Kineton Parkes, "A Classical Sculptor in America: John Gregory," *Apollo* 17 (February 1933): 28–31.

Parrish Art Museum, Southampton, NY: *Fauns and Fountains: American Garden Statuary, 1890–1930*, 1985.

ISABEL BISHOP
ANA 1940; NA 1941
Cincinnati, Ohio 1902–1988 Riverdale, New York

As a child growing up in Detroit, Bishop began her training attending Saturday classes at the Wicker Art School. In 1918 she moved to New York to pursue her studies, initially at the New York School of Applied Design for Women, with the intention of becoming an illustrator, but in 1920 transferring her goal and studies to painting classes at the Art Students League.

After working briefly under Max Weber and Guy Pène du Bois, she found her mentor in Kenneth Hayes Miller, who was a close friend as well as teacher. With Miller, and Reginald Marsh she was drawn to New York's Union Square as a working base, maintaining her studio in the area from 1926. This closely knit group of artists, which included Edward Laning and others and was referred to as "the Fourteenth Street School," shared a common focus on the lower-middle-class office and shop workers and the drifters and derelicts who populated the area.

Bishop's work began to attain recognition in the 1930s; her paintings, drawings, and etchings were shown regularly at the Midtown Galleries, with which she was associated from 1932, as well as in such prominent and competitive institutional exhibitions as the Carnegie International, Corcoran Gallery Biennial, Whitney, and Academy annuals. Among prizes and honors she received were: First Prize, American Society of Etchers, 1940; William A. Clark Prize, Corcoran Biennial, 1945; Walter Lippincott Prize, Pennsylvania Academy of the Fine Arts Annual, 1953; the National Arts Club Gold Medal, 1968; and from the Academy, the Isaac N. Maynard Prize, 1936; the Adolph and Clara Obrig Prize, 1942; Andrew Carnegie Prize, 1945; the Joseph Isidor Medal, 1957; Benjamin Altman Prizes, 1955 and 1973; and in 1966, the Samuel F. B. Morse Medal.

Isabel Bishop was elected to membership in the National Institute of Arts and Letters in 1944, and became the first woman member to hold one of its officerships when she was elected vice president in 1946. She served as recording secretary of the Academy, 1948–49. Major retrospectives of Bishop's work were organized by the University of Arizona Museum of Art, Tucson, and by the Whitney Museum of American Art, New York, in 1974 and 1975, respectively.

ABG

REFERENCES
Brooklyn (NY) Museum: Una E. Johnson and Jo Miller, *Isabel Bishop*, 1964.

University of Arizona Museum of Art, Tucson: Sheldon Reich, *Isabel Bishop*, 1974.

Karl Lunde, *Isabel Bishop* (New York: Harry N. Abrams, 1975).

NUDE STUDY [1934]
Oil on canvas, 15×18
Inscribed lower left: *Isabel Bishop*
NA diploma presentation, February 17, 1942

The painting is a fully developed study for the work entitled *Nude*, in the collection of the Whitney Museum of American Art, New York, which is 33×40 in dimensions, and is dated 1934. Ms. Bishop informed the Academy that this study was also executed in 1934. While nudes are not rare in Bishop's oeuvre, they were a significantly less common subject interest for her than working women—and in later years, students—shown in character of their occupations and preoccupations.

149

ALPHAEUS PHILEMON COLE

ANA 1930; NA 1941

Jersey City, New Jersey 1876–1988 New York

As the eldest of four sons of the wood engraver Timothy Cole, Alphaeus Cole was largely raised in Europe where his father was executing a commission from the Century Company to make an extensive series of reproductions of old master paintings. The family went abroad in 1883, living first in Florence, where Alphaeus began his studies in drawing. They spent periods in various other Italian cities, including Venice, and in Holland, Spain, France, and England. In Paris he studied at the École des Beaux-Arts and at the Académie Julian under Jean Paul Laurens and Jean-Joseph Benjamin-Constant.

Cole exhibited his first picture, *Dante Watching the Building of the Florentine Cathedral*, at the Paris Salon of 1900; the following year the same painting received an honorable mention at the Pan-American Exposition, Buffalo, New York. At about this time he moved to London, where he established a successful practice as a portaitist and was an exhibitor in the Royal Academy shows. In 1908 married the English sculptor Margaret Ward Wamsley.

Cole returned to New York in 1911, where he continued to pursue his work in portraiture, and became active in the New York art scene. He first visited the Old Lyme, Connecticut, art colony in the 1920s, drawn there by his friendship with Eugene Higgins. Shortly after he bought a home there; this was his summer residence and workplace until 1979 when it burned. Cole was so associated with the town that he was made honorary dean of the Old Lyme Academy of Fine Arts.

He had first been represented in an Academy annual exhibition in 1910, and he rarely missed showing with the Academy every year through 1973, the last annual to which he submitted work. In 1922 an exhibition of his decorative portraits was given by the Braus Gallery; the latest one-man exhibitions of his work were presented by the Clayton and Liberatore Art Gallery, Bridgehampton, New York, in 1971 and 1980.

Cole taught still life and portrait painting at the Cooper Union from 1924 to 1931 and at the Grand Central School of Art from 1927 to 1929. He served as president of the New York Water Color Club from 1931 to 1941 and president of the Allied Artists of America from 1952 to 1953. The Academy elected Cole its recording secretary from 1949 to 1951 and returned him to the Council for a three-year term in 1962.

Cole survived his first wife and in 1961 married Anita Rio Higgins, widow of Eugene Higgins; she died in 1973. He made his home at the Chelsea Hotel in New York from 1963, and it was there he died at the age of 112.

RP

REFERENCES

Alphaeus P. Cole, "Development of Realism in Venetian Art," *American Magazine of Art* 20 (October 1929): 571–78.

Alphaeus P. Cole, "The New York Water Color Club," *The London Studio* 6 (November 1933): 255–63.

Alphaeus P. Cole and Margaret Ward Cole, *Timothy Cole, Wood Engraver* (New York: Pioneer Associates, 1935).

Alphaeus P. Cole, "An Adolescent in Paris: The Adventure of Being an Art Student Abroad in the Late 19th Century," *American Art Journal* 8 (November 1976): 111–15.

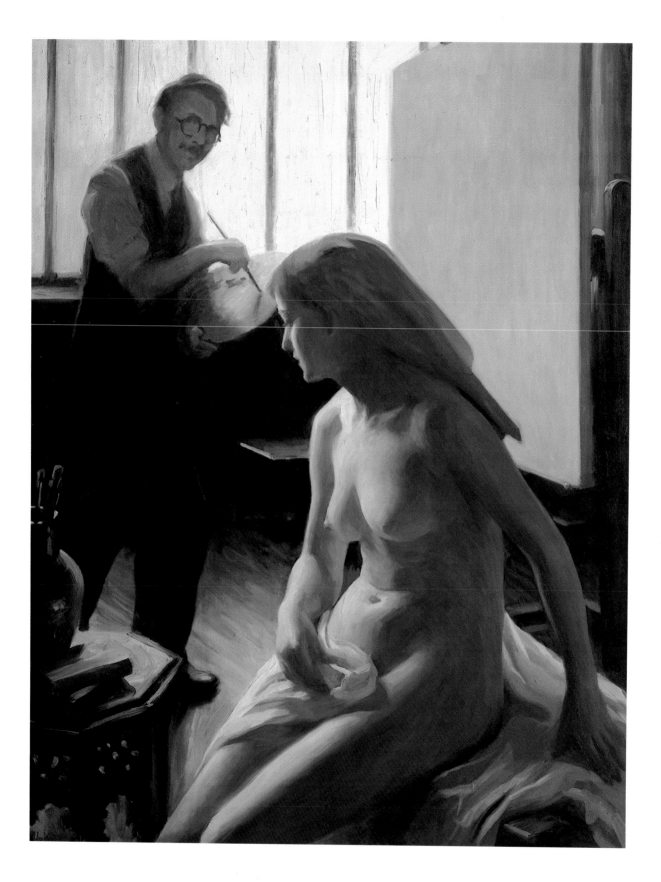

THE BLANK CANVAS [1937]
Inscribed lower left: *Alphaeus P. Cole*
Oil on canvas, 48¼ × 37⅜
NA diploma presentation, May 6, 1941.

JOHN STEUART CURRY

ANA 1937; NA 1943
Dunavant, Kansas 1897–1946 Madison, Wisconsin

Curry's parents were college-educated, staunch Scotch Covenanters, and hard-working farmers. His childhood was disciplined by the rigors of daily farm chores while his imagination was stirred by the revival meetings, the severe storms, and other aspects of the indigenous life of a Kansas farm community. In his mature work he turned that experience into a heighten realist imagry expressive of the spiritual values of America's heartland. Curry, with Thomas Hart Benton and Grant Wood, formed the triumverate known as the Regionalists, who represented the survival of a strong realist tradition in American painting in the twentieth century.

In 1916 Curry went to study at the Kansas City Art Institute, but remained only a month. He worked a short time on the railroads, earning enough to go to Chicago and study at the Art Institute. After serving in World War I he finished his education at Geneva College in Beaver Falls, Pennsylvania. In 1919 he went to Leonia, New Jersey, where he trained in illustration under Harvey Dunn and began illustrating adventure stories for the popular magazines.

Following his marriage in 1923, and a year living in New York's Greenwich Village, he settled in Westport, Connecticut. By 1925 Curry's artistic aims had gone beyond illustration work. He made trips home to Kansas and to upstate New York for subjects for paintings. In 1926, recognizing a need to improve his drawing skills, Curry went to Paris. He lived in the studio of the American sculptor, Hunt Dietrich, drew in the academy of the Russian artist Basil Schoukhaieff, copied in the Louvre, and painted Paris street and cafe scenes.

Arriving home in 1927 via London, Curry completed his first major work, *Baptism in Kansas* (Whitney Museum of American Art, New York), which received favorable reviews when it was exhibited at the Corcoran Gallery, Washington, D.C. The following year he became a member of the Whitney Studio Club in New York, which provided a stipend. He continued to work from models and attended anatomy lectures at the Art Students League. His first one-artist show at the Whitney Studio Club in 1930 estalished his reputation as a major painter.

During the 1930s Curry was much occupied in teaching, at the Cooper Union, 1932–34, and the Art Students League, 1932–36, and with mural commissions, the work with which he is most associated. Among his murals in this period are *Tragedy and Comedy* in true fresco for the Westport High School, 1934, and *Ancient Industry and Modern Hat Industry* for the Norwalk (Connecticut) High School, 1936.

Curry's completed lunette murals, *Movement of the Population Westward* and *Law Versus Mob Rule*, for the U.S. Department of Justice Building, Washington, D.C., were installed in 1937, but only after major revisions had been made in the latter because of controversial content. In 1942, after he had been appointed artist-in-residence at the Agricultural College, University of Wisconsin, Madison, he was able to realize his original intention in his mural, *Freeing of the Slaves*, for the Law School library. Other murals in Washington, D.C. include *Rush for the Oklahoma Land 1889* and *Homesteading* for the U.S. Department of the Interior, 1939. In 1938 Curry began a series of murals for the Kansas State Capitol at Topeka, which he considered the crowning achievement of his career, but were left incomplete because of adverse public reaction.

RP

REFERENCES
American Artists Group, New York: Laurence E. Schmeckebier, *John Steuart Curry's Pageant of America*, 1943.

Kansas State Capitol, Topeka: *John Steuart Curry: A Retrospective Exhibition*, 1970.

Cedar Rapids (Iowa) Art Center: Joseph S. Czestochowski, *John Steuart Curry and Grant Wood: A Portrait of Rural America*, 1981.

BELGIAN STALLIONS, 1938

Inscribed lower right: *John Steuart Curry / 1938*
Oil on panel, 30 × 25 ½
NA diploma presentation, October 4, 1943

As soon as Curry arrived at the University of Wisconsin to begin his artist-in-residence appointment, he headed for the stock pavilion to sketch the Percheron stallions, which were being prepared for a coming stock show. This painting was developed from a drawing that appeared on the April 1938 cover of the student publication *Wisconsin Country Magazine*. Curry repeated the image in a lithograph of 1938.

REFERENCES
Schmeckebier, 190–91.

Thérèse Diamand-Rosinsky, in NAD: *From All Walks*, 38.

ABRAHAM LEON KROLL

ANA 1920, NA 1927

New York 1884-1974 Gloucester, Massachusetts

Leon Kroll began his career as an artist at the age of fifteen, assisting Charles Yardley Turner in drawing plans and elevations of the grounds and buildings of the Pan-American Exposition to be held in Buffalo, New York, in 1901. Turner was then president of New York's Art Students League and when the exposition project was finished, he directed Kroll to study at the League and helped him get an office job there so he could cover expenses. His first teacher at the League was John H. Twachtman. He entered the Academy school in 1904, where he studied with Charles C. Curran, Francis Coates Jones, George W. Maynard, Charles W. Mielatz, and Hermon MacNeil over the next four years. The summer of 1906 he had a scholarship that allowed him to go to Woodstock, New York, where he painted with Paul Daugherty and John Burroughs. He was able to pass the next summer painting in Maine; there he had occasion to meet Winslow Homer and receive the senior artist's comments on his work, which greatly impressed him. Kroll won most of the prizes the Academy school offered, and in 1908 he received the premier award it had to give: the Edward L. Mooney Traveling Scholarship. With this financial support he went to Paris and studied with Jean Paul Laurens at the Académie Julian. He continued to win school prizes at the Académie, exhibited at some of the major Paris shows, and came under the influence of the Impressionists and especially Cézanne.

Upon his return from Europe in 1910, Kroll, as a Mooney scholarship recipient, was allowed to mount a one-man exhibition of works he had done in Paris at the Academy. Like the many one-man exhibitions he would subsequently have, it was a critical as well as financial success. He also began his first period of teaching at the Academy school in 1910, which continued into 1918. Kroll began to paint views of New York, especially the bridges and Central Park. One of this series, *The Brooklyn Bridge*, was admired by George Bellows who saw it hanging at an Academy exhibition. This was Kroll's first contact with the artists associated with The Eight and soon he was exhibiting with them at the MacDowell Club.

Kroll was invited to exhibit in the 1913 Armory Show; the work he showed, *Weehawken Heights*, was purchased by Arthur Jerome Eddy. In general his work was beginning to sell, and he could afford to return to Europe in 1914. He painted at Fontainebleau and Barbizon and visited Spain. On his return home later that year he renewed his relationships with William Glackens, John Sloan, Eugene Speicher, Robert Henri, and George Bellows, who was a particularly close friend and strong influence on the character of his work. Kroll was again in France in 1923 and there married Genevieve Maria Therese Domec, to whom he had been introduced by Robert and Sonia Delaunay. With this reinforcement of ties with France, throughout the 1920s he passed extended periods abroad. It was following his marriage that Kroll began the life-long habit of summering at Folley Cove on Cape Ann in Massachusetts.

Kroll's popularity was at its height in the 1930s. He won numerous awards at the major annual exhibitions of contemporary art mounted by museums, the most notable being the first prize in the Carnegie Institute International Exhibition of 1936. In Academy exhibitions he had won the Thomas B. Clarke Prize in the annual of 1921; Benjamin Altman Prizes in the winter exhibitions of 1922 and 1932; and received another Altman in the annual of 1935. (He would continue to receive honors from the Academy throughout his long history of participation in its annuals: the Adolph and Clara Obrig Prize, 1943; Anonymous Prize, 1949; Altman prizes, 1965 and 1969; and the Saltus Gold Medal, 1966.) The 1930s also saw Kroll's second period of teaching at the Academy school; he was again a faculty member from 1931 into 1938.

Like so many American painters in this period, Kroll turned to mural painting in the later 1930s and proved exceptionally successful in these monumentally scaled compositions. Among his works in this form are: lunettes, *Defeat* and *Triumph of Justice*, for the Attorney General of the United States's office, Justice Department Building, Washington, D.C., 1935–37; the World War I Memorial Chamber, Worcester (Massachusetts) Auditorium, 1939–41; a mosaic for the dome of the chapel at Omaha Beach, Normandy, France; and on an Abbey Mural Fund commission administered by the Academy, three panels on history, agriculture, and industry for the Senate Chamber of the Indiana State Capitol, Indianapolis, 1953.

Among Kroll's many memberships and honors were presidency of the American Society of Painters, Sculptors, and Engravers, 1931–35; election to the National Institute of Arts and Letters, and in 1943, its vice presidency; and election to the American Academy of Arts and Letters in 1954. In 1956 he was made a Chevalier of the French Legion of Honor. He served on the Academy Council from 1943 to 1947, and returned to its school faculty in 1959, the year in which the school was revitalized with the opening of its present building; he remained one of its most influential teachers until his retirement in 1968. In 1971 the Academy conferred on Kroll its President's Gold Medal.

Kroll's admiration of the work of Poussin, Renoir, and Cézanne is reflected in the classically articulated solid forms of his landscapes, complex figural compositions, portraits, and especially his studies of the nude.

RP

REFERENCES

James W. Lane, "Leon Kroll," *American Magazine of Art* 30 (April 1937): 219–23.

Leon Kroll, "National Academy School," *National Academy Bulletin*, (November 1937): 6–8.

Leon Kroll (New York: American Artists Group, 1946).

Index to 20th Century Artists 1933–37 (New York: reprint Arno Press, 1970), 82–87, 89, 91, 93.

Leon Kroll, "Modern and Traditional Ways of Teaching Painting, II," *College Art Journal* 11 (Spring 1952): 185–87.

Fredson Bowers and Nancy Hall, eds., *Leon Kroll: A Spoken Memoir* (Charlottesville: University of Virginia, 1983).

THE CONVERSATION, n.d.
Inscribed lower right: *Leon Kroll*
Oil on canvas, 28×42
NA diploma exchange presentation, October 2, 1961

Kroll's initial NA diploma presentation, accepted in 1928, was
a painting titled *Bryant Park*. It was damaged in the fire that
occurred in Academy headquarters at West 109th Street in
1941. An attempt was made—probably by Kroll, himself—to
repair the work, as it was noted in NAD minutes that it "could
not be restored satifactorily" at the time *The Conversation* was
accepted.

PETER HURD

ANA 1941; NA 1942
Roswell, New Mexico 1904–1984 Roswell

Hurd's parents had moved to Roswell from Boston. His father was a leading lawyer and his mother a prominent figure in the social life of the community. Hurd attended the New Mexico Military Academy in Roswell and responded well to the discipline of cadet life; he was successful in his studies, adept at the trumpet, a jovial prankster, and an indefatigable sketcher in the style of the magazine illustrators of the time. He entered the United States Military Academy, West Point, New York, in 1921, but resigned his commission after his second year, having decided to devote himself to art. He completed his education at Haverford College, in suburban Philadelphia, and studied at the Pennsylvania Academy of the Fine Arts in the city. In the summer of 1924, he apprenticed himself to N. C. Wyeth for training in illustration.

Hurd easily entered the artistic and cultural life of the Wyeth family in Chadds Ford, Pennsylvania, working in illustration and landscape; soon he became engaged to Wyeth's oldest child Henriette. Before their marriage in 1929, Hurd made frequent visits home, where he painted in a studio on his father's land. On one of these visits he began to paint in a thick impasto that freed him from the illustration style of his father-in-law and to develop a style of painting landscape that owed much to the work of George Inness.

Settling in Chadds Ford, the Hurds established an active family and social life, which included entertaining, raising horses, fox hunting, and polo. Longing for New Mexico, Hurd in 1934 purchased forty acres on the Ruidoso River near Roswell, where the family settled into ranch life. This removal from Chadds Ford was accompanied by a transition to an artistic style based on experiments in the early Renaissance technique of painting in tempera on gesso ground derived from the texts of Cennino Cennini. He made this technique his own and later introduced it to N. C. and Andrew Wyeth. He also began to work in lithography during this period, at first as a way to supplement his income. Life in New Mexico also intensified his committment to the land, and he became active in the conservation movement and studied botany.

During World War II Hurd was an artist war correspondent for *Life* magazine and went on assignment to England and to India. It was during this period that he began to work in watercolor. Hurd also executed murals, among them a depiction of the history of the Southwest for the New Mexico Military Institute (no longer extant); *Old Pioneers* for the Big Spring, Texas, post office, 1938; *Sun and Rain, Sorghum,* and *Yucca* for the Federal Building, Alamagordo, New Mexico, 1940; *Eastbound Mailstage, Air Mail Over Texas,* and *Pioneer Homebuilders,* Dallas (Texas) Parcel Post Building, 1940; and *The Lubbock Pioneers,* Texas Technological College, Lubbock. Hurd returned to the role of illustrator for two novels by Paul Horgan, his friend from student days at the New Mexico Military Academy.

Hurd was primarily a recorder of the landscape, customs, and people of New Mexico. He depicted its land, especially its dramatic contrasts: the huge mountain ranges and level plains; the calm cloudless sky and sudden bursts of rain. He also depicted ranch life—repairing fenceposts, cowboys riding the range, and local events—however, the human element is always subordinated to the context of the natural setting. Yet

Hurd's portraits of his family and neighbors are highly refined in expressing the individuality of the sitter.

Inevitably, Hurd's remote place of residence and reluctance to be long absent from it, meant he had little contact with the Academy. He received the Issac N. Maynard Prize in the annual exhibition of 1953.

RP

REFERENCES
Paul Horgan, "The Style of Peter Hurd," in *New Mexico Artists* (Albuquerque: University of New Mexico Press, 1952).

Paul Horgan, *Peter Hurd* (Austin: University of Texas Press, 1964).

Baker Gallery, Lubbock, Texas: *Peter Hurd—The Lithographs,* 1968.

Evening in the Sierras, n.d.
Inscribed lower left: *Hurd*
Egg tempera on gessoed panel, 24¼×42
NA diploma presentation, February 3, 1947

The painting was exhibited in April 1939 and is therefore estimated to have been executed within the previous year.

THEODORE VAN SOELEN

ANA 1933; NA 1940

Saint Paul, Minnesota l890–1964 Santa Fe, New Mexico

Van Soelen completed high school and then left Saint Paul to explore the West. He worked as a cowhand on cattle ranches in Utah, Nevada, and Montana. Returning to Saint Paul he began formal artistic training at the Saint Paul Institute of Arts and Sciences in 1908. After another period spent working in Utah and Nevada, he continued his studies in Philadelphia at the Pennsylvania Academy of the Fine Arts, where he was awarded the Cresson Traveling Fellowship, which enabled him to spend the year 1913–14 in Europe painting.

At the outbreak of World War I, Van Soelen was in Holland. On his trip home, he was shipwrecked off the coast of Ireland, which resulted in pneumonia followed by tuberculosis. Settling in Philadelphia he exhibited at the Pennsylvania Academy and at the Corcoran Gallery of Art in Washington, D. C.; in 1916 he made his first sale, *Summer Morning*, to the Pennsylvania Academy. That year, on the advice of his physician, he relocated to the Southwest. Van Soelen found New Mexico to his liking and following his marriage in 1921 to Virginia Morrison Carr, a daughter of an old Albuquerque family, the couple settled in Tesuque Valley near Santa Fe.

Van Soelen painted portraits, landscapes of the Southwest, and scenes of the daily life of the cowboy on the range. He and his wife spent winters in the East during the years their children were attending schools there, which yielded landscapes of a very different character. In the late 1930s and early 1940s, like so many American artists, he participated in the federal art projects. He painted murals for the Grant County Courthouse, Silver City, New Mexico; *Buffalo Range* for the Portales, New Mexico, post office, 1938; *Wild Geese* for the Waurika, Oklahoma, post office, 1939; *Landscape* and *Buffalo Hunting* for the post office at Livingston, Texas, 1941. In 1947 he began to work in lithography. He limited his work in this medium to a series on cowboy life in the premechanized Southwest.

His work was handled in New York by Ferargil Gallery, where his western paintings were exhibited in 1935 and landscapes painted in Litchfield, Connecticut, in 1940. A retrospective of his work was presented by the Museum of New Mexico Art Gallery, Santa Fe, in 1960. Van Soelen's awards included a bronze medal in the Philadelphia Sesqui-Centennial Exposition, 1926, and in Academy exhibitions, a J. Francis Murphy Memorial Prize, 1927, and Benjamin Altman Prize, 1930.

Van Soelen served on the Art Advisory Committee for the Fine Arts Museum of the Museum of New Mexico; on the board of the School of American Research; and on New Mexico's State Police Board, State Appeals Board, and Selective Service Board.

RP

REFERENCES

Denver Art Museum: *Picturesque Images from Taos and Santa Fe*, 1974, 201-6.

WINTER EVENING, n.d.
Inscribed lower left: *Van Soelen*
Oil on canvas, 25×30
NA diploma presentation, June 21, 1940

GERTRUDE KATHERINE LATHROP
ANA 1932; NA 1940
Albany, New York 1896–1986 Connecticut

Lathrop began her studies in 1918 with Solon Borglum, first at the Art Students League in New York, and then, in 1920–21, at Borglum's own school of sculpture. She spent 1923 traveling throughout Europe, extending her artistic knowledge. Her final period of formal study was the summer of 1925, which she passed working with Charles Grafly in Gloucester, Massachusetts. Lathrop's reputation as an *animalier* began to develop even before she had completed her formal training. She first had her work accepted in an Academy annual exhibition in 1921. Admiration for Lathrop's work grew rapidly, and she enjoyed a long and successful career.

She specialized in sculpting the smaller creatures of the animal world, both wild and domesticated, but also worked in portraiture. She designed the 18th Issue of the Society of Medalists in 1940 and the Brookgreen Gardens Medal in 1947. Among her public works are the World War Memorial Flag Pole for Memorial Grove, and the Leonard Woods Richardson Memorial Tablet at the New York State College for Teachers, both in Albany, New York.

Among Lathrop's many awards were four presented by the Academy: the Helen Foster Barnett Prize in the winter exhibition of 1928; the Julia A. Shaw Memorial Prize in the winter exhibition of 1931; the Ellin P. Speyer Memorial Prize in the annual exhibition of 1936; and the Saltus Gold Medal in the annual of 1970. She exhibited a bust of her mother, Ida Pulis Lathrop, in the Academy annual of 1935.

Lathrop was a member of the National Sculpture Society, the National Association of Women Painters and Sculptors, and the Society of Medalists.

DBD

REFERENCES

"Sculpture by Gertrude K. Lathrop," *American Artist* 6 (October 1942): 16–17.

Beatrice Gilman Proske, *Brookgreen Gardens Sculpture* (Brookgreen, SC: Trustees of Brookgreen Gardens, 1968), 408–13.

SILVER MARTEN RABBIT, 1940
Inscribed on attached wooden base: *G. K. Lathrop, 1940*
Bronze with brass inlay, 14⅜ × 14¾ × 6
NA diploma presentation, December 16, 1941

The sculptor has used subtly blended inlays of a contrasting metal on the underside of the piece to represent the change of color of fur typical of members of the marten family for which the silver marten rabbit was named.

REGINALD MARSH

ANA 1937; NA 1943
Paris 1898–1954 Dorset, Vermont

Marsh was born in an apartment over the Café du Dome occupied by his artist-parents, Fred Dana Marsh and Alice Randall, during the five years they lived in Paris. He was brought up in Nutley, New Jersey, and then in New Rochelle, New York. After attending a military academy and the Lawrenceville (New Jersey) School, he entered Yale College, New Haven, Connecticut, in 1916. Marsh began his career executing illustrations for *The Yale Record*. On graduating from Yale, he turned the experience to advantage by earning his living in New York as a freelance illustrator; from 1922 to 1925 he was on the staff of the *New York Daily News*, and was a regular contributor to *The New Yorker* magazine from its founding in 1925 to 1931. The subject matter of his illustration assignments—the life of the city of New York—would remain central to his art throughout his life.

In 1922 Marsh attended New York's Art Students League, taking a month's instruction under George Luks, George Bridgeman, and Kenneth Hayes Miller, each in turn. He then began to work in earnest in painting media and in 1924 had his first one-man exhibition of works in oil and watercolor at the Whitney Studio Club. The following year he made the first of his frequent visits to Europe; he spent most of the six-month sojourn in Paris, and in the Louvre studying and copying the old masters.

Marsh returned to the League for a term's study with Kenneth Hayes Miller in 1927–28. Miller became a close friend and important influence. The so-called Fourteenth Street School—an unstructured group of artists, including Isabel Bishop, Raphael Soyer, and Edward Laning, who had their studios in the Union Square area and focused on the human and architectural scenery of that somewhat seedy part of the city for subject matter—centered on Miller. Marsh took his first studio on 14th Street in 1929 and would maintain a working space in the neighborhood thereafter. Like Miller, Marsh took the city and its people for his subject, but where Miller and a number of the other Fourteenth Street School artists depicted the middle-class shopper and worker seen along the Street, Marsh went further afield, to Coney Island and the Bowery, and generally further down the social scale for his characters.

Marsh also followed Miller's example in the study of anatomy, in teaching, and in the mastery of varied techniques. He studied anatomy at the New York College of Physicians and Surgeons, 1931, and Cornell University Medical College, New York, 1934; in 1945 his *Anatomy for Artists* was published. Marsh frequently taught summer classes at the Art Students League from the mid 1930s, became a member of the regular faculty in 1942, and remained so throughout his life.

In the late 1920s Marsh began to work in lithography and in the 1940s added etching to his repertoire of media after a period of study with William Stanley Hayter; he began painting in egg tempera in 1929. In the 1940s he first studied with Jacques Maroger to master the special painting medium he had developed, based on old master techniques, and then experiment in combined use of the Maroger medium and egg tempera. Under the U.S. Department of the Treasury program to commission murals in public buildings, Marsh executed two frescoes in the Post Office Building, Washington, D.C., 1936, and the rotunda mural in dry fresco in the U.S. Customs House at Bowling Green, New York, 1936–37. He did not embark on these commissions, however, until he had studied the fresco technique with Olle Nordmark.

From 1931 Marsh's paintings were regularly included in most of the major national competitive annual or biennial exhibitions. He also enjoyed a long association with New York's Frank K.M. Rehn Gallery, which almost annually presented one-man exhibitions of his work from 1930 through 1953. He won a substantial number of prestigious awards, including the Academy's Thomas B. Clarke Prize in 1937. During his lifetime Marsh did not attain any great popular admiration, essentially due to the often distasteful nature of his preferred subjects. His extraordinary mastery of the figure and a style rooted in an illustrator's command of line served to enhance exactly those characteristics in his work that most offended narrow-minded critics.

Marsh married the sculptor and daughter of Bryson Burroughs, Betty Burroughs, in 1923; they lived in the Burroughs's Flushing, Long Island, home until their divorce in 1933. The next year he married Felice Meyer, also a painter, and daughter of the painter Herbert Meyer; they lived in New York and kept a summer weekend home in Dorset, Vermont. Marsh served one year on the Academy Council, 1944–45.

RP

REFERENCES

Lloyd Goodrich, *Reginald Marsh* (New York: Harry N. Abrams, Inc., 1972).

Edward Laning, *The Sketchbooks of Reginald Marsh* (Greenwich, CT: New York Graphic Society, Ltd, 1973).

Norman Sasowsky, *The Prints of Reginald Marsh* (New York: Clarkson N. Potter, Inc., 1976).

BARREL OF FUN, 1943

Inscribed lower right: *Reginald Marsh / 1943*
Oil on composition panel, 24 × 29¾
NA diploma presentation, April 3, 1944

The entrance to Brooklyn's Coney Island amusement park on the ocean-front was through a huge revolving cylinder, the Barrel of Fun.

REFERENCES

Laurene Banks, in NAD: *From All Walks*, 67.

EDWIN WALTER DICKINSON

ANA 1948; NA 1950
Seneca Falls, New York 1891–1978 Wellfleet, Massachusetts

Dickinson grew up in Buffalo, New York, in the cultured atmosphere provided by his father, a Presbyterian minister, and
spent summers in the dramatic landscape of the Finger Lake
region at Sheldrake, New York.

In the autumn of 1910 he entered the Pratt Institute in
New York, where he studied for one year. The following year
he studied at the Art Students League under William Merritt
Chase and Frank Vincent DuMond; in December 1912 he
was admitted to the Academy school, but was suspended at the
close of term for not submitting a drawing for examination—
a not uncommon practice among NAD students. Dickinson
returned home in the academic year 1912–13 to study at the
Buffalo Fine Arts Academy. But the more significant aspect of
Dickinson's period of training was his off-season experience.
The summer of 1912 was his introduction to the Cape Cod
School of Art and working under Charles Hawthorne; he was
back in Provincetown the next summer and remained there
until 1917 except for the summer of 1916 when he taught at
the Buffalo Fine Arts Academy. Dickinson always credited
Hawthorne with being his most influential teacher.

Dickinson's first one-man exhibition was at the Mac-
Dowell Club in New York in 1917. With America's entrance
into World War I in 1917, Dickinson was in New York studying telegraphy; he then enlisted in the Navy and served on active duty until 1919. He then spent a year in Paris, studying
at the Académie de la Grande Chaumiere, and visited Spain
before returning to Provincetown in 1920, where he essentially remained, except for a season spent teaching at the Art
Students League, 1922–23, into the mid-1930s. For the year
1937–38 he was in France; and he was again teaching at the
Buffalo Fine Arts Academy, 1938–39.

Yet when not away traveling or teaching, Dickinson returned to Cape Cod. In 1939 he made his commitment to the
area permanent with the purchase of a home in Wellfleet,
near Provincetown, where he remained year-round until
1944. Thereafter Dickinson passed winters in New York,
where he was intensely involved in teaching: at the Art Students League, 1945–66; at Cooper Union, 1945–49; and at
the Brooklyn Museum School, 1950–58. For the year 1954–
55 he was a member of the Academy Council.

Dickinson's somber-toned, introspective paintings, characterized by complex perspective spaces and compositional
juxtapositionings that suggest relationships to both Cubism
and Surrealism, steadily gained an appreciative audience.
The Albright Gallery, Buffalo, presented a one-man exhibition of Dickinson's work in 1929; in New York his work was
shown annually by the Passedoit Gallery from 1936 to 1942.
He was represented in an Academy exhibitions only twice
prior to his election to membership: in the winter exhibition
of 1922, and in the winter exhibition of 1929, when he submitted one of his most important works, *The Fossil Hunters*
(Whitney Museum of American Art, New York), which was
awarded an Altman prize. In the annual exhibition of 1949
he received the Evelyn Clair Lockman Prize and in 1958 a
Benjamin Altman Prize. In 1965 the Academy again honored
the artist by nominating him to receive the Florence Brevoort-
Eickemeyer Prize, which is awarded once every five years by
Columbia University for the lifetime achievment of an artist
selected by the Academy.

RP

REFERENCES

Whitney Museum of American Art, New York: Lloyd Goodrich, *Ed-win Dickinson*, 1965.

Burchfield Center, State University College at Buffalo, New York:
Frances Dickinson, *Tribute Exhibition, Emphasizing the Buffalo and Sheldrake Years*, 1977.

Hirshhorn Museum and Sculpture Garden, Smithsonian Institution,
Washington, D.C.: Joe Shannon, *Edwin Dickinson: Selected Land-scapes*, 1980.

NAD: *Edwin Dickinson: Draftsman/Painter*, 1982.

Eliot Adler, "Observations on Edwin Dickinson," *Arts Magazine* 56
(April 1982): 124–26.

Helen Dickinson Baldwin, "Edwin Dickinson," *Provincetown Arts* 4
(1988): 64-67, 168–69.

SELF-PORTRAIT, 1949

Inscribed upper left: 1949 / E. W. Dickinson ANA
Oil on canvas, 23 × 20⅛
ANA diploma presentation, November 7, 1949

The painting received the Evelyn Clair Lockman Prize for
portraiture in the Academy annual exhibition of 1949, which
opened to view just four days following the Council's formal
acceptance of the work and confirmation of Dickinson's election as Associate.

Helen Baldwin, the artist's daughter, in describing the
creation of the portrait, tells much about Dickinson's structured reordering of reality in his paintings:

> The *Self Portrait* of 1949 was painted in a New York studio
> and I say "a" New York studio advisedly because over the
> years he had so many there. . . . In this self portrait he
> adapted the actual room to suit the painting. He arranged
> the walls of his "space" to suit himself and brought the sky-
> light into the picture by using tilted mirrors. He was accus-
> tomed to drawing on the studio's bare walls as he worked out
> exercises in perspective, and so he painted in one of those
> drawings, but also foreshortened it so that the cube drawn
> on the wall appears in the painting as a diamond.

Dorothy Adlow, in writing about Dickinson's art and, in
particular, this portrait at the time it was introduced in the
Annual exhibition of 1949 said:

> The artist has worked with complete independence of cur-
> rent vogues of a rebellious nature. He has held to a long tra-
> dition of chiaroscuro, using it to independent and emotional
> ends. His *Self Portrait* calls attention to a great American
> tradition which has fallen unhappily into disuse or neglect,
> the art of personal portraiture. Mr. Dickinson brings to it the
> benefits of sound technique, good taste and imagination.

Dickinson frequently borrowed this painting from the
Academy to represent his work in informal faculty exhibitions
and presentations related to fellowship competitions.

REFERENCES

Dorothy Adlow, "Self Portrait": A Painting by Edwin Dickinson,"
Christian Science Monitor, Boston, 19 December 1949.

Baldwin, 169.

RAPHAEL SOYER

ANA 1949; NA 1951
Borisoglebsk, Russia 1899–1987 New York

Raphael Soyer, with his twin Moses, was brought to America by his parents in 1912. The family lived first in Philadelphia and then settled in the Bronx, New York. The twins and their younger brother, Isaac, drew and painted from childhood. Soyer studied at the Cooper Union from 1914 to 1917, then entered the Academy's school where he studied with Charles Curran and George Maynard. He was much quoted as saying that the first thing he did on leaving the Academy school was to forget everything he'd been taught there. In an article written shortly before his death, however, he tempered that statement to a description of the instruction as "dull," but noted his debt to the Academy library for his discovery there of the work of Edgar Degas. Soyer finished his study at the Academy in the spring of 1922. He had studied under Guy Pène du Bois, whom he considered the teacher who most influenced him, at the Art Students League for a few months in the 1920–21 season, and returned to his class, again for a few months, in 1923; his last period of study at the League was a month under Boardman Robinson in 1926.

In the first years after finishing his formal study, Soyer worked at various jobs to earn his living and painted at night. Alexander Brook introduced him to the Whitney Studio Club, where he had his first opportunity to show in group exhibitions. His first solo exhibition was at the Daniel Gallery in New York in 1929; sales from it enabled him to give up his odd jobs, and turn fully to painting. From the early 1930s when his work began to be regularly included in the major annual and biennial exhibitions around the country, his career developed steadily. His first award was received in the 1932 annual exhibition of the Art Institute of Chicago. He first received an Academy award, the Thomas B. Clarke Prize, in the 1945 annual exhibition; it was followed by Adolph and Clara Obrig prizes in 1947 and 1952, the Clarke Prize again in 1948, the Andrew Carnegie Prize in 1949, and the Joseph S. Isidor Gold Medal in 1975.

Soyer first taught at the John Reed Club, New York, in about 1930. He was teaching at the Art Students League for the season of 1933–34, and returned to teaching at the League, 1935–42. After the Second World War he taught for several years at the American Artists School and then was on the faculty of the New School for Social Research from 1957 through 1962. His last period of teaching was two season, 1965–67, with the Academy school.

Soyer came to be considered America's leading exemplar of the realist tradition, although his somber figure studies, portraits, and city street scenes were definitely of a twentieth-century aesthetic in their muted color harmonies and softened outlines. While he wrote and spoke widely of his dissatisfaction with the rising tide of abstraction in its various forms, it was as a steadfast spokesman for an older tradition, not narrow, polemical attack against any opposition. In 1953 in an open letter he at once expressed his criticism of abstractionist art and the motivation of his own art: "This arbitrary exploitation of a single phase of painting encourages a contempt for the taste and intelligence of the American public. . . . We believe that texture and accident, color, design and all the other elements of painting are only the means to a larger end, which is the depiction of man and his world."

RHL

REFERENCES
Moses Soyer, "Three Brothers," *Magazine of Art* 32 (April 1939), 201–7, 254.

Whitney Museum of American Art, New York: Lloyd Goodrich, *Raphael Soyer*, 1967.

Lloyd Goodrich, *Raphael Soyer* (New York, Harry D. Abrams, Inc., 1972).

Raphael Soyer, *Raphael Soyer—Life Drawings and Portraits* (New York: Dover Publications, 1986).

Obituary, New York Times, November 5, 1987.

Raphael Soyer, "Résumé of an Aged Artist," *Art & Antiques* (January 1988): 69–73, 104–6.

SELF-PORTRAIT, 1950

Inscribed lower left: *Raphael Soyer / 1950*
Oil on canvas, 24½ × 20⅛
ANA diploma presentation, March 6, 1950

Like Rembrandt, one of the artists he most revered, Soyer from youth through old age regularly took stock of himself in the execution of self-portraits. The wistfulness of portraits done in his student days is long gone in this image taken in middle age and well after he had attained a highly successful career, yet—in a departure from Rembrandt's self-image at a similar point—he shows himself without a trace of vanity. Soyer was in Los Angles in 1985, at the same time the Academy's exhibition of a selection of its artists' portraits was being presented at the Los Angeles County Museum of Art. He hastened to write to report on the general good effect of the show, and added: "It gave me pleasure to see again my self-portrait of 40 years ago. Much to my satisfaction it hangs next to Edwin Dickinson's."

REFERENCES
NAD archives, Raphael Soyer, undated postcard.

JOHN KOCH
ANA 1953; NA 1954
Toledo, Ohio 1909–1978 New York

Koch was raised in Ann Arbor, Michigan. At the age of four-teen, without the encouragement or technical guidance of any teacher of art, he began to paint. Summers of 1927 and 1928 spent on Cape Cod, Massachusetts, provided an oppor-tunity to observe Charles Hawthorne's classes at work. Later in 1928 Koch went to Paris to continue his independent study of art. There he gave great attention to the old master paint-ings in the Louvre, being particularly influenced by the great colorists of the Baroque, such as Rubens and Tintoretto. On his return to America in 1933, he settled permanently in New York. His first one-man exhibition was presented by the Krau-shaar Galleries, New York, in 1939; Kraushaar would re-mained his principal representative throughout his life.

Koch's favored subject was social gatherings in well-appointed Manhattan apartment interiors, where the grace and ease of the occasion was complemented by the objets d'art and paintings that characterized the settings. For a number of years Koch and his wife, the concert pianist Dora Zaslavsy, held a Sunday afternoon "salon" in their Manhattan home, which was attended by a number of their friends from the world of art, music, and literature, among whom were Leo Lerman, Virgil Thompson, Roger Bacon, and Maurice Gros-ser. Several of his paintings depicted these occasions, with all the figures being portraits. Koch's work was essentially freely brushed, academic realism in style. In his particular attention to the rendering of the light of interior spaces he reflected more an admiration and study of the Dutch and Flemish mas-ters, such as Vermeer, than of Impressionism. Koch also worked extensively as a portraitist and was known for his im-ages of the wealthy and celebrated, among whom were H.R.H. Princess Margaret of Great Britain, and the composer Richard Rogers.

Koch was an active member of the Academy's Council, serving three terms as assistant treasurer from 1957 to 1960, as assistant corresponding secretary for the year 1962–63, and first vice president from 1963 to 1965. He taught at the Art Students League from 1944 to 1946, and although never a member of the Academy school's faculty, he chaired its school committee for a part of the period of his Council service.

For paintings shown in Academy annual exhibitions he received Benjamin Altman Prizes in 1959 and 1964; the Sal-tus Gold Medal, 1962; the Samuel F. B. Morse Medal, 1968; and the Michael M. Engel Memorial Artists Fellowship Medal, 1972. His work was also honored by the Audubon Art-ists; the Lotos Club, New York; and the Butler Institute of American Art, Youngstown, Ohio. Koch was a member of the National Institute of Arts and Letters, the Royal Society of Artists, and the International Academy of Literature, Arts and Sciences.

RHL

REFERENCES
Museum of the City of New York: *John Koch in New York, 1950–1963*, [1963].

Obituaries, *New York Times*, April 20, 1978; *New York Post*, April 20, 1978.

Therese Lichtenstein, in NAD: *From All Walks*, 57–58.

Kraushaar Galleries, New York: *John Koch 1909–1978, A Memorial Exhibition*, 1980.

INTERIOR: LEO LERMAN, [1953]
Inscribed lower left: *Koch*
Oil on canvas, 20¼×24
NA diploma presentation, May 3, 1954

Mr. Lerman recalls sitting for this portrait at the artist's re-quest, in the spring or early summer of 1953, in the living room of the Koch apartment: "I sat some five times. He worked with astonishing facility, and sitting for him was a great pleasure. We were, of course, great friends."

REFERENCES
Therese Lichtenstein, in NAD: *From All Walks*, 57–58.

Letter, Leo Lerman to NAD, June 20, 1989.

WALTER STUEMPFIG

ANA 1951; NA 1953
Germantown, Pennsylvania 1914–1970 Ocean City, New Jersey

Stuempfig, who spent most of his life in the Philadelphia area, studied in that city at the University of Pennsylvania and at the Pennsylvania Academy of the Fine Arts, from 1931 to 1934. The Pennsylvania Academy, awarded him a Cresson Traveling Scholarship in 1933. He was later a professor of composition at the Pennsylvania Academy where he taught for over twenty years. He married the artist Lila Agnes Kennedy Hill in 1935. His first solo exhibition occurred in New York in 1943. He was known as a painter of romantic, sometimes melancholy, landscapes, and, later in his career, of still lifes and cityscapes.

At the National Academy Stuempfig won the Benjamin Altman Prize in 1952 and in 1953; the Adolph and Clara Obrig Prize in 1956; the Samuel F. B. Morse Medal in 1962; and the Isaac N. Maynard Prize in 1963. He was a member of the National Institute of Arts and Letters.

RHL

REFERENCES
Obituary, New York Times, 2 December, 1970.

FIELD GRASS, n.d.
Inscribed lower right center: *Stuempfig*
Oil on canvas, 25 × 30
NA diploma presentation, January 9, 1956

AARON SHIKLER
ANA 1962; NA 1965
B. Brooklyn, New York, 1922

Shikler studied at New York's High School of Music and Art; at the Barnes Foundation, Merion, Pennsylvania, 1941–43; at the Tyler School of Fine Art of Temple University, Philadelphia, 1943–48; where he received B.F.A., B.S.Ed., and M.F.A. degrees; and at the Hans Hoffman School in New York, 1949–51. His work was first included in a group exhibition in 1948; his first one-person exhibition was presented by the Davis Galleries, New York, in 1953. Since that time his work has been regularly featured in gallery exhibitions, and at one-person shows mounted by, among others, the New Britain (Connecticut) Museum of American Art, 1964; California Palace of the Legion of Honor, San Francisco, 1970; and the Lyme Academy Art Gallery, Old Lyme, Connecticut, 1986.

He was the recipient of a Louis Comfort Tiffany Award in 1957, and a United States Department of State Travel Grant in 1976. Among his many awards are those for works exhibited in Academy annuals: Thomas R. Proctor prizes in 1958 and 1960; the Thomas B. Clarke Prize, 1961; and a Benjamin Altman prize in 1976. Shikler was elected to a three-year term on the Academy Council in 1970 and as second vice president of the Academy; he continued to serve on the Council from 1973 to 1975.

Shikler draws and paints figure studies and portraits in a clear, luminous style that is at once classic and appealing in its realism. His portraits of distinguished persons, among them President and Mrs. John F. Kennedy, Mrs. Lyndon Baines Johnson, Senator Abraham Ribicoff, and Mrs. Ronald Regan have brought him considerable celebrity. He resides in New York and is represented by Davis and Langdale Company.

RHL

REFERENCES
Brooklyn Museum: *Paintings and Drawings by David Levine and Aaron Shikler*, 1971.

PORCELAIN CATS (or) MAURICE VAN GUENS, 1957
Inscribed lower left: *Shikler '57*
Oil on canvas, 38¼×28
NA diploma presentation, May 3, 1965

Edward Fenno Hoffman III
ANA 1969; NA 1978
B. Philadelphia, Pennsylvania, 1916

Hoffman was a student at the Pennsylvania Academy of the Fine Arts, Philadelphia, from 1946 to 1950. The Pennsylvania Academy's Cresson Traveling Scholarship, which he was awarded in 1948, and a Tiffany Foundation Grant, received in 1951, allowed him to continue his studies in Europe. From 1952 to 1955 he worked at La Napoule, France, with the La Napoule Art Foundation. He was a student of Walker Hancock, Harry Rosin, and Charles Rudy; for a time he served as an assistant to Paul Manship.

Among his early commissions were a war memorial for the Pennsylvania Hospital, Philadelphia, and gateposts for St. Alban's Church, Newtown Square, Pennsylvania. In 1955, he established a studio in Wayne, Pennsylvania. He was commissioned to execute a series of portrait reliefs for Weightlifters' Hall of Fame in York, Pennsylvania. Several major commissions for religious subjects followed the purchase of his *Descent From the Cross* for Saint John's Church in Southampton, New York.

Hoffman has been the recipient of many awards. Those which have been presented by the Academy for works exhibited in its annual exhibitions are the Helen Foster Barnett Prize, 1951; the Samuel F. B. Morse Medal, 1966; the Artist's Fund Prize, 1969, the latter for *Reaching*; the Elizabeth N. Watrous Medal, 1972; and the Thomas R. Proctor Prize, 1982.

DBD

REFERENCES
Beatrice Gilman Proske, *Brookgreen Gardens Sculpture* (Brookgreen, S.C.: Trustees of Brookgreen Gardens, 1968), 468–72.

REACHING, 1963
Inscribed on top of base: *Edward F. Hoffman III 1963*
Bronze, 15 × 12¾ × 7
NA diploma presentation, May 1, 1978

PHILIP PEARLSTEIN
ANA 1980; NA 1988
B. Pittsburgh, Pennsylvania, 1924

The first of Pearlstein's many honors were the first and third prizes he received in *Scholastic Magazine*'s 14th National High School Art Exhibition in 1941; Reginald Marsh was a member of this awards jury. Upon graduation from high school in 1942, he enrolled in the Carnegie Institute of Technology, but the draft limited his attendance to one year. After discharge from the army in 1946 he returned to Carnegie, where he studied with Robert Lepper, Balcomb Greene, and Samuel Rosenberg and received his BFA degree in 1949. He then immediately moved to New York and obtained work as a graphic designer producing catalogues of plumbing fixtures, which provided financial support for the next eight years. In 1950 he began graduate studies at New York University's Institute of Fine Art. Two years later his paintings were shown in a group exhibition at the Tanager Gallery, an artist's cooperative; in 1954 Clement Greenberg selected his work for a group show at the Kootz Gallery, New York, titled *Emerging Talent*; and in 1955—the same year he received his Master's degree from the NYU Institute—Pearlstein's first one-man exhibition was presented at the Tanager Gallery.

In 1958 Pearlstein was awarded a Fulbright grant, which supported a year of travel and painting abroad, passed mostly in Italy. In September 1960 a one-man exhibition of his paintings and drawings was held at the Allan Frumkin Gallery in Chicago, followed by another at Frumkin's New York gallery in the spring of 1961, beginning a long association with the Frumkin Gallery. Through the late 1950s Pearlstein's paintings had focused primarily on landscape rendered with an emphasis on abstract patterning. In about 1962, however, he turned his attention to the classical subject of the studio-posed nude and began producing the extended series of paintings with which he is most identified: models shown singly or in pairs at intentionally unsettling angles, often truncated, and always with extreme objectivity of realism.

Pearlstein frequently contributes analytical articles on contemporary art to major art journals. He also has been a dedicated teacher throughout his career: at Pratt Institute, Brooklyn, New York, 1959–63; visiting artist and lecturer at the Skowhegan School of Painting and Sculpture in Maine, summers of 1965 and 1967; and member of the resident faculty, Boston University summer program, Tanglewood, Massachusetts, 1969; and his primary teaching affiliation, Brooklyn College of the City University of New York. He joined the Brooklyn College faculty in 1963 as an assistant professor and was appointed a distinguished professor in 1977.

Among Pearlstein's honors are a National Endowment for the Arts grant, 1968; a Guggenheim Foundation fellowship, 1969; and election to the American Academy and Institute of Arts and Letters, 1982.

Pearlstein also works extensively in drawing, lithography, etching, and watercolor. He resides in New York, where he is represented by Hirschl & Adler Modern.

RHL

REFERENCES
Jerome Viola, *The Painting and Teaching of Philip Pearlstein* (New York: Watson-Guptill Publications, 1982).

Milwaukee (Wisconsin) Art Museum: *Philip Pearlstein: A Retrospective*, 1983.

NUDE TORSO, 1963
Inscribed lower left: *Pearlstein 63*
Oil on canvas, 37¼×45¼
NA diploma presentation, May 6, 1988

JANE FREILICHER
ANA 1980; NA 1982
B. New York, 1924

Freilicher completed her undergraduate education at Brooklyn College of the City University of New York in 1947. The next year she studied at the Hans Hofmann schools in New York and in Provincetown, Massachusetts. She also attained a Master's degree in art education from Columbia University, New York.

The first exhibition solely of her work was presented by the Tibor de Nagy Gallery, New York, in 1952. Despite her adherence to an essential realism during the period of Abstract Expressionism's dominance, her work was regularly presented by that gallery through the 1960s and in group shows including the Whitney Museum of American Art Annual of 1955 and at the Rhode Island School of Design, Providence, the same year. Over the succeeding three decades her lyrical, painterly landscapes and still lifes have enjoyed ever-widening audience and recognition. Her subject matter is consistently drawn from her immediate visual experience of New York's Greenwich Village, where she lives in the winter months, but more frequently of Water Mill, Long Island, where she passes summers.

In addition to easel painting, Freilicher has given particular attention to illustrating books in collaboration with poets John Ashbery, Kenneth Koch, and James Schuyler. She has been a visiting lecturer and critic at the University of Pennsylvania, Philadelphia; Skowhegan (Maine) School of Painting and Sculpture; Carnegie Mellon Institute, Pittsburgh, Pennsylvania; and the Maryland Institute of Art, Baltimore. Freilicher served a three-year term, 1985–88, on the Academy's Council.

She has received an American Association of University Women Fellowship, and in 1976, a National Endowment for the Arts grant. She was elected to the American Institute of Arts and Letters in 1989. The Academy awarded her its Saltus Gold Medal in the annual exhibition of 1987.

Freilicher has been represented by the Fischbach Gallery, New York, since 1975.

RHL

REFERENCES
Gerrit Henry, "Jane Freilicher and the Real Thing," *Art News* 84 (January 1985): 79–83.

Currier Art Gallery, Manchester, NH: *Jane Freilicher Paintings*, 1986.

Michael Brenson, "Jane Freilicher Casts Her Landscapes in a Special Light," *New York Times*, 21 September 1986.

Telephone Poles, 1963

Inscribed lower right: *Jane Freilicher*; reverse, on stretcher: *o/c 1963*
32½ × 40½ "Telephone Poles"—Jane Freilicher
Oil on canvas, 32½ × 40½
NA diploma presentation, November 1, 1982

Robert Winthrop White

ANA 1979; NA 1982
B. New York, 1921

White is a son and grandson, respectively, of the architects Lawrence Grant White and Stanford White; his own son, Christian White, executed the oil portrait with which his father confirmed election as an Associate of the Academy. His work in sculpture extends into the time and idiom of the mid-twentieth century the family's long tradition of creative expression in classical form.

White studied wood carving with Josef Weisz and painting with Hans Grad in Munich, in 1933–34. He took up the study of sculpture with John Howard Benson at the Portsmouth Priory, Rhode Island, from 1935 to 1938 and then continued as a pupil of Benson at the Rhode Island School of Design, Providence, to 1942. In 1945–46 White returned to RISD for study with Waldemar Raemisch, John Frazier, and Gordon Peers. His first one-man exhibition was presented at the Suffolk Museum, Stony Brook, New York, in 1948. White was a resident of the American Academy in Rome from 1952 to 1955, having won its Rome Prize three years in succession.

Among his major commissions are a bronze fountain on Martha's Vineyard, 1957; a bronze figure of the saint for the Saint Anthony of Padua School, Northport, New York, 1959; three life-size figures in wood of the Holy Family for Saint Michael's Roman Catholic Church, Bedford, Massachusetts, 1960–66; a bronze relief of Joseph Wilson for the Xerox Corporation, Stamford, Connecticut, 1972; a monument to Bishop Cranmer for Saint James Episcopal Church, Saint James, New York, 1977; and an eight-foot bronze representing General Pershing in Washington, D.C., 1983.

White has taught at the Parson School of Design, New York; the State University of New York, Stony Brook; the American Academy in Rome; and the Skowhegan School of Painting and Sculpture, Maine. He is a Fellow of the American Academy in Rome and a trustee of the Saint-Gaudens Memorial, Cornish, New Hampshire. For works exhibited in Academy annual exhibitions he has been awarded the Thomas R. Proctor Prize in 1962, 1981, and 1987. White was first elected to the Council in 1985, when he began two terms as Academy's second vice president; from 1987 to 1989 he held the post of first vice president; and in 1989 was elected the Academy's corresponding secretary.

DBD

References
Graham Modern, New York: *Robert White*, 1987.

The Drinker [1964]
Inscribed at rear: *Robert White / I*
Bronze, 28 × 20 × 16
NA diploma presentation, October 4, 1982

Valentin Tatransky, in a December 1983 *Arts* magazine article, described the facts of the creation of this piece and its sensibility:

> In 1959–60 White created a series of sculptures of men drinking in a bar. The originality of this group owes a lot to how he used the technique of direct-plaster. He made these figures about the same time as George Segal's first plaster-cast sculpture, *Man Sitting At a Table* (1961). Neither one knew about the other's work.
>
> White was inspired by what he saw happen to the human body in the bar. He says he was impressed by the "ritual character" of the bar. He saw how drinking creates a language of the body, otherwise absent in daily life. To create the circumstances of the bar, he composed an ensemble of four figures. He worked directly in plaster from memory, without models.

References
Graham Modern, 1987.

WILL BARNET
ANA 1974; NA 1982
B. Beverly, Massachusetts, 1911

Barnet studied painting with Philip Leslie Hale at the school of the Museum of Fine Arts, Boston, and print making with Charles Locke at the Art Students League, New York. The first of his many one-man exhibitions occurred in 1938; the most recent was in 1988 at Kennedy Galleries, New York, which represents him.

A regular participant in Academy annual exhibitions, he has been awarded a Benjamin Altman Prize, 1977, Thomas R. Proctor Prize, 1984, and Gladys Emerson Cook Prize, 1986. Among other awards are those from the Carnegie Institute, Pittsburgh, Biennial; the Ford Foundation; and the Pennsylvania Academy of the Fine Arts. He has been a member of the faculties of the Art Students League, the Cooper Union, the New School for Social Research, all in New York; Yale University, New Haven; the University of Minnesota, Duluth, Cornell University, Ithaca; and the Pennsylvania Academy of the Fine Arts, Philadelphia.

Barnet is a member of the American Academy and Institute of Arts and Letters and many artists' organizations. He served as recording secretary of the Academy from 1985 to 1989 and was elected vice president in 1989. He resides in New York.

RHL

REFERENCES

Wichita Art Museum, Wichita, Kansas: Howard E. Wooden, *Will Barnet: Paintings & Prints 1932–1982*, 1983.

Robert Doty, *Will Barnet: Paintings* (New York: Harry Abrams, 1984).

Avis Berman, "Artist's Dialogue: Will Barnet, from Maine to Infinity," *Architectural Digest* 43 (March 1986): 62.

KIESLER'S LAST REQUEST, n.d.
Inscribed upper right: © *Will Barnet '82*
Oil on canvas, 40 × 34
NA diploma presentation, October 3, 1984

In a letter of September 25, 1984, to the Academy Barnet describes the circumstances underlying this imaginative double portrait:

> The origin of this painting began when Kiesler, in 1964, asked me to do a portrait of him and his bride, Lillian. Kiesler, an acclaimed architect and sculptor and a very good friend was about four feet and some inches tall and Lillian about 5 ft and four inches or more.
>
> His reaction to the finished painting "Kiesler and Wife," which is now in the collection of the Metropolitan Museum [of Art, New York] was very favorable. However, he requested that I do another painting—only this time enlarge his stature and diminish Lillian's size. . . . Unfortunately he soon became gravely ill and had difficulty posing. The painting reflects the foreboding of the finality of his life. . . . The Painting was finally completed several years after his death [in 1965].

GYORGY KEPES
ANA 1973; NA 1978
B. Selyp, Hungary, 1906

Kepes studied under Istvan Csok at the Academy of Fine Arts in Budapest from 1924 to 1929. While still a student he was member of the group of avant-garde Hungarian artists known as Munka. In 1930 he turned to film as a medium of artistic expression, abandoning painting. He worked first in Berlin and then in London with Laszlo Moholy-Nagy, among others, in film, and in stage, exhibition, and graphic design. In 1937 he joined Moholy-Nagy in coming to the United States to develop Chicago's New Bauhaus, which became the Illinois Institute of Design. Kepes headed the New Bauhaus's Light Workshop. His *The Language of Vision*, a summary of educational ideals and methods developed from his years of teaching, was published in 1944 and remains a standard work in the field. Another landmark publication was *The New Landscape in Art and Science*, 1956, which reflected his growing interest in a convergence of art and science. In 1945 Kepes joined the faculty of the Massachusetts Institute of Technology, Cambridge, to teach visual design. In 1967 he created MIT's Center for Advanced Visual Studies, which he directed until his retirement in 1974.

He had returned to working in the painting medium in 1950, and shortly thereafter began to be the subject of frequent one-man exhibitions of his design concepts and paintings held throughout the country. Kepes also executed designs for a number of murals and stained glass windows for major buildings including Walter Gropius's Graduate Center, Harvard University; Church of the Redeemer, Baltimore, Maryland; Manufacturer's Trust, Time-Life Building, New York.

Among Kepes's many honors are a Guggenheim Memorial Fellowship, 1958; Silver Medal of Honor awarded by the Architectural League of New York, 1962; Fine Arts Medal awarded by the American Institute of Architects, 1968; and honorary degrees from Loyola University, Chicago; the University of Mexico, Mexico City; Carnegie Mellon University, Pittsburgh; and the University of Design, Budapest. He is also a member of the American Academy and Institute of Arts and Letters and a Fellow of the American Academy of Arts and Sciences.

RHL

REFERENCES
Museum of Science, Boston: Erik H. Erikson, *Works in Review*, 1973.

Hayden Gallery, Center for Advanced Visual Studies, Massachusetts Institute of Technology, Cambridge: *The MIT Years: 1945–1977*, 1978.

Nature Structure, 1969
Inscribed reverse: 1969
Oil and sand on canvas, 24×20
ANA diploma presentation, November 5, 1973

GEORGE CLAIR TOOKER

ANA 1968; NA 1970
B. Brooklyn, New York, 1920

Tooker was raised in the fairly rural atmosphere of Bellport, New York, on Long Island. At the age of seven he began two years of painting lessons with a family friend and neighbor, Malcolm Fraser. He attended local public schools, but the final two years of his secondary education where taken at Phillips Academy, Andover, Massachusetts, from which he graduated in 1938. Andover, although adhering to a strict and conventional curriculum was unusual in offering art instruction and making studio art facilities available to students; Tooker made the most of the opportunity. The next four years he attended Harvard College, Cambridge, Massachusetts, graduating in 1942. Although he immediately entered the armed forces, he was discharged within a few months because of aggravation of a long-standing stomach ailment.

In the spring of 1943 he entered the Art Students League, New York, for two years of study under Kenneth Hayes Miller, Reginald Marsh, and Harry Sternberg. It was his meeting with Paul Cadmus in 1944, and somewhat later with Jared and Margaret French, that had lasting impact on his art. Cadmus was a strong influence on the formal character of Tooker's work (termed Magic Realist), but more important it was Cadmus who introduced him to the Renaissance technique of egg tempera on gessoed panel, which he has consistently practiced since 1945.

Tooker began to achieve recognition in 1950, when perhaps his most well-known painting, *Subway*, was acquired by the Whitney Museum of American Art, New York, and, with Cadmus and French, he was selected for inclusion in Lincoln Kirstein's exhibition, *Symbolic Realism*. His first solo exhibition took place in New York the next year. Thereafter his work was regularly seen in group shows as well as in periodic solo exhibitions. A major survey of his work was organized by the Fine Arts Museums of San Francisco in 1975.

Tooker taught at the Art Students League from 1965 to 1968. He was elected to the American Academy and Institute of Arts and Letters in 1983. Since 1960 he has made his home in Hartland, Vermont, although he maintains a studio on Long Island, and frequently spends time in Spain. Tooker is represented in New York by the Marisa del Re Gallery.

RHL

REFERENCES

The Fine Arts Museums of San Francisco: Thomas H. Garver, *George Tooker*, 1974.

David Tunkl Gallery, Los Angeles, California: Merry A. Foresta, *George Tooker*, 1980.

Thomas H. Garver, *George Tooker* (New York: Clarkson N. Potter, Inc., 1985).

Robert Hull Fleming Museum, University of Vermont, Burlington: Ildiko Herrernan, *George Tooker: Working Drawings*, 1987.

Thomas H. Garver, *George Tooker* (New York: Rizzoli, 1987).

VOICE II [1972]

Inscribed lower right: *Tooker*
Egg tempera on gessoed panel, 17½ × 11½
NA diploma presentation, October 2, 1972

Voice I (private collection), a slightly more naturalistic rendering of essentially the same composition, was executed in 1963 and was the first in a series of paintings showing people separated or confined by walls that Tooker did over approximately the next twelve years. These works, which focus on the futility of human communication, are among Tooker's most powerful commentaries on the frustration and isolation of contemporary man. Tooker has pointed out that the two figures—one so anxious to be heard, the other straining to hear, but seemingly neither achieving satisfaction—are identical. He repeated this image in a lithograph in 1977.

The artist wrote the Academy, July 28, 1972, that he had "just finished" the painting he wished to submit as his NA diploma presentation.

REFERENCES
Garver (1987), 77, 126.

ANNE POOR

ANA 1972; NA 1975
B. New York, 1918

The daughter of the writer Bessie Breuer, Poor began her artistic studies in 1935 in New York at the Art Students League, where her teachers were Alexander Brook, Yasuo Kuniyoshi, and William Zorach. She attended Bennington College in Vermont from 1936 to 1938 and continued her studies under the auspices of Bennington in Paris at the Académie Julian and the École Fernand Léger. She also studied in Paris with Jean Lurçat and Abraham Rattner.

Poor became expert in painting in the true fresco technique by assisting her stepfather, Henry Varnum Poor, in the execution of murals for the U.S. Departments of Justice and of Interior, Washington, D.C., in the late 1930s and at Pennsylvania State University, 1940. On independent commissions from the Public Works Administration she then executed murals for post offices in Gleason, Tennessee, and Depew, New York, in 1941 and continued to do mural work through the 1950s. Her paintings began to be included regularly in exhibitions around the country in 1942; however, in 1943 she joined the Women's Army Corps, and served as an artist-correspondent in the Army Air Force in the Pacific Theater. Poor's first solo exhibition was of her work resulting from this experience, and was mounted at the American British Art Center, New York. New York's Graham Gallery presented its first solo exhibition of her paintings in 1957; the Gallery continues to represent her to the present time.

She was an instructor and one of four directors of the Skowhegan School of Painting and Sculpture in Maine from 1947 to 1961, has served on the school's Board of Governors and Board of Trustees, and in 1978 returned to the school to teach a special course in fresco painting. In connection with the Skowhegan School, she executed a fresco mural in the South Solon (Maine) Free Meeting House. She was elected to the American Academy and Institute of Arts and Letters in 1987. Among her awards are the Edwin Austin Abbey Memorial Fellowship for Mural Painting, 1948; and from the Academy, Benjamin Altman prizes in the annual exhibitions of 1971, 1981, and 1987.

Poor lives in the home built by her stepfather in New City, New York.

RHL

REFERENCES
Sylvia Moore, "Anne Poor," *Woman's Art Journal* (Fall 1981/Winter 1982): 50–53.
Telephone interview with the artist, 1989.

DERRICKS ON THE HORIZON, HAVERSTRAW, n.d.

Inscribed lower left: *Anne Poor*
Oil on canvas, 30×45
NA diploma presentation, October 3, 1979

The artist, in responding to Janet Rosenthal's inquiries, said of this painting: "The area around Haverstraw is very close to me. I've lived near the river all my life. It's always magic to go down there, by the river, particularly during the winter or the fall, when the Hudson is buried in snow. At Haverstraw there is something special in the light and the way it lies out in the middle of the river. . . . I like to work on a painting until the subject has been annihilated, until only the substantial parts are left. I don't want to be too dependent on the actual objects in it."

REFERENCES
Janet Rosenthal, in NAD: *Next to Nature*, 204.

CHARLES WILBERT WHITE
ANA 1971; NA 1974
Chicago, Illinois 1918–1979 Los Angeles, California

White's career in art could probably be said to have begun with the gift of a set of oil paints received on his seventh birthday. A scholarship to the school of the Art Institute of Chicago gave him his first formal instruction in 1937. His work was first shown at the the Institute's annual exhibition the following year. In 1939 and 1940, under the Federal Arts Projects, he executed the mural *Five Great American Negroes*, George Cleveland branch of the Chicago Public Library, and by the commission of the Associated Negro Press, a mural, *History of the Negro Press*, for the American Negro Exposition, Chicago. In 1942–43 he did a mural, *The Contribution of the American Negro to American Democracy*, for Hampton Institute, Virginia; this project was carried out with the support of a Julius Rosenwald fellowship and with study of mural techniques with Harry Steinberg at the Art Students League in New York.

Drafted into the Army in 1944, his service was cut short when he developed tuberculosis. The following year he was appointed artist-in-residence at Howard University, Washington, D.C. A long-held wish to visit Mexico was realized in 1947. There White met the great muralists David Siqueiros and Diego Rivera and attended the Escuela de Pintura y Escultura la Esmeralda and the Taller de Grafica, in Mexico City. This experience had a profound affect not only on the stylistic character of his art, but on its motivation. While his work had been appearing in group shows at museums around the country since 1941, 1947 also brought his first one-man show, held at the Barnett-Aden Gallery in Washington.

Returning from Mexico he settled in New York in 1949, and with others formed the Committee for the Negro Arts in New York City, a group concerned with assisting Black artists. He had one-man shows at New York University and Hunter College of the City University of New York that year. The next year he began teaching at the Workshop School of Advertising Art and exhibited the first of many times at New York's A.C.A. Gallery. In 1951 he made a tour of Europe. Because of poor health, White moved to Los Angeles in 1956, where he remained for the rest of his life. In 1965 he began an association as a teacher with the Otis Art Institute, Los Angeles, that was sustained throughout his remaining years. The twenty years from 1959 to his death were filled with honors, awards, and exhibitions from all parts of America and Europe—among them the Academy's Isaac N. Maynard Prize in 1972, and Adolph and Clara Obrig prizes in 1971 and 1975, the latter for *Mother Courage II*.

White, who worked extensively in lithography and drawing as well as painting, portrayed only Blacks—with a skill and a restrained dignity and respect for their character and heritage that won him wide-ranging admiration. He told an interviewer for the *Negro History Bulletin* (quoted in the *New York Times* at White's death), "I like to think that my work has a universality to it. I deal with love, hope, courage, freedom, dignity—the full gamut of human spirit. When I work, though, I think of my own people. That's only natural. However, my philosophy doesn't exclude any nation or race of people."

RHL

REFERENCES
High Museum of Art, Atlanta, GA: *The Work of Charles White: An American Experience*, 1976.

Obituary, *New York Times*, October 6, 1979.

The Studio Museum in Harlem, New York: Peter Clothier, *Images of Dignity: A Retrospective of the Works of Charles White*, 1982.

John Oliver Kiltens, "Charles White: The People's Artist," *The Georgia Review* 40 (Summer 1986): 449–72.

MOTHER COURAGE II, 1974
Inscribed lower right: *Charles White '74*
Oil on canvas, 49¾ × 39⅞
NA diploma presentation, March 3, 1975

John Barnes Dobbs
ANA 1973; NA 1976
B. Passaic, New Jersey, 1931

Dobbs studied at the Rhode Island School of Design, Providence, at the Brooklyn Museum Art School, and the Skowhegan School of Painting and Sculpture in Maine. The Academy has awarded him the Thomas R. Proctor Prize, 1974; a Benjamin Altman Prize, 1978; the Leila Gardin Sawyer Prize, 1983; and the Grumbacher Art Award, 1989, for paintings shown in annual exhibitions. He has taught at the Brooklyn Museum School, the New School for Social Research, New York, and John Jay College of Criminal Justice, City University of New York. Dobbs resides in New York City and is represented by the ACA Gallery. He served on the Academy Council, 1984–87.

RHL

Sᴍ ғᴏʀ Rᴀᴘʜᴀᴇʟ, n.d.
Inscribed lower right: *Dobbs*
Oil on canvas, 28⅛ × 32
NA diploma presentation, April 2, 1979

WOLF KAHN

ANA 1979; NA 1980
B. Stuttgart, Germany, 1927

Kahn had some private art instruction as a child in Frankfurt. He arrived in America in 1940 and in New York in 1943, where he attended the High School of Music and Art for two years. After a year of service in the U.S. Navy, he returned to New York and began his artistic studies in classes given by Stuart Davis and Hans Jelinek at the New School for Social Research. It was his study with Hans Hofmann in New York and in Provincetown, Massachusetts, 1947–49, that was more influential, however. Kahn then attended the University of Chicago, receiving his bachelor's degree in 1951.

Back in New York the following year, he established his studio and began to exhibit his paintings, initially with the cooperative Hansa Gallery of which he was a participant founder. The first of a long series of one-man exhibitions presented by the Grace Borgenicht Gallery occurred in 1956; the Borgenicht Gallery continues to represent Kahn. In 1957 Kahn was included in the exhibition *New York School—The Second Generation*, organized by the Jewish Museum, New York.

From 1955, a year passed living and working in Mexico, to 1968, when he acquired a farm in West Brattleboro, Vermont, Kahn frequently took up temporary residence elsewhere than New York: he lived in Venice, 1957–58; was a visiting professor at the University of California, Berkeley, 1960; with a Fulbright award, lived in Milan and Rome, 1963–64. Summers in this period were spent in Martha's Vineyard, Massachusetts, or Deer Isle, Maine. For the past twenty years his time has been more consistently divided between New York and Vermont, which is a major source of his highly simplified landscapes composed in terms of brilliant color.

Kahn's paintings have been widely shown in one-man exhibitions organized by museums and commercial galleries throughout the country, including the Munson-Williams-Proctor Institute, Utica, New York; the Chrysler Museum, Norfolk, Virginia; the San Diego Museum of Art; the Meredith Long Gallery, Houston, Texas; and the Thomas Segal Gallery, Boston. Among his honors are a Guggenheim Memorial Fellowship, 1966; American Academy and Institute of Arts and Letters award, 1979; and membership in the Institute, 1984. In Academy annual exhibitions his paintings have received a Mikhail and Katernya Shatalov Award, 1985; Saltus Gold Medal, 1986; and Andrew Carnegie Prize, 1989. Kahn has served on the Academy Council since 1982, initially a three-year term as a member, becoming assistant corresponding secretary in 1985, and treasurer in 1989.

RHL

REFERENCES

Helen Raye, in NAD: *Next to Nature*, 209–11.

Art Club of Chicago: Martica Sawin, *Wolf Kahn: 10 Years of Landscape Painting*, 1981.

Grace Borgenicht Gallery, New York: *Wolf Kahn: Pen, Pencil and Pastel 1946–1986*, 1986.

Grace Borgenicht Gallery, New York: *Wolf Kahn: New Work, 1987–1989*, 1989.

POND IN NOVEMBER, 1977
Inscribed lower right: *W. Kahn*; reverse: *#69 1977*
Oil on canvas, 29 × 36
Gift of Donald S. Crook, accepted as artist's ANA diploma presentation, February 4, 1980

Stephen Greene

ANA 1980; NA 1982
B. New York, 1918

Greene studied at the Academy school, the Art Students League, New York, and with Philip Guston at the University of Iowa, Iowa City. An abstractionist in his mature work, he is noted for his creation of a personal vocabulary of symbols, expressive of essential themes of Christianity, and explorations of the dark side of human psychology.

He received a Prix de Rome, providing study and residence at the American Academy in Rome, 1952–54, and again passed two years in Rome, 1972–74. Other awards and grants were received from the Corcoran Gallery of Art, 1965; the Council of Arts and Letters, 1966; and the American Institute of Arts and Letters, 1967. In Academy annual exhibitions he has received the Andrew Carnegie Prize, 1971; the Paul Puzinas Memorial Award, 1981; the Saltus Gold Medal, 1983; and the Adolph and Clara Obrig Prizes, 1985 and 1989. He has taught at Princeton University; the Art Students League; the Tyler School of Art, Philadelphia; and the Skowhegan School of Painting and Sculpture, Maine.

Greene's paintings are held in major public and corporate collections throughout America and abroad. Major retrospectives of his work have been held at the Corcoran Gallery, Washington, D.C., in 1963, and at the Akron Art Institute, in 1978. In 1988 Greene was elected to a three-year term on the Council. He resides in Valley Cottage, New York, and is represented by the Marilyn Pearl Gallery, New York.

RHL

REFERENCES
Martica Sawin, "Stephen Greene's Recent Paintings," *Arts Magazine* 50 (September 1975): 83-85

Akron (Ohio) Art Institute: Robert Doty, ed., essay by Dore Ashton, *Stephen Greene: A Decade of Painting*, 1978.

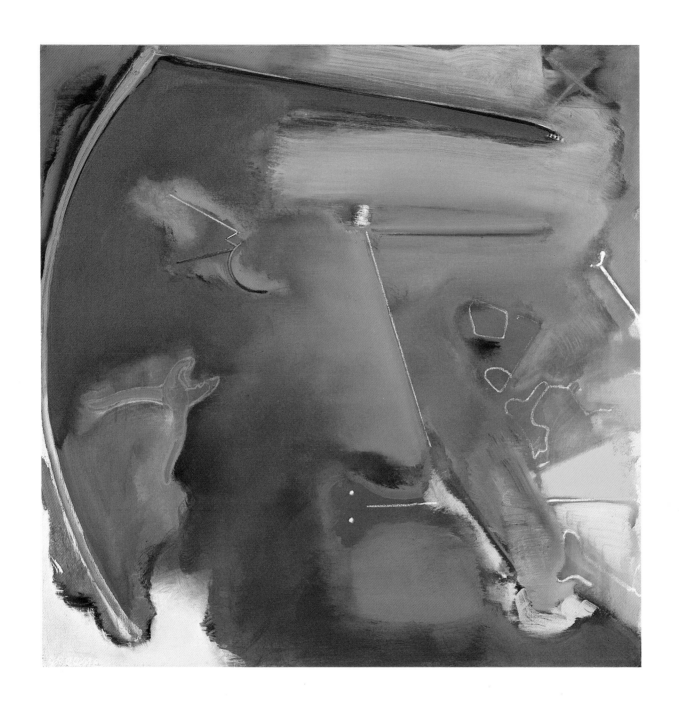

FERMATA #2, n.d.
Inscribed lower left: *Greene*
Oil on canvas, 34×34
ANA diploma presentation, April 6, 1981

Jean Donner Grove

ANA 1980

B. Washington, D. C., 1912

Jean Donner received her bachelors degree from Wilson Teachers College, Washington, D.C., in 1939, and was given her first solo exhibition by the College that year. Further study and training were taken at the Hill School of Sculpture, the Corcoran Gallery School of Art, and Catholic University of America, all in Washington, D. C.; Cornell University, Ithaca, New York; and the Philadelphia Museum of Art. Her teachers at these institutions were Clara Hill, Hans Schuler, Heinz Warneke, and Fritz Janschka. She has executed commissions for Artists Equity, Philadelphia, and the Fine Arts Commission of Philadelphia. A number of her portraits, garden, and fountain figures are in private collections. She has collaborated with her husband, Edward Grove, on several works including the *Communion of Saints*, a mural for the Church of the Holy Comforter, Drexel Hill, Pennsylvania, and *The American Express Goldpiece* of 1982. She has won many awards among which is the 1976 Tallix Foundry Award from the National Sculpture Society, an organization of which Grove is a member. She and her husband maintain their studio and home in West Palm Beach, Florida.

Torso

Marble, 14¾×9×8¼

ANA diploma presentation, December 7, 1981

TORSO
JEAN DONNER GROVE, SC.

MARIANNA PINEDA

ANA 1982
B. Evanston, Illinois, 1924

Pineda studied at the Cranbrook Academy, Bloomfield Hills, Michigan, under Carl Milles, 1942; at the University of California, Berkeley, under Raymond Puccinelli, 1943–45; at Columbia University, New York, under Oronzio Maldarelli, 1945–46; and at the Ossip Zadkine School of Sculpture in Paris, 1949–50. It was in Paris in 1951, that her first works were realized in bronze. In an article written for the *Radcliffe Quarterly*, Pineda has said: "After years of relatively academic art training (a tradition already considerably diluted), I fully expected, like most of my contemporaries, to work in an abstract mode. However, I had become so enthralled by the formal problems and the metaphorical possibilities of the human form that I have never felt compelled to move away from it."

One-person exhibitions of Pineda's work have been presented by the Walker Art Center, Minneapolis, Minnesota, 1952; and by the Honolulu Academy of Arts, 1970. Among major works she has created are a bronze medallion for the Jan Veen Dance Library of the Boston Conservatory of Music, 1965; a relief for Newton College of the Sacred Heart, Massachusetts, 1975; a figural piece, *Twirling*, for the Boston Redevelopment Authority, 1976; the statue of Queen Lili'uokalani for the city of Honolulu, 1982; and *Aspect of the Oracle: Rapturous*, for Radcliffe College, Cambridge, Massachusetts. In 1962 Radcliffe awarded her a Bunting Institute fellowship, in support of two years of intensive work. She has taught at Boston University, 1975–83, and Newton (Massachusetts) College of the Sacred Heart, 1972–86. Pineda makes her home in Boston with her husband, the sculptor Harold Tovish; she is represented by the Judi Rotenberg Gallery, Boston.

DBD

REFERENCES
Marianna Pineda, "Sculpture Is An Act of Faith," *Radcliffe Quarterly* 70 (June 1984): 29–30.

Who's Who in American Art (New York: R. R. Bowker, 1986), 799.

PORTRAIT OF GERTRUDE S., n.d.
Inscribed at right: *M. Pineda*
Bronze, 7⅝×7×7¾
ANA diploma presentation, December 6, 1982

The subject of this imagined portrait is the celebrated expatriate American writer Gertrude Stein.

Richard Estes
ANA 1971; NA 1984
B. Kewanee, Illinois, 1936

Estes studied at the School of the Art Institute of Chicago
from 1952 to 1956. He worked in advertising and publishing
for a decade before giving full-time attention to painting. His
first one-man exhibitions occurred in 1968 at the Hudson
River Museum, Yonkers, New York, and the Allan Stone Gallery, New York. Since that time, as a recognized leader in the
contemporary movement dubbed Photo-Realism, Estes's work
has been seen with ever-increasing frequency in exhibitions
presented by museums and galleries throughout the United
States and Europe. He employs numbers of photographs he
has taken himself in composing his highly finished, intensely
"real" paintings and silk screen prints of excerpts of urban
scenery. He has been quoted in the catalogue of the major
exhibition of his work, organized by the Museum of Fine
Arts, Boston, in 1978, as saying: "The abstract quality of reality is far more exciting than most of the abstract painting that
I see."

Estes resides in New York and continues to be represented by the Allan Stone Gallery.

RHL

REFERENCES
John Canaday and John Arthur, *Richard Estes: The Urban Landscape*
(Boston: Museum of Fine Arts, and New York Graphic Society,
1978).

Parking Lot, n.d.
Oil on composition panel, 23¾ × 36
NA diploma presentation, January 7, 1987

MORTON WAYNE THIEBAUD
ANA 1985; NA 1987
B. Mesa, Arizona, 1920

Wayne Thiebaud was raised in California. While still a teenager, in 1936–37, he worked briefly in the animation department of Walt Disney Studios, Los Angeles. He attended the Frank Wiggins Trade School, Los Angeles, to study commercial art in 1938. From 1942 to 1945 he served in the U.S. Army Air Corps. Based in Sacramento, he was assigned to duty that employed his skills as an illustrator and filmmaker. Following military service he returned to work as a cartoonist and animator. In 1949 Thiebaud turned to painting and returned to completion of his formal education, attending San Jose State University in 1949 and then California State University, Sacramento, where he received his B.A. in 1951 and M.A. in 1952. The first of his many one-man exhibition was presented by the Crocker Art Gallery, Sacramento, California, in 1951.

He began teaching at Sacramento Junior College (now Sacramento City College) in 1951 and served as chair of the art department there several times during the 1950s. He also taught at the San Francisco Art Institute; in 1960 he joined the faculty of the University of California at Davis, where he continues to hold the rank of professor. In addition, Thiebaud has been a visiting professor and artist-in-residence at a number of educational institutions.

Thiebaud first came to prominence representing a West Coast outpost of the Pop Art movement of the earlier 1960s. His renderings of food stuffs, frequently of the more luscious variety—pastries, ice cream, and candy—painted in equally enticing colors, shared this movement's radical return to the faithful, realistic representation of the inanimate models. His overtly painterly style was sharply different from the main body of Pop artists, however, who strove to suppress all evidence of the artist's hand. Thiebaud has since expanded his subject interest to include city and landscape and other themes.

He has received many awards and honors. Among these are the Osborn Cunningham Award to create a mural for the Sacrmento Municipal Utility District Building, an Honorary Ph.D. degree from the California College of Arts and Crafts, Oakland, and in 1985 election to the American Academy and Institute of Arts and Letters. He is also a filmmaker and works in graphic media.

RHL

REFERENCES
San Francisco Museum of Modern Art and University of Washington Press: Karen Tsujimoto, *Wayne Thiebaud*, 1986.

TENNIS PLAYER (SELF PORTRAIT), 1985

Inscribed upper right: *Thiebaud / 1985*; upper left: *Tennis Player*; reverse:
Thiebaud 1985; "Tennis Player" (Self Portrait) / l hour December 21 '85
Oil on plywood panel, 12 × 11½
ANA diploma presentation, October 1, 1986

CHARLES F. CAJORI

ANA 1982; NA 1987
B. Palo Alto, California, 1921

Cajori studied at the Colorado Springs (Colorado) Art Center and the Cleveland (Ohio) Art School before coming to New York in 1946, where he briefly attended Columbia University. Cajori pursued his studies at the Skowhegan School of Painting and Sculpture in Maine. In 1955 he was a participant in the establishment of the Tanager Gallery, where his first one-man exhibition was held the following year. Cajori has been termed a "second generation Abstract Expressionist," who renewed concern for formal problems, which for him has focused on the classical female nude.

Among his distinctions have been grants or awards from the National Endowment for the Arts; the Louis Comfort Tiffany Foundation; the American Institute of Arts and Letters; the Ford Foundation; and Yale University. In Academy annual exhibitions he has received Benjamin Altman Prizes, 1983 and 1987; the Andrew Carnegie Prize, 1984; the Ralph Fabri Prize, 1985; and the Joseph S. Isidor Gold Medal, 1988.

Cajori has served on the faculties of the American University, Washington, D.C.; Cornell University, Ithaca, NY; the Philadelphia Museum of Art School; and the University of California, Berkeley. In New York he has taught at the Cooper Union, 1956–65, and Queens College, 1965–86; in 1964 he became a founding member of the faculty of the New York Studio School. In 1988 Cajori was elected to a three-year term on the Academy Council. He resides in Watertown, Connecticut.

RHL

REFERENCES
Joseph Dreiss, "Charles Cajori," *Arts Magazine* 50 (June 1976): 15.

SHIFTING DOWN, n.d.
Inscribed reverse: *Cajori "Shifting Down"*
Oil on canvas, 65¾×48
NA diploma presentation, October 7, 1987